A Textbook of Insurance Broking

EDITED BY
RODERICK CLEWS, FCII, FCIArb
Formerly Chairman, UK Operations, Glanvill Enthoven & Co. Ltd.

Second edition

WOODHEAD-FAULKNER
in association with
THE BRITISH INSURANCE BROKERS' ASSOCIATION

Published by Woodhead-Faulkner Limited
Fitzwilliam House, 32 Trumpington Street,
Cambridge CB2 1QY, England
and
27 South Main Street, Wolfeboro,
New Hampshire, 03894-2069, USA
in association with
The British Insurance Brokers' Association
BIBA House, 14 Bevis Marks,
London EC3A 7NT

First published 1980
Second edition 1987

© The British Insurance Brokers' Association 1980, 1987

ISBN: 0-85941-405-1

Designed by Geoff Green
Typeset by Goodfellow & Egan, Cambridge
Printed in Great Britain by St Edmundsbury Press, Bury St Edmunds, Suffolk

Contents

The Chartered Insurance Institute professional examinations
and activities. Examinations for those with lower academic
attainments. The Insurance Industry Training Council.

Editor's introduction

RODERICK CLEWS, FCII, FCIArb

Formerly Chairman, UK Operations, Glanvill Enthoven & Co. Ltd

A Textbook of Insurance Broking is intended as an introductory guide for those who are already working or considering working within the insurance broking industry and introduces the reader to insurance generally and to the duties and knowledge required by an insurance broker. It will also be of assistance to those working in related spheres such as insurance companies, banks and other sectors of finance and commerce.

The first edition was the first publication in the United Kingdom which set out to describe the profession of insurance broking. It was written at the suggestion of the British Insurance Brokers' Association which has as one of its principal aims the raising of insurance broking standards in the United Kingdom.

The book does not attempt to replace those more detailed technical publications dealing with the law and practice of insurance matters. However, each chapter is contributed by an acknowledged specialist in the field and further references for additional reading are included.

The business of insurance broking is widely diversified, both in terms of the varying sizes of firms and of the types of business dealt with. At one end of the spectrum is the multinational company, employing thousands worldwide and at the other, the local high street brokerage, often run by one or two individuals. Their business is equally diverse and the practice of marine insurance, for example, demands a very different range of skills and procedures from those necessary for the placing of individual life business.

Successful insurance brokers need to have an understanding of a number of subjects, among them the practice of insurance, the law, economics and the workings of industry and commerce. It is hoped that the reader will gain an insight into the principles governing the work of an insurance broker and the specialist fields of activity in which he or she may become involved. In addition, the book provides information on the organisational and other background aspects that are broadly common to all types of insurance broking.

The book begins by tracing the history of insurance broking – already a recognised feature of the commercial scene by the eighteenth century – and Chapter 2 goes on to explain the role of the present-day broker in terms of the services offered to his clients. Chapter 3 looks at the responsibilities of the broker with special reference to the law of agency and Chapter 4 provides an account of the structure of Lloyd's and the procedures that are observed by brokers in that institution.

Chapter 5 summarises the basic elements and principles of insurance and this is followed by five contributions (Chapters 6 – 10) which each examine a separate class of business from the broker's viewpoint – insurances of the person, property and interruption insurance, credit insurance, insurance of liabilities and insurances of transportation. The next part of the book (Chapters 11-14) deals in a similar manner with the specialist areas of risk management, corporate pension plans, reinsurance and the London market placing operation.

The need for insurance brokers to pay sufficient attention to promoting their services is given due prominence in Chapter 15 on marketing, while Chapter 16 points to the business that can be obtained through the broker's ingenuity in formulating special schemes suited to particular circumstances. Chapter 17 deals with the major accounting disciplines as they affect insurance brokers and Chapter 18 demonstrates how a broker's efficiency can be improved by the proper organisation of office personnel and systems. Chapter 19 highlights the increasing importance of education and training in insurance broking and the glossary contains explanations of terms frequently encountered in the profession.

Since the book was first published, there have been many developments affecting all insurance intermediaries; the most important, however, is the Financial Services Act. This received Royal Assent on 6 November 1986 though its main provisions affecting insurance brokers will not come into effect until 1 January 1988. From that date, any firm wishing to deal in or advise on investments, and this includes life and pensions policies and unit trusts, must be authorised. There are three main routes to authorisation: direct authorisation from the Securities and Investments Board (SIB), membership of a Self Regulatory Organisation, of which the Financial Intermediaries, Managers and Brokers Regulatory Association (FIMBRA) is at present the obvious and popular route for most insurance brokers, or membership of a recognised professional body. It is predicted that compliance with the high standards embodied by the various provisions of the Act will have a fundamental effect on the day-to-day conduct of the insurance broker's business.

Other areas in which recent developments have affected insurance brokers include credit insurance and the insurance of liabilities, where directors' and officers' liability insurance has become an important feature. The increasing use, in the early 1980s, of computers and electronic data processing equipment has also produced changes in many brokers' offices.

Education and training have become increasingly important in recent years and several initiatives have been seen in this area. The British Insurance Brokers' Association introduced their own 'Certificate of Competence in Basic Insurance Knowledge' in 1983 which is aimed at those people working in a broker's office who do not have the necessary academic qualifications for entry to the Chartered Insurance Institute's professional examinations and therefore offers an alternative route to these exams. The Chartered Insurance Institute launched their 'Certificate of Proficiency' in 1987 with much the same intention for candidates throughout the industry. Furthermore, from January 1986 anyone new who wishes to trade in the Room at Lloyd's must pass the 'Lloyds Introductory Test' within fifteen months of obtaining their ticket to Lloyd's.

A further appendix (Appendix 2) has been added to the book, giving two extracts from the Insurance Companies Regulations 1981 which have particular reference for the insurance broker. The two sections given deal with the contents of advertisements and with intermediaries: connected persons.

Finally, I should like to thank all the contributors, both old and new, for their work so willingly performed, and in particular the members and secretariat of the British Insurance Brokers' Association Education Committee for their encouragement and advice. It is to be hoped that this publication will succeed in its aim of acquainting its readers with the basic techniques and procedures of our industry and thereby play a small part in ensuring that insurance brokers in the future will offer their clients a level of service compatible with the highest professional standards.

CHAPTER 1

A *history of insurance broking*

S. D. CHAPMAN, BSc(Econ), MA, PhD
Department of History, University of Nottingham

Insurance brokers were already an established feature of the London commercial scene by the beginning of the eighteenth century. They came into existence because the insurance of ships (hulls and cargoes) emerged slowly as the part-time occupation of a large and disorganised group of private individuals, some with specialised knowledge such as merchants, shipowners and bankers, but including a wide penumbra of people whose only common characteristic was that they had capital to speculate. This miscellaneous group included, at one time or another, such diverse figures as Samuel Pepys, the Admiralty civil servant and famous diarist, and Daniel Defoe, the celebrated journalist and novelist, but no doubt there were hundreds (if not thousands) of others who, in the gambling spirit of the age, were willing to put their signature to (i.e. underwrite) a list of people sharing a risk. Because of the hazardous nature of marine insurance, no one would gamble more than a fraction of his (or her) fortune on any particular vessel, and so someone had to run round the City to assemble a list of names to provide cover for each of the ships leaving port. As Gibb writes in his *Lloyd's of London*, the brokers were 'the fixed point in a floating market'; it was they who were the professionals, the full-time men who depended on insurance for their daily work and livelihoods, who kept recognised offices, knew the responsible underwriters and, through long experience, were best informed on the nature of marine risk.

Over the next 250 years or so, the evolution of insurance broking saw many ups and downs, but was characterised by three outstanding features: the growth, diversification and, most recently, amalgamation of firms. In order to provide a survey in a few paragraphs, we may summarise each of these features in turn.

Until very recently, anyone could call himself an insurance broker, and so it is difficult to encapsulate the numbers and organisation, much less the scale of the business. The most that can be done is to examine the London directories over a long period of time. The best of these reference works begin to have a comprehensive look about them from 1763, and the detail becomes richer as new publishers entered the field, with insurance brokers recorded among long lists of merchants and tradesmen. However, it was not until after the French Wars, with the appearance of Johnstone's *Directory* of 1817, that we have any separate classification and enumeration of insurance brokers. At this date 105 insurance brokers and 166 ship and insurance brokers were listed, but this does not give a comprehensive view of all those involved in the industry. London then had some 1,650 merchants, many of whom were sporadically involved in underwriting, while the small group of merchants who were evolving into merchant banks – Barings, Rothschilds, Huths and others – were active in placing business. Insurance broking as a specialism distinct from shipping and banking was still in the early stages of its emergence and, in the manner of nearly all City firms of the day, was founded on the fluctuating interests of the family owners.

At the middle of the nineteenth century, when the annual series of Post Office Directories begins, the structure of the industry was still recognisably similar. Insurance brokers were listed in three separate sections: 'Brokers (Insurance)' contained 95 names, 'Brokers (Ship and Insurance)' contained 191 names, and a long list of about 1,700 'Merchants' included some 42 names who were identified as both merchants and insurance brokers. In other words, although there was a distinct profession of insurance broker at this time, more than two-thirds of the practitioners were involved in other activities complementary to their insurance activities.

Fifty years later, the London *Post Office Directory* of 1900 offered the same threefold classification of insurance brokers, but the length of the lists had changed quite significantly. Those who described themselves as insurance brokers pure and simple had nearly tripled their numbers to 277, while the ship and insurance brokers were up by about a half to 300 names. However, there were only 13 merchants who were also brokers, but among them were at least three firms that subsequently rose into the premier league of Lloyd's brokers: Hogg & Robinson, which had shipping interests in Australia and Canada; Alexander Howden, which owned ships sailing to North and South America, the West Indies, Africa and later India; and C. T. Bowring, the owners of a shipping line to Newfoundland that later extended to other parts of North America. Insurance and other broking activities emerged slowly as an ancillary activity, gathering momentum during the so-called 'Great Depression' in British shipping in the 1880s and 1890s. Moreover, as ships grew in scale with the change to iron construction and steam power, the old family firms could no longer raise the capital and limited liability companies took their place as shipowners. However, this long process of evolution has left a wide variety of species that found different solutions to the changes in economic climate, so that even today there is a small but distinguished group of merchant houses and shipping lines that retain a minor interest in insurance by keeping broking departments within their organisation. The best known of these are Cayser Irwin, Sime Darby, Blue Star (Vestey Group), Brook Bond, Andrew Weir and Furness Withy.

The depression in world shipping was probably the main reason for the beginning of the diversification of the interests of Lloyd's underwriters and brokers. For most of the nineteenth century both confined themselves to marine risks, and were slow to notice the opportunities that were beckoning in fire, life, accident and other branches. The initiative here was taken by the companies, with the pace set by the Sun Fire Office (founded 1710), the Royal Exchange Co. (1720), the London Co. (also 1720), the Phoenix (1782) and other City ventures. Between the 1860s and 1880s numerous new companies were floated, some of them launched by Lloyd's men. The volume of business flowing through Lloyd's actually declined during the first half of the nineteenth century as the companies found their way into the marine market, and Lloyd's was slow to respond to growing opportunities for another generation after that. Insurance against fire risk was by no means unknown at Lloyd's after 1865 (when Gladstone reduced the duty to a penny a policy) but it was a sideline cultivated by a few marine underwriters; many others would have nothing to do with it. According to the memories of staff at Sedgwick Collins, 'Until the present century, risks other than marine were hardly known at Lloyd's, and they were not encouraged by the Committee.'

The old and narrow conception of the insurance broker's function began to change slowly from the mid-1880s under the leadership of a handful of outstanding underwriters and brokers. Cuthbert Heath is the widely recognised pioneer, accepting reinsurance for a major company's portfolio of fire risks (1885), and leading with the first policies to cover burglary (1889) and earthquakes (1895), credit insurance, householder's comprehensive, professional indemnity, riots and civil commotions, and many other imaginative ideas. Heath brought to Lloyd's not only new ideas but a new outlook, what has been called 'the tradition of the open mind'. New proposals should not be greeted with 'Is there any reason why I should write it?' but rather 'Is there any reason why I should not write it?'

While Heath was winning the laurels for his imaginative ideas, little-known rivals were moving into profitable new fields of business abroad. In the 1890s the Bowring family began to enter the North American marine insurance market, though it was not until 1903 that a separate subsidiary was formed. In 1882 Henry Willis & Co. (one of the components of the present Willis Faber & Dumas) were appointed as underwriters for the Italia Company of Genoa, and in 1899 their successors, Willis Faber & Co., were appointed as underwriting agents for the Tokio Company and Johnson & Higgins of New York. Meanwhile Charles Price, the grandson of the first secretary of the important Dissenters' Life and Fire Office (1837), was creating a fire insurance market at Lloyd's; his firm eventually merged with another to form Price Forbes.

During the 1920s and 1930s the world shipping market was again depressed and new challenges met with a more rapid response at Lloyd's. Bowrings developed their connections in the United States, Japan, India, Germany and other countries, and secured the fleet insurance policy for Imperial Airways. Price Forbes and Leslie & Godwin were among the pioneers of motor vehicle insurance. Willis Faber & Co. took a dramatic initiative in 1922 by buying out a large firm of provincial brokers with offices in Bristol, Cardiff and Birmingham, and immediately after World War II they acquired local brokers in Sheffield, Glasgow and Warrington. Bowrings and Price Forbes, not to be outflanked, advanced into the provinces soon afterwards. From their new bases they were able to secure many of the big industrial corporations for their clients, and in the era of amalgamations and rationalisation of industry between the wars the brokers' business grew in pace with that of their more successful clients. Other brokers that missed this opportunity found it difficult to make up lost ground.

The extending activities of C. E. Heath, the Bowrings, Willis Faber and Price Forbes are sufficient to make the point that the pace and direction of City insurance broking was set by a handful of hereditary leaders with entrepreneurial flair. However, it is important to add that their energy and insight did not preclude the rise of new men, either within existing firms or starting from scratch. The well-known Lloyd's broker Bland Welch (subsequently Bland Payne, now amalgamated with Sedgwicks) dates from 1895, when two senior clerks, John Bland and Alexander Welch, assumed the ownership of a firm founded 65 years earlier. The Stenhouse Group began in 1904 when A. R. Stenhouse returned from six years in American insurance to introduce their pushing professionalism to Glasgow and Edinburgh. Another leading Lloyd's broker, J. H. Minet, was founded as recently as 1929. John Minet, after a period of experience in the United States, migrated to Lloyd's to introduce a volume of direct American non-marine business, superseding the established practice of taking such lines only through reinsurance. In these and other ways, many of them still unchronicled, Lloyd's and its leading brokers became world-famous for their flexibility and enterprise, and the diversity of their interests within the insurance world. The rising generation of families connected with Lloyd's, and eager competitors from outside, could not fail to recognise that the success of enlarged syndicates and prospering brokers was the product of new enterprise at home and abroad, and young adventurers scoured the world to rake in new business from the Americas, the Far East, Australia, South Africa and Europe. Gibb writes of the period from 1908 to 1930 as a golden age for Lloyd's men, a period of dynamic enterprise when Lloyd's insurance was stretched round the globe.

New interests and contractions in the marine market also brought the first mergers and takeovers between insurance brokers and the growth in size of underwriting syndicates. Last century most brokers were small family businesses carried on from one generation to another and employing no more than a handful of clerks, and the early mergers were characteristically between friends with complementary interests. They were no doubt encouraged by the continuing growth in the scale of their clients' businesses, and in particular by the period of mergers, takeovers and 'rationalisation' that was a feature of the international economy towards the end of last century, between the wars and again in the late 1950s and early 1960s. Here we can chronicle only a few early examples that took the headlines in their day and set a precedent for rivals to observe and evaluate.

The 1893 merger that created Price Forbes was a union between two third-generation family firms, with Forbes having a traditional interest in the marine cargoes and Price being a pioneer of fire and life insurance at Lloyd's. Similarly, Sedgwick Collins was launched in 1912 as a union of Sedgwick's marine interests with F. L. H. Collins's firm of fire insurance brokers, the latter a product of the genius and enterprise of a self-made man who began his career as a clerk in a City textile warehouse. Henry Willis & Co. amalgamated with Faber Brothers in 1898 because the former had systematically cultivated the companies for business while the Fabers had given the preference to Lloyd's. In 1922 Bowring bought out Crawley Dickson & Co. to secure a better footing in the non-marine market and Willis Faber amalgamated with Dumas & Wylie in 1928 for similar reasons. Other firms were merged for the more traditional reasons of retirement of the partners without heirs or successors in the firm.

While mergers and takeovers were a sporadic feature of the insurance scene from the end of the last century, the post-war years have witnessed a sustained attempt by a small number of Lloyd's brokers to gobble up smaller firms in the City, the provincial centres and around the world. This continuing process has created a premier league of about a dozen very big brokers, all public companies and multinational in their range of activities, and often maintaining subsidiaries in associated financial, shipping, travel or other industries. These leaders are constantly jostling for the premier positions so that any record of their order is likely to be outdated before it can be published. However, at the time of writing, this group includes (in alphabetical order) C. T. Bowring, C. E. Heath, Hogg Robinson, Jardine Glanvill, Leslie & Godwin, J. H. Minet, Sedgwicks, Alexander Stenhouse, Stewart Wrightson and Willis Faber. On the other hand, in an industry which lives on personal service, size is not always a guarantee of efficiency and success. Almost all of the big mergers of recent years have created internal tensions which have led to the resignation of some senior managers, sometimes using their expertise and connections to launch their own firms. For this reason, the core of multinational brokers continues to be in competition with scores of smaller rivals whose principals make a living, in the traditional City way, on entrepreneurial flair and the network of personal connections. Between these Goliaths and the Davids there stands a range of medium-sized brokers (typically employing 20 to 30 people) in the major provincial centres. Many offer special services appropriate to their locality such as farming or engineering insurances, and they often compete with the branches of the big London brokers in their own regions.

Of course, this rush for size is not motivated purely by the desire to break out of the chrysalis of the old family patrimonies; nor is it to be seen simply as a species of empire building. The most rational explanation is the accelerating growth and increasingly international nature of the businesses that insurance broking exists to serve. It is not merely a question of the scale of industry and commerce in Britain. In recent years the American market has provided half of Lloyd's business and so dominated the horizons of City brokers. Most of the bigger firms have long since developed close connections with brokers in New York and in the late 1970s several market leaders started the move to forge formal financial links with their American business associates. Lloyd's initial response was to block such moves, and in 1978 tried unsuccessfully to prevent Leslie & Godwin's plans to merge with Frank B. Hall, one of the largest US brokerage firms specialising in casualty and property. Lloyd's acted under a rule that ostensibly banned 'non-Lloyd's insurance interests', but this line did not hold. Leslie & Godwin were absorbed by Frank B. Hall in 1978 and the majority of the larger Lloyd's brokers have followed suit. C. T. Bowring was taken over by the biggest US broker, Marsh & McLennan in July 1980 and Alexander Howden was bought by the second biggest, Alexander & Alexander, in 1982. In 1985 Reed Stenhouse were also taken over by Alexander & Alexander, and although Willis Faber are still independent, they do have a 'gentlemen's agreement' with the American brokers Johnson & Higgins, which has been in force now for nearly 100 years. Johnson & Higgins also own 5 per cent of Willis's shares.

Traditionally, brokers in London and New York differed in one respect, in that part of the City brokers' income arose from the management of Lloyd's underwriting agencies. The agencies administer the work of Lloyd's underwriting syndicates, the groups of private individuals who actually shoulder the risks of insurance. Originally, the syndicates used to consist typically of a few rich families, but with the rise of taxation and death duties on the one hand and the increase in scale of international insurance on the other the syndicates have grown to as much as three or four hundred names, and the authority of the agencies has correspondingly increased. Numbers of syndicates consisted, until recently, of the directors of insurance broking firms, formally acting in their private capacities, a development encouraged by the increasing prosperity of brokers in the post-war years.

In recent years, however, there has been a growing uneasiness about the power of the big brokers at Lloyd's and this was one of the subjects investigated by the committee chaired by Sir Henry Fisher. The Fisher Report was published in 1980 and urged Lloyd's to deal with what it saw as a potential source of conflict; that Lloyd's brokers, whose business it was to place insurance, should also act for underwriting agencies and therefore be providers of insurance was seen as anomalous. The Fisher Report therefore urged Lloyd's to ensure brokers divested themselves of their underwriting agencies. In 1982, an important year for Lloyd's, not only did this divestment become mandatory, but in June of that year an Act was passed in Parliament revising the structure of the Council of Lloyd's and its constitution. A further step to self-regulation has been seen with the publication of the Neill Report in January 1987, which has once again altered the constitution of the Council of Lloyd's. The report also recommended that the Fisher Report's proposals for the regulations of Lloyd's brokers be adopted and, at time of writing, this is expected to have a considerable effect on brokers in the Lloyd's market.

Lloyd's brokers have increasingly placed business around the world and draw more and more income from professional consultancy fees rather than brokerage. Further diversification in recent years has sometimes been less easy to understand. The extensive losses suffered at Lloyd's in the late 1960s persuaded some brokers to diversify into adjacent financial activities, and a few into industrial investment. Brokers have traditionally handled large sums of money on behalf of insurers (premiums in transmission) and with their own retained earnings this has given them long experience of short- and long-term investment. Among the more publicised examples, Bowrings moved into merchant banking, Stewart Wrightson and Clarksons into ship broking, and Hogg Robinson into the retail travel business. In the early 1970s H. C. Stenhouse feared the nationalisation of the insurance industry and so acquired a group of companies in electrical and general engineering. His forebodings were widely shared and no doubt added fuel to the diversification movement. Simultaneously, there was a strong merger movement in the City prompted by the merchant banks, which thought they were being threatened by the clearing banks' growing interest in traditional accepting house activities. The accepting houses (the name given to the 17 leading merchant banks) decided to diversify their activities, and nearly all of them moved into insurance, an activity close to their traditional expertise. The characteristic entrée to the new interest was by acquisition of successful companies, often from the founding families. In this way some of the bigger brokers became part of financial conglomerates: Bland Welch of Samuel Montagu, Lowndes Lambert of Hill Samuel, and Glanvill Enthoven of Charterhouse Japhet. The larger City brokers joined in the fury of takeovers and mergers by gobbling up numerous smaller firms in London and the provinces, all to often suffering from heavy indigestion in the process.

If there is little information on the history of City insurance brokers, those in provincial centres are recognised by historians merely as *terra incognita*, so that it is possible to discern only a few tendencies in their development. From the early eighteenth century, London insurance companies, beginning with the Sun Fire Office, began to appoint provincial agents and by the end of the century numerous country offices were jostling for attention in the advertisement columns of the local newspapers. In the second half of the nineteenth century the companies proliferated, and agents began to serve complementary firms or became managers of branch offices. It seems to have been a common practice for agents and managers to act on their own account as brokers; certainly several of the best-known provincial brokers began in this way, including William Heap & Son of Manchester (established 1876), A. W. Bain & Sons of Leeds (1879), P. F. Scanlon, now Russell, Sons & Scanlon of Nottingham (c. 1881), Macalaster & Alison of Glasgow (1890) and Sydney Packett & Sons of Bradford (1920).

Provincial brokers evidently built up a diverse folio, but those that achieved eminence characteristically did so by specialising in some regional industry that required a particular expertise; for instance, Heaps specialised in handling insurances for firms in the textile-finishing industry, Scanlon in coal-mining, Bains and Packetts in the West Riding wool trade and industry, and

Macalaster & Alison in paper-making. The slowness of the tariff
companies to revise their terms to meet the development of fire
sprinklers created opportunities for several firms, and it seems
likely that the large companies suffered from other rigidities.
Provincial brokers secured access to Lloyd's through City brokers,
with whom they often developed close business ties. Since World
War I these connections have often culminated in acquisitions or
mergers as the growing concentration of British industry com-
pelled City firms to reach out into the provinces and provincial
brokers to pursue clients to new centralised headquarters in
London.

FURTHER READING

There is no history of the insurance-broking industry as such and the
various histories of Lloyd's and the companies pay scant attention to
brokers. The only useful historical background is D. E. W. Gibb, *Lloyd's of
London: A study in individualism* (Corporation of Lloyd's, 1957), a book
written by an insider mainly for other insiders, but useful for context and
on Cuthbert Heath as an innovator. Several of the leading City brokers have
had potted histories written, with one exception all for private circu-
lation. The exception, David Keir, *The Bowring Story* (1962), is better on
the firm's earlier mercantile and shipping activities than on insurance
and finishes in 1954. The private published works which have been
consulted are as follows:

Anon.: *Irons in the Fire: A record of the Matthews Wrightson Group of
    Companies 1901-51* (1951).
Anon.: *And at Lloyd's: The story of Price Forbes & Co. Ltd* (1954).
Anon.: 'The Stenhouse Group' (typescript 1979).
Brown, Anthony, *Cuthbert Heath: Maker of Modern Lloyd's of London*
    (David & Charles, 1980).
Chapman, S. D.: 'Hogg Robinson: the Rise of a Lloyd's Broker' in O. M.
    Westall ed., *The Historian and the Business of Insurance* (Manchester,
    1984).
Collins, B. R.: *The History of Sedgwick Collins & Co. Ltd* (1969).
Dawe, Donovan: 'History of Alexander Howden' (typescript 1979).
    Typescript at Guildhall Library.
Head, V.: *Two's Company: A history of Leslie and Godwin 1885-1985* (1985).
House, J.: *Macalaster & Alison the Insurance Brokers 1877-1977* (1978).
Maufe, G.: 'A Short History of Willis Faber & Dumas Ltd', *Willis Faber
    Review* (1970).
Packett, C. N.: *Diamond Jubilee History of Sydney Packett & Sons* (1980).

As much of this material is now badly dated, it has been necessary to
cover recent developments by reference to the BIBA, to press reports,
the reviews of the special stockbrokers (notably Sheppards & Chase and
W. Greenwell & Co.) and private information.

CHAPTER 2

The role of an insurance broker

G. N. CROCKFORD, BA, FCII
Information Services Manager, Bowring Services Ltd

INTRODUCTION

There is no such thing as a typical insurance broker. There are far too many possible permutations of size, type of client, class of insurance, marketing approach and services offered for generalisations about 'the broker' ever to be more than approximately true.

With the coming into force of the Insurance Brokers (Registration) Act 1977, only those who comply with the standards required for registration may legally call themselves insurance brokers, but a registered broker may be anything from a one-man business, operating in a single town, to a large multinational company, with branches, subsidiaries and associated companies all over the world. A broker may operate primarily in the Lloyd's market or he may be a provincial broker representing many insurance companies, but without direct access to Lloyd's. Some brokers have diversified and have subsidiaries offering other financial services; others are themselves owned by banking organisations or by shipping or industrial companies.

There are brokers who are equipped to service the whole range of a client's insurance needs – from life and pensions to marine and aviation insurance – and others who specialise in a very restricted range of covers. The clients they serve may be ordinary individuals, who know very little about insurance and who probably have only a sketchy idea of what their insurance needs really are, or they may be large industrial or commercial companies, which often employ specialist insurance managers with an expert knowledge of insurance, and which know precisely what they want.

A broker may see himself as being essentially a placer of insurance on behalf of his clients, or he may offer many kinds of additional service, from information about savings and pensions to fire, burglary or safety surveys.

The difference between the work of one broker and that of another may thus be enormous, but there is one thing that they all have in common. Each of them is an expert adviser to his clients on insurance matters, a link between the client's need for cover and the insurers who can meet that need. The broker's skill lies in finding as good a match as possible for his client's needs from among the display of competing insurance products on the market and, where necessary, stimulating insurers to modify their policies or to create new covers in order to meet the client's needs better.

This means that not only must the broker understand the insurance market, which is the basic specialist skill he is offering to the public, but he must also understand his client. This is not simply a matter of finding out what kind of insurance the client is looking for; it is also one of discovering what particular needs underlie the request. A broker has thus to be very well informed about both sides of the market he serves, and this necessity is often a sound reason for specialisation, particularly for the smaller broker.

The market sector chosen may be determined by some specialist knowledge of particular classes of insurance which the broker's staff have, or the size of his firm may lead the broker to concentrate on a particular type of client. Large broking firms seek to provide service to clients both large and small, but it may be uneconomic to handle insurances for individuals side by side with those of large industrial clients. The solution usually adopted is to set up subsidiaries or branches specially designed to serve the individual. This avoids the difficulty inherent in trying to serve both markets with the same organisation, namely that, since the broker's remuneration is normally by commission calculated as a percentage of the premium, the overheads involved in providing all the services needed to deal with the insurance needs of large companies might rule out handling small premium business.

Some brokers have neither individuals nor industrial companies as their main clients, but insurers, for whom they place reinsurance. This may be an important part of the business of a large broker, or it may constitute the whole activity of a smaller specialist broking firm.

The broker's main role – that of a skilled intermediary using his special knowledge to help his client to obtain the best from the insurance market – will be the same in every case, but the way he goes about it will vary according to the type of client he chiefly serves. Let us therefore consider in turn the needs of the individual, of the industrial company and of the commercial or professional concern.

INSURANCES OF THE INDIVIDUAL AND THE FAMILY

The individual is not, on the whole, very insurance-conscious He is aware of a few of the commoner forms of insurance but will probably have no conception of the enormous variety of covers which the insurance market provides. He may be prepared to concede that the idea of insurance is a good one, but he still tends to be a reluctant purchaser.

His reluctance is perhaps understandable when one thinks that he is being asked to pay out money in return for which he receives no immediate tangible benefit. All he gets is a promise and a piece of paper – the insurance policy – which embodies that promise. The policy is a legal document and as such is written in a style and language which the insured may find difficult to understand.

The agreement is an odd one because not only may a very long time elapse before there is an opportunity to test the promise that has been given, but also that opportunity will usually arise only in unpleasant circumstances which the insured would rather not think about. It is, in short, an agreement which both parties would rather never came into effect, and so it is hardly surprising that most insurance for individuals is bought as a result of either compulsion or persuasion.

Compulsory insurance, as far as the individual is concerned, means motor insurance, and many brokers base their business on individual motor policies. The motorist must have cover, and he does not know how to find the best insurer. That, in a nutshell, is the problem that the broker solves for him. The broker is able to find the best combination of rates and conditions for the particular circumstances of his client among the many on offer, and to recommend a sound insurer to him. If the insured has a motor accident, it is to the broker that he turns for guidance and help through the formalities of making a claim upon his insurers, and possibly for assistance in making an uninsured loss claim against the other motorist.

This is one of the simplest illustrations of the role played by a broker in arranging an insurance and in making sure that the insured obtains the full benefit from it when he comes to make a claim, but it can lead to a very successful relationship between broker and client. Just how close the relationship can be is shown by the number of clients who find it very difficult to remember the name of their insurer but who have no difficulty in recalling that of the broker.

If motor insurance tends to be the result of compulsion, life assurance often depends upon persuasion. A broker has to be a good salesman to be successful in life assurance, but he has to be much more than that. He must also be a financial adviser to his client, recommending the best forms of cover for the client's particular circumstances. These will decide whether it will be protection of the client's family in the event of his death or life assurance as a means of investment which will be emphasised.

The relationship built up through meeting these more readily recognisable needs of the client is often the starting-point for the broker to introduce his client to other forms of insurance because, where the individual is concerned, the broker's role must to some extent be that of an educator in insurance matters. The client, who probably has many things he would rather think about than insurance, will often need prompting to consider the need to insure his possessions against loss and to make sure that his family would have a continuing income not only in the event of his death but also if he were involved in an accident or suffered a major illness.

The broker needs to do more than merely introduce his client to the forms of cover he requires. He must keep in touch with his client to ensure that the insurances he has are still appropriate as his way of life or family circumstances change. In these days of inflation, too, the broker has a duty to remind his client of the necessity to make sure that the sums insured on his policies are regularly adjusted so that the cover remains adequate.

In arranging insurances for individuals, the broker's task will largely be to select the most appropriate cover from a range of standardised policies. Some, particularly those which set out to package several insurances in one policy, may offer a range of options which between them will meet the needs of a very large majority of the general public, but there is comparatively little scope for designing a 'tailor-made' policy for a particular individual. Insurance is, of course, based on the principle of a fund built up from the contributions of many people, out of which the losses of a minority of them can be paid. There must be a certain minimum of premium to be derived from a form of insurance before it becomes economic to offer it, so that the individual who wants a cover applicable to himself alone is unlikely to find it. Nevertheless, it is the broker's job to search the market to find as close an approximation to a 'tailor-made' cover as possible at a reasonable premium, provided that it is offered by an insurer in whose security and reputation the broker has absolute confidence. However good the cover may look on paper, its value is diminished if there are unwarranted difficulties or delays in claims settlement, and it is worthless if the insurer becomes insolvent.

INSURANCES OF INDUSTRIAL CONCERNS

Businesses come in all sizes, and the role of the broker will vary in some respects with the size of the client company and the amount of insurance expertise it has available among its own staff. The approach to insurance of a small engineering workshop in a side-street will not be the same as that of a huge multi-national corporation which may number an insurance company among its subsidiaries. The essentials of the broker's task will be the same, however, for the largest company as it is for the individual: to use his knowledge of insurance and of the insurance market to help his client to arrange a sound insurance programme which, to the maximum extent possible, meets the client's particular insurance needs.

The broker will handle the insurances of a small company in a manner very similar to those of an individual. The relationship is likely to be a personal one with the directors of the business, and they can be considered, in a way, as individuals who have a different, and more extended, set of insurance needs because of their involvement with the company.

The first essential will be for the broker to ensure that his clients have the compulsory insurances which they need for their business to be carried on legally. Employer's liability cover to protect the workforce must be arranged, and motor insurance is also likely to be a necessity. If the business has plant or machinery which must have a periodical statutory inspection, it will be usual to arrange for this to be done by a specialist engineering insurer under the terms of an engineering inspection contract, with or without insurance.

Fire insurance will be very important, as will consequential loss insurance to protect the firm against loss of earnings during the period following a fire until it is fully back in business. Then there will be all the other insurances which a business needs – public and products liability, theft and money insurance, goods in transit and perhaps marine insurance, all-risks covers, fidelity guarantee and possibly others. The broker may also be asked to provide insurance covers for staff, a group life and pensions scheme, or personal accident or permanent health insurance for example.

The range of insurances which may be needed, and the variety of problems which may be associated with them, place great demands on the broker with an industrial firm as his client, and make it much less possible for him to be a specialist in one or two types of insurance only. The individual may be happy to consult a broker for life or motor insurance only, but the industrial company is likely to want a single source of advice for all its insurance problems.

The larger the client company is, the less it will be interested in buying standardised insurance covers, and the more it will want policies which match its own specific needs. This calls for a very deep understanding of the client's business on the part of the broker, matched by creativity in designing insurance solutions to the problems posed. The broker's negotiating skills may also be called upon to persuade an insurer to accept what may be an entirely new approach to a particular insurance need.

The problems of a small spread of risk may be overcome because the company is large enough to be rated on its own past record rather than as a member of a trade which is rated as a class. When it reaches this size, a company may be interested in extensive self-insurance, and these days it is part of the broker's role to help such clients develop appropriate self-insurance plans and to advise on risk management measures to ensure that the risk that is being retained is reduced as far as is economically possible.

Risk management will be discussed in detail in a later chapter but the broker's role in assisting his client company to identify and manage the risks that threaten it should be noted here. This help may include the identification and evaluation of those risks, so that the correct action can be taken to limit their effects or to provide for the cost of loss. Many risks can only be eliminated completely by incurring unacceptable costs or inconvenience, but it may be possible to reduce them to an acceptable scale. Loss control measures may operate to reduce the probability of loss – as, for example, the separation of areas of high-fire risk by fire-resistant partitions – or to reduce the severity of loss once it occurs – for example by the installation of sprinklers.

Although a risk has been controlled in this way, there may still be a residual risk which would be too great to be borne comfortably by the company. In such cases, the risk may be transferred by insurance or financed when it occurs, either by raising loans or by meeting it from the company's own resources. This may be done by establishing a self-insurance fund from which losses can be paid as necessary. The modern broker must be prepared to advise his client not only on insurance matters but also on loss prevention and on these alternatives to insurance.

Larger companies will almost certainly employ a risk manager or insurance manager, and his knowledge of the company's operations may relieve the broker of much of the basic investigation of the client company's insurance needs. The risk manager is himself an insurance specialist, and can be expected to take over much of the broker's task to act as an interpreter between the worlds of industry and insurance. The broker is not, however, relieved of his responsibility to suggest new covers, or new forms of old ones, and to point out needs which appear not to have been met.

The broker, looking at the company from the outside, may see things that the risk manager has missed, and the broker's connections with the insurance market, which are likely to be more extensive and more frequent than those of the risk manager, may suggest innovations or lines of enquiry which may result in a better insurance programme for the client.

A large company will probably have overseas operations, and will wish to co-ordinate the insurance arrangements of all its branches and subsidiaries as far as possible. This means that the broker must be able to provide service, either through his own organisation or through a network of correspondent brokers, wherever his client may be operating.

The emphasis with larger clients is likely to be on catastrophe risks – perhaps the threat of fire or explosion to a vast industrial complex, the risks of a major construction contract, or the possibility of a huge award being made in a products liability case. In cases such as this, the broker may have to go to markets beyond the British one in order to find sufficient capacity. The broker who has large companies and multinationals as his clients cannot therefore think in purely national terms.

Many large clients these days are interested in forming an insurance subsidiary – a so-called 'captive' insurance company – usually in an offshore tax haven. The broker's role thus becomes extended to carrying out a feasibility study on such a proposal, advising on suitable locations, and setting up, managing and arranging reinsurance programmes for the captive.

INSURANCES OF COMMERCIAL AND PROFESSIONAL CONCERNS

In many respects, the role of the broker with a client in commerce or the professions will be similar to his function as broker to an industrial company. He must be able to understand the intricacies of his client's business, so that he can recommend the best insurance programme from among all the available options. The range of covers from which the choice is to be made will be the same as for an industrial company, but the relative importance of covers will not be the same.

For smaller companies, some form of package policy covering most of the risks of shops or offices in a single document may be appropriate. It will be part of the broker's duty to examine how well a cover of this kind, with its standardisation, meets the particular needs of his client firm, and to recommend the stage at which it would be better served by separate policies designed to cover the client's individual circumstances.

The insurances of larger companies will be handled in the same way as those of an industrial company, with the same combination of expert placing of the risk in the insurance market and advice on means of preventing or minimising loss. In large retail organisations security will assume particular importance. There will inevitably be a substantial amount of cash in transit, and losses through theft by shoplifters or by staff can, if unchecked, assume serious proportions. The broker should be equipped either to give advice on risks of this kind himself or to draw his client's attention to the need for loss prevention, and perhaps to indicate some other sources of specialist advice.

The presence of the public on the insured's premises leads to risks which the industrial client is unlikely to have to face to anything like the same extent. Liability insurances, both public liability and products liability, which will provide cover against liabilities incurred through products sold or supplied, will be important, and the broker must ensure that his client has insurance protection which is both adequate in amount and wide enough to cover all the types of business in which he is engaged. Subsequently, the broker must remind his client of the necessity of ensuring that the limits of liability under his policies are reviewed periodically so that they remain adequate as inflation and court awards rise.

Liabilities will also be very much in the broker's mind in advising clients in the professions. The major risk in this case will be that of professional negligence. Substantial professional indemnity cover is now a condition of being permitted to practise many professions, including that of an insurance broker. The public is entitled to expect that persons or firms holding themselves out as possessing particular professional skills will in fact exercise them, and the trend is towards the extension of liability to include persons other than those with whom the professional person is in a contractual relationship.

Placing the professional indemnity risk may call for the exercise of just such a professional skill on the part of the broker, for the financial consequences of an error may be far greater than any other risks the professional person may face. Apart from professional indemnity, his insurances may be no more complicated than those of a simple office risk.

It is in alerting his client to major risks of this kind which may be concealed in what appears to be a comparatively risk-free occupation, as well as in the skilful placing of insurances both complicated and simple, and in helping the client to obtain a speedy and fair settlement when a claim comes along, that the broker earns his money.

Although he will normally be remunerated by the insurer through a commission based on the amount of the premium, and although he will be for some purposes the agent of the insurer, there is no doubt where the broker's chief loyalty lies. Above all other considerations he must put the interests of his client first.

CLAIMS

The client cannot see the result of those insurances for which he has paid until he makes a claim. He will expect and be entitled to immediate and expert attention. He should receive guidance on how to make the claim and how to deal with insurers and loss adjusters when they are appointed. The limitations and extent of the client's policy must be fully explained to him and the insurance broker should be active in safeguarding the interests of his client.

FURTHER READING

Cockerell, Hugh, and Shaw, Gordon: *Insurance Broking and Agency: The law and the practice* (Witherby, 1979).

Economist Intelligence Unit and Corporation of Insurance Brokers: *A Study of the Requirements, Internal Practices, Attitudes and Expectations of Insureds in Obtaining Insurance* (Corporation of Insurance Brokers, 1971).

Shaw, G. W., Mitchell, J. K., *et al.*: 'The Insurance Broker', fourteen-part series in *Post Magazine and Insurance Monitor* (10 June 1971 – 9 September 1971).

CHAPTER 3

Insurance brokers and the law of agency

ALAN TEALE, ACIS, ACII, MInstAm
Formerly Director, Technical Services and Overseas Affairs, BIBA

Revised by Ronald L. Peters, ACII
Director, UK Technical and Education, BIBA

The use made of the terms 'agent' and 'agency' within the context of the insurance world and applied to those involved in the provision of insurance services gives rise to apparent anomalies and frequent confusion. This is irritating to those who are trying to understand the true status of the insurance intermediary with whom they are dealing and yet paradoxically the lack of precise definition is frequently of substantial benefit to everyone involved.

In many countries beyond British influence the insurance industries have largely avoided such problems of uncertainty. Their insurance companies (Lloyd's being unique to the United Kingdom) have long appointed intermediaries to work for them and these specifically are called their agents. It is at once clear that these agents look to the insurance company concerned as their first principal rather than the buyer of insurance, the eventual policyholder.

Outside of the United Kingdom and the Commonwealth, the emergence of the form of insurance intermediary called an 'insurance broker' has largely been a later development; for example, agents found that they needed more freedom and became insurance brokers. Within the Untited Kingdom, the ranks of intermediaries have been much more intermingled in the past and without a sharp division.

THE 'INSURANCE BROKER'

Historically, a broker of any kind has been a 'go-between' for buyers and sellers, whose origins lay in commodities and who has differed from a factor by not having possession of the goods for sale. The term has been extended into the insurance world, largely through Lloyd's underwriters who soon after their emergence in the seventeenth century became accustomed to dealing only through brokers. Gradually, others have adopted the description and a massive industry has developed.

'Insurance broker' describes someone who is normally the agent of the insured: *Shee* v. *Clarkson* (1810), *Rozanes* v. *Bowen* (1928), *Anglo-African* v. *Bayley* (1969). These are all examples of judgments evidencing this responsibility. Such judgments provide a substantial body of law to which reference can be made establishing this fundamental point. It is from this important concept that an attempt to clarify what 'insurance agency' might mean must begin.

'A broker . . . is an agent employed to make bargains and contracts between persons . . .': *Fowler* v. *Hollins* (1872). What has occurred is that custom and practice have progressively caused the *insurance* broker seeking to provide a service to his first principal (the insured) in the making and fulfilment of the insurance contract to accept certain additional responsibilities for insurers also. As this has occurred, insurers not unnaturally have wished to protect themselves and have enforced conditions on the insurance broker by enforcing acceptance of agency agreements which define the relationship between broker and company.

It is significant that the insurer by whom an insurance broker may be called upon most for assistance (the Lloyd's underwriter) does not, except in special circumstances, demand this form of written agreement.

WHAT LAW MAY GOVERN AN AGENCY RELATIONSHIP?

It is important from a legal standpoint that 'insurance brokers' do clearly identify themselves precisely as such, for using just the term 'broker' is now an anachronism. It can mean anything, and an entirely different body of law and privileges may apply.

The insurance broker is subject to five different sources of law in determining what status he may have in any particular circumstance:

1. The law of agency itself, which covers all forms of agency relationship.

2. Judgments on specific insurance broker problems.
3. The Insurance Brokers (Registration) Act 1977 (and in particular the Code of Conduct).
4. The developing body of EEC law.
5. Miscellaneous law found in the following legislation:
   Marine Insurance Act 1906 (ss.52–54) (the responsibility of the marine insurance broker);
   Misrepresentation Act 1967 (holding out that a position exists that does not);
   Powers of Attorney Act 1971 (authority given under seal);
   Corporate Bodies Contracts Act 1960 (contracts entered into by corporations);
   Fair Trading Act 1973 and the restrictive trade practices legislation;
   Insurance Companies Act 1982 (ss.73–75) (law relating to intermediaries);
   Consumer Credit Act 1974 (licensing and responsibilities of credit brokers);
   Policyholders Protection Act 1975 (calls on life brokerages);
   Supply of Goods and Services Act 1982.

Additionally, insurance brokers frequently commit themselves to individual company agency agreements, letters of appointment by clients, and internal agreements between partners and directors affecting their responsibility.

Ascertaining the standing of a broker's appointment and assessing his responsibility for acts subsequently carried out may well involve reference to one or more of the above authorities. It is essential to examine each question which may arise specifically and to take no generalised view.

THE LLOYD'S BROKER

Only specially approved insurance broking companies have access to Lloyd's Underwriting Room and the companies undergo a detailed examination by the Committee of Lloyd's before inclusion on the list of Lloyd's brokers. These brokers are committed in consequence to additional responsibilities on behalf of Lloyd's underwriters beyond normal insurance-broking practice and within the general law of agency.

Such responsibilities include the preparation of policies which are submitted to Lloyd's Policy Signing Office for checking and signature on behalf of underwriters. Accounting between Lloyd's brokers and underwriters is transacted under a unique central accounting scheme which inevitably necessitates the application of procedures which vary the brokers' position in law by comparison with their dealings with insurance companies.

While therefore Lloyd's brokers in their company business would look to the general law of agency for an understanding of their status, within Lloyd's the additional factors deriving from their relationships with Lloyd's underwriters and Lloyd's practices necessitates a separate study. All new users of the Room at Lloyd's are now required to pass Lloyd's Introductory Test within fifteen months of obtaining permission to use the Room.

APPOINTMENT AND TERMINATION OF 'AGENCY'

Insurance brokers are the agent of the insured, although in practice or by custom they may accept such appointments or responsibilities from others also.

The appointment of an agent may be:
(a) by an agreement in writing (i.e. by express agreement);
(b) by implication or conduct or by the situation of the parties;
(c) by necessity;
(d) by imposition.

Agents may in turn be:
(a) special (for a specific act only);
(b) general (empowered to do anything within certain limits);
(c) universal (unlimited powers).

In practical terms this means the following:
1. *By express agreement.* Either orally or in writing a specific appointment will be made which may contain conditions, e.g. a letter of appointment by a client or an insurance company's agency agreement. Sometimes a contract under seal will be made (a power of attorney).
2. *By implication or conduct.* Someone may permit another to obtain or do things for him and commonly approve of what is done: e.g. a client may accept renewals automatically made on his behalf. A principal may be prevented also from denying the fact of agency if he fails to intervene when the agent has apparent power to act (the doctrine of estoppel).
3. *By necessity.* It may be impossible to get a principal's instructions, and a necessity arises forcing an agent to deal with the events.

4. *By imposition.* Some deeds or leases impose an agency relationship on a principal (who may be unwilling). This is a relationship in which circumstances can well emerge whereby the principal will challenge the position of the agent concerned. If an agent does not have authority to contract for his principal or has exceeded his powers, then there is no binding contract.

It may be possible for the agent to obtain ratification of his acts without authority later, but if this is not possible a personal responsibility may well remain in the absence of some defence being available.

Should it be wished to terminate the relationship between a principal and an agent this may be accomplished by mutual agreement, revocation or operation of the law.

A mutual agreement to end a relationship should nevertheless deal with all aspects of the severance. There is no set procedure, but an exchange of letters or a record of conversations is important to avoid future liabilities being imposed on the agent. This record of events should indicate the date of termination, how the disposal of information and documents will be carried out, what responsibilities remain and how unpaid debts will be met.

An insurance broker subject to an insurance company agency agreement should also deal with responsibilities which may exist between him and the insurer on the business of his clients. Written termination is to be commended to avoid subsequent dispute: termination clauses in such agreements must be reviewed, for they differ and some include provisions which are severe in their effect.

Revocation of an agency relationship may well include equal need for care. If there has been some alleged breach of the contract of agency in either direction leading to revocation, loss of remuneration may lead to damages being claimed. A principal should, therefore, be expected to be precise in the terms of the revocation and if the agent has been allowed to assume some authority (e.g. debt collection) then the revocation may be invalid unless any third party is informed. In the event of an insurer's revocation not being clear, the 'agent' should consider a letter stating his position to be desirable.

Operation of the law may terminate agency relationships where:
(a) the period of appointment has expired;
(b) a particular transaction for which the agent was appointed has been completed or an agreed event has taken place;

(c) the agency has become unlawful;
(d) there has been death or insanity;
(e) there has been bankruptcy or liquidation.

DUAL RESPONSIBILITY

The dual responsibility of the insurance broker most often accepted to the total advantage of the insurers has nevertheless led to some criticism in the courts. It is said that the insurance broker has violated a tenet of the law of agency that an agent must not serve two principals. Megaw J dealt with the point in the *Anglo-African* v. *Bayley* judgment in 1959 when he held that an insurance broker could not argue he had authority to act relating to an insurance claim when the instruction to do so had come from the insurers unless he could show it had been agreed he should do so.

The judgment is, of course, limited to a particular situation, but it is indicative of the care an insurance broker needs to exercise to ensure that he is acting properly. If there is some suspicion that he is not acting in the total interests of his principal then careful attention should be given to the possible need for consent to do so. Many factors exist which may well ensure that principals are indeed fully aware of the role being played, but if doubt should exist it is better that the precaution of asking for consent is taken.

The impression might be gained that insurance brokers are unique in their dual representation and thus no other precedents exist. However, they are not and the dual concept extends on occasions, for example, to auctioneers, solicitors and shipbrokers as well. As the responsibilities of insurance brokers and others grow, so also may classical agency law have to change.

A glimmering of a trend towards this occurred in the case of *McNealy* v. *Pennine* (1978), where the insurance broker had accepted a liability accompanying his completing a proposal form for his client, but had not given warning that the insurance company imposed special terms on certain types of proposer.

In *Stockton* v. *Mason* (1978) an insurance broker was held to have been acting as the agent of the insurer when confirming over the telephone that the required insurance cover existed; the insurance broker was empowered to do so, and was speaking as agent of the insurer at that moment.

The undertaking of certain responsibilities on behalf of insurers by an insurance broker is inevitable: a document produced more quickly when needed or action taken on an insurer's behalf for the purposes of speed are valuable assets for those who use an insurance broker's services.

THE INSURANCE BROKERS (REGISTRATION) ACT 1977

Some of the uncertainties which existed in the past are disappearing as a result of the effects of the Insurance Brokers (Registration) Act 1977.

The Act was deliberately drafted not to have a direct effect on the law of agency but first to achieve a vital identification of who is an insurance broker. Those who register or enrol are seen to be 'insurance brokers' and those who do not indicate that they wish to be known as some other form of intermediary. In this manner, there has emerged a body of people and organisations clearly known to the public and others for what they have elected to be.

The statutory responsibilities of insurance brokers and the rules governing their identification so that their names will appear in a public register are becoming increasingly well known to policyholders. This vital foundation when linked to developing law has grown and will continue to grow into a definitory pattern governing insurance brokers.

There is also no definition in the Act of an 'insurance broker': one is not needed, for those whose names are listed in the register will have indicated their commitment to the Act. The Code of Conduct adopted under s. 10 of the Act coupled with custom, practice and judgment law will provide a framework. Much of the Code of Conduct is drawn from the general law of agency and applies it to insurance brokers in a manner previously not possible. In consequence they are assessable as to their responsibilities and duties in law more clearly. Breach may constitute unprofessional conduct and deletion from the register, a serious additional penalty.

For the Act to have attempted to resolve the current agency anomalies in some other way would have led to endless argument preventing its passage, but the foundation has been laid for the future.

The drafters of the Act also took note of past attempts to produce a definition of an 'insurance broker', none of which has been successful. The only known recognised definition appears in the EEC Intermediaries Directive (1976), where it is accompanied

by the definition of an agent. In order that the differences
between the two are illustrated, both are quoted:

> (a) *Insurance broker.* 'Professional activities of persons who, acting
> with complete freedom as to their choice of undertaking, bring
> together, with a view to the insurance or reinsurance of risks,
> persons seeking insurance or reinsurance and insurance or reinsu-
> rance undertakings, carry out work preparatory to the conclusion
> of contracts of insurance or reinsurance and, where appropriate,
> assist in the administration and performance of such contracts, in
> particular in the event of a claim.'
> (b) *Agent.* 'Professional activities of persons instructed under one
> or more contracts or empowered to act in the name and on behalf
> of, or solely on behalf of, one or more insurance undertakings in
> introducing, proposing and carrying out work preparatory to the
> conclusion of, or in concluding, contracts of insurance, or in
> assisting in the administration and performance of such contracts,
> in particular in the event of a claim.'

The prime difference is that an agent answers directly to the
insurer; the insurance broker relates to the policyholder. To this
extent therefore the term 'agent' has come to have a special
meaning beyond the simple 'agent' dealt with in the law of
agency, and it is the different uses of the word in insurance circles
that so often cause the anomalies and confusion suffered.

DOES DEFINITION HAVE ANY REAL VALUE?

The twin EEC definitions are important, for they will be used
within the Community and they are already accepted in the
general discussion of insurance law as providing a view of the
functions various intermediaries perform.

They do not, however, at present have an acceptance in
national law beyond the directive and it is not possible when
considering their purpose to acknowledge a real value within the
United Kingdom. They are designed for the specific purpose of
separating the types of intermediary within the context of the
EEC.

OTHER FORMS OF INTERMEDIARY

From the point of view of those who use the services of insurance
intermediaries, it is notable that in recent years further terms
have been invented beyond 'agent': 'insurance consultant',
'insurance adviser' and 'direct selling agent' are a few.

It is not really known what responsibilities any of these intermediaries might have or what security they offer their principals, but in the absence of some specific acceptance of responsibility they may possess none at all. It is difficult to understand how being a 'consultant' relates to the responsibilities readily accepted by an insurance broker and, at this time, it appears that the public will remain unprotected where general business is concerned. Legislation has recently been passed in the form of the Financial Services Act which will require authorisation by a self-regulatory authority of, *inter alia*, all intermediaries transacting investment business which includes life and pensions business. When the Act becomes effective, authorised businesses will have to comply with certain statutory requirements whether they are registered brokers or not. The rules of the various authorities concerned have not, at the time of writing, been approved. (Reference is made to the Financial Services Act later in the chapter.)

Some exceptions to the regulatory framework are offered to pension trustees. Advice given by pension consultants, however, must meet the requirements of authorisation as outlined above.

AGENCY AGREEMENTS

The most common form of express agreement found in the insurance industry on appointment of an agent is the company agency agreement. Many insurance companies are at present not prepared to accept business from an insurance broker unless the latter has signed such an agreement. While these agreements differ in terms they all commonly lay down the conditions of the relationship between the two parties. A number of insurers vary the terms of their agency agreement as between practising insurance brokers and unregistered intermediaries.

The position at Lloyd's is different, as Lloyd's brokers commit themselves to special responsibilities, except in the case of a binding authority which empowers the holder to accept business automatically on behalf of underwriters subject to specified limitations and terms which vary according to class.

Agreements are, however, required by many Lloyd's *brokers* before they will undertake to accept business from non-Lloyd's intermediaries for placement with Lloyd's. This is particularly so for motor business where, unusually, direct contact between the Lloyd's underwriters and non-Lloyd's intermediaries does exist.

The Committee of Lloyd's requirements for such business insist, however, that even in these cases a Lloyd's broker is involved and that he protects his own interests by seeking a written agreement from the actual producers. This is an example of insurance brokers or intermediaries becoming principals and agents between themselves.

Certain clauses tend to be common for company, Lloyd's and Lloyd's broker agreements. Provision is made not only for the authority the insurance broker may have but also for the contractual relationships involved. Conditions controlling the dealings between the two parties are laid down, and commonly agreements provide for the following:

1. The scope of the authority of the insurance broker on behalf of the insurer.
2. Terms of remuneration.
3. The method and periods of settlement of monies and the basis on which settlement is to be made (e.g. balance or otherwise).
4. The handling of documentation arising from insurance contracts entered into.
5. How the relationship may end and what happens to the business in those circumstances.
6. A right of cancellation of the agreement.

Some insurance companies request personal guarantees from directors of corporate insurance brokers which enable the company to seize the personal belongings of directors. Such provisions when imposed give rise to opposition, and complaints of harsh treatment are common. While it is a matter for decision by an individual whether he is prepared to sign, there is often little option if he wishes to deal with the insurance company concerned. An insurance broker may also find that on termination of an agreement he has no right to renewal commission on what he had thought was his business but which the company lays claim to as theirs. On the death of a sole trader or partner what had been imagined to be a legacy for wife and family may disappear if the company claims a portfolio, as some agreements allow them to do. These requirements are harsh but if the agreement is with a corporate body some difficulties may be avoidable, for the agreement is normally with the company and not the individual.

Should a bankruptcy of a client occur, an insurance broker will need to study any agreement into which he has entered and he may find that he has no right of access to refunds of monies to the client whereas the terms of agreement signed may hold him responsible for the premium. Similar situations arise should an insurer become insolvent and rights of offset in account may be lost by application of clauses dealing with accounting transactions.

Fortunately, most problems may be resolved by negotiation, but the potential effect of an agency agreement, if strictly imposed, is considerable. A number of insurance companies have updated and are continuing to update the terms of their agency agreement by the use of modern wordings which more accurately reflect current market practice.

The situation was somewhat improved following the Registration Act: companies had claimed in the past that they had to have reassurance on the terms of their relationships, the Act was of assistance in rectifying shortcomings which they felt had previously called for specific terms. The British Insurance Brokers' Association is pressing for changes to continue and believes that the Financial Services Act may further influence existing arrangements.

DUTIES OF AN AGENT

The general law of agency requires that beyond a specific duty accepted as the result of, say, an agency agreement, an insurance broker assumes responsibilities which require him:

(a) to exercise due diligence in carrying out instructions on the responsibilities which he has undertaken;
(b) to exercise any skill he professes to have;
(c) to ensure the principal is aware of factors likely to affect his judgement in fulfilment of the contract;
(d) to render an account and not make any secret commission or profit beyond normal remuneration;
(e) to maintain confidentiality;
(f) not to delegate authority without specific permission.

The similarity between these general duties and the Insurance Brokers Registration Council Statutory Code of Conduct (see Appendix 1), expressed in the examples contained in the Code, indicates an intention that failure may also constitute unprofessional conduct in the future. Some illustrations follow:

Failure to carry out duties

An insurance broker employed to arrange insurance cover or

effect a renewal may fail to do so without telling his principal. Circumstances may affect the general liability incurred by this failure (e.g. the insurances required are illegal or impossible), but prompt notice even in such cases is essential.

Instructions may also be deemed to have arisen from usage and, in the event of there being known reliance on the insurance broker, the absence of express instructions could well not be a barrier to a successful action for failure.

Brokers have a duty to advise clients of forthcoming expiry dates of policies and failure to seek renewal instructions places the broker in a vulnerable situation. Out of court settlements have resulted from breaches of this duty and it is, therefore, essential that a broker should have an efficient system to enable him to fulfil his duty at renewal.

Skill

An assessment of the exercise of skill is normally made by comparing the skill exercised by persons of equal standing. For example, the motor expert purporting to have life assurance expertise is vulnerable if he has held himself out as a professional adviser and has not taken reasonable care in the exercise of his responsibility.

The Hedley Byrne judgment of 1964 (see below) resulted in the demand for considerable care in the giving of advice, but previous cases such as *Sarginson* v. *Moulton* (1943), when it was incorrectly stated that a risk was uninsurable, are also evidence of the degree of responsibility demanded.

Failure to communicate

An insurance broker may fail to pass on a communication indicating a change or adjustment required by an insurer. A subsequent loss may be unprovable and a liability on the insurance broker arises.

Accounting

Most relationships are governed by terms set by insurers, or by customs and practice, but a general duty to account to a principal with diligence and in accordance with the principal's instructions exists.

Confidentiality

The confidentiality of the information held on behalf of clients is paramount and must not be abused. Similarly, information held in confidence on behalf of insurers must be respected: *North & South* v. *Berkely* (1970).

The provisions of the Rehabilitation of Offenders Act 1974 and the Data Protection Act 1984 should also be borne in mind. Any breaches of these Acts could give rise to legal actions.

Delegation

In the absence of specific authority or a known custom, an agent may not delegate. Exceptions appear in some forms of underwriting authority and where a Lloyd's broker must be employed to gain access to Lloyd's underwriters.

THE INSURANCE BROKER AND RESPONSIBILITY FOR NEGLIGENCE

A factor which distinguishes insurance brokers sharply from other forms of intermediary is their acceptance of responsibility for negligent acts. If an insurance broker errs he pays and he is required to insure substantially against the possibility.

It is for this reason that the duties of care exercised are high and this was emphasised in 1964 when in *Hedley Byrne* v. *Heller* it was held that care on advice given had to be exercised by persons even without any formal contract. An insurance broker must be certain of the advice he gives in addition to carrying out specific and required acts on behalf of his principal.

Judgments supporting the need for a duty of care to be performed are numerous and much reported, but fundamentally whether the required degree of skill has been exercised depends in each case on the circumstances. An insurance broker thus may suffer penalty at the hands of his principal if he fails in this duty and also be subject to the Statutory Code of Conduct.

The acceptance of this level of responsibility is important: it is a reassurance matching the independence an insurance broker claims to have.

THE CONSEQUENCES OF A BREACH OF DUTY

In the absence of a ratification of an unauthorised or negligent action, remedies may be sought by disappointed principals and these are common to both agents and insurance brokers.

The right of dismissal is inherent irrespective of express terms and this may be summary (as in *Swale* v. *Ipswich Tannery* (1906)). To this may be added liability for loss occurring from the breach of duty and a principal is entitled to seek redress for actual loss incurred (*McNiell* v. *Millen* (1907)), wilful failure to insure (*Cock Russell* v. *Bray Gibb* (1920)) and failure to notify lack of cover (*Charles* v. *Altin* (1854)). In these instances the liability is for damages and not for the amount the insurer might have paid. A criminal responsibility may arise in the area of alleged corruption or fraud or under the Marine Insurance (Gambling of Policies) Act 1909.

While the normal remedy is the award of damages for negligence, forfeiture of all rights including commission may also arise. This may occur where the agent has made a secret commission, and not only may that commission be lost but also the right to normal commission payable. In the event of an insurance eventually proving to be abortive by reason of breach of duty, any linked commission or even expense incurred is forfeit.

A breach of the long-term agreement may also result in the award of damages against the offender.

THE RIGHTS OF AN INSURANCE BROKER

The right of an insurance broker to support from his principal in the carrying out of his responsibilities as agent of the insured is frequently undermined by his acceptance of specific responsibilities without redress. However, it is the duty of a principal to indemnify his agent for acts lawfully done and liabilities incurred in the carrying out of the responsibilities involved.

The right to the commission earned is fundamental and the fact that physically the commission is usually paid by the insurer by deduction does not make the broker into the agent of the insurer: *Bancroft* v. *Heath* (1900), affirmed 1901.

The right to commission is earned when the premium is paid. The agency which is the effective cause of an insurance contract being placed with an insurer is entitled to that commission. It is not necessary that the premium be paid via that agency for commission entitlement to attach.

Also a general right of lien exists under the law of agency (which becomes a right of offset in a liquidation in respect of accounting matters which arose prior to the liquidation), but the lien can be lost if the insurance broker relinquishes possesssion of the policy or has otherwise conceded his right. This, for example, frequently occurs by the terms of agency agreements, which may dictate that the rights of insurance brokers are given up.

The probability that an insurance broker has a right to deduct outstanding premiums which he may be committed to pay (e.g. in marine insurance or under an agency agreement) from monies due to an insured has been supported in cases involving marine insurance, e.g. *Fairfield* v. *Gardner Mountain* (1911). Other instances of practical application of offset have occurred during liquidations of insurers when the method of account settlement was taken into consideration.

The matter currently rests that, dependent on circumstances, lien should not be lightly discarded, or rights otherwise held easily abandoned, for the unwary might incur a heavy responsibility without any possibility of support.

RESPONSIBILITY FOR PREMIUM

A policy lien has a particular importance when premium is unpaid, and has long been a specific subject of the law relating to marine insurance, where insurance brokers were traditionally and in law responsible for unpaid premium before the codification carried out by the Marine Insurance Act 1906. The first traceable judgment is in *Airey* v. *Bland* (1774).

For other classes of business the general view is that in the absence of a specific commitment (as in the case of a specific agency agreement), liability for premium does not under normal conditions arise. Life assurance is also an exception, but the premium collection methods normally avoid dispute.

The most recent substantiation of this view arose in *Wilson* v. *Avec* (1974), in which an insurance broker was under pressure to pay a liquidator of an insurance company and decided to pay from his own funds. Subsequently, the insurance broker was unable to recover the monies from the client. The judge could find no authority supporting the possibility of 'the agent' being responsible for the premium due.

The insurance broker may nevertheless incur a general responsibility by not informing the insurer immediately difficulty arises on premium collection; and, if he fails to do so or fails to inform the insurer of some other factor detrimentally affecting payment, the insurer could well claim that negligence had occurred and seek damages for breach of duty.

By virtue of the terms of an agency agreement a broker may also incur responsibility for premium payments if, for instance, he has issued a certificate of insurance or a new policy or has failed to return renewal documentation within a specified period and without first having collected the insurance premium from his client.

IMPUTATION OF KNOWLEDGE

Those who deal with agents rely upon the general assumption in law that the principal has passed on all the facts and information necessary for the transaction involved. Thus, an insurer may rely upon the insurance broker's presentation of the case for his client and the principal cannot rely on the possible ignorance of the insurance broker: *Webster* v. *Foster* (1795), *Bufe* v. *Turner* (1815), *Mackintosh* v. *Marshal* (1843).

Equally, it may be assumed that an agent has communicated facts to the principal: this is effective at the point in time when the communication should have occurred: *Proudfoot* v. *Montefiore* (1867). The conditions on which this general rule is dependent are that the agent was actually aware of the fact involved and that he was operating for the principal on the matter. Further, the agent may have indicated he did not intend to pass on the fact, thus relieving himself of responsibility.

These general rules are important when considering matters of non-disclosure, for it is the duty of the agent to inform the insurer of material facts within the agent's knowledge which in given circumstances may also be 'however acquired': *Bancroft* v. *Heath* (1901). The entitlement to voidance of a contract for non-disclosure arises from failure to disclose and is a heavy penalty for the principal (the proposer) who has delegated duties of disclosure to the insurance broker. It is a frequent cause of the accusations that are made of claims being rejected because of 'the small print'. Actions for negligence may well lie in such circumstances, but it is incumbent on the proposer to advise his insurance broker of all information essential to the negotiation.

The general doctrine extends also to each stage of the insurance contract where it is material for facts to be disclosed, but it does not extend to those transactions with which the insurance broker had no concern.

The most common point at which problems arise is on completion of a proposal form. It is a condition precedent that the facts stated are completely accurate and in consequence the completion of the proposal by the client or a statement verifying accuracy is a vital protection for the insurance broker. It is more difficult to allege that a principal has failed to disclose something material, thus reducing the chance of liability being imposed, if the form is completed on the proposer's behalf.

The physical conveyance of the proposal by the insurance broker to the insurer does not revalidate the imputation of knowledge (*Parsons* v. *Bignold* (1846)), but the commonly accepted status of the insurance broker completing proposals is that he is the agent of the proposer and thus the agent's knowledge cannot be directly imputed to the insurer. The proposer in turn is entitled to rely on the insurance broker as having guided him properly on completion of the proposal. Thus the insurance broker is vulnerable from both sides.

The imputation of knowledge of his agent to the insurer is (with the exception of the area of proposal forms) a less well-tested field. Broadly, for such knowledge to be imputed, it must be known that the agent (insurance broker) was in fact the agent of the insurer at that time. Additionally the agent must have authority to acquire the knowledge involved. In this context lies an important example of the difference between insurance broker and insurance agent, emphasising the vital nature of the former working primarily for the insured.

FINANCIAL SERVICES LEGISLATION

Proposals to regulate the financial services industry in the United Kingdom are now enacted under the Financial Services Act. These provide for the setting up of a Securities and Investments Board and within the provisions of this legislation this Board will be responsible for the authorisation of all those who wish to conduct any form of investment business, including life and pensions business. All insurance brokers and other intermediaries who conduct life and pensions business and who offer other investment services must therefore be authorised to do so from a date yet to be decided. It is expected that FIMBRA (Financial Intermediaries Managers and Brokers Regulatory Association) will be the appropriate self-regulatory authority from which brokers and other intermediaries should seek authorisation.

CHAPTER 4

Insurance brokers at Lloyd's

RODERICK CLEWS, FCII, FCIArb

Formerly Chairman, UK Operations, Glanvill Enthoven & Co. Ltd

INTRODUCTION

The history and development of Lloyd's has been well documented, and this is not the place to take more than a cursory look at its progress. Suffice it to say that Lloyd's originated in a coffee house belonging to a certain Edward Lloyd which was the haunt of those concerned with maritime trade.

For many years business transacted at Lloyd's was confined to marine insurance. In the nineteenth century, however, a large non-marine business began to be built up, particularly business from overseas, and Lloyd's is now a major market in this field.

THE STRUCTURE OF LLOYD'S

This organisation is unique in the world. The Council of Lloyd's, established under the 1982 Lloyd's Act, is the governing body and activities under its jurisdiction are governed by Acts of Parliament. Statutory regulations aimed at preserving the solvency and integrity of Lloyd's underwriters differ from those applicable to insurance companies, though the intent is the same. The reader who wishes to know more about this matter is referred to the Lloyd's Acts 1871–1982. The systems used for issuing policies, collecting and accounting for premiums, and dealing with claims also differ from those adopted by insurance companies. Only accredited Lloyd's brokers can place insurance at Lloyd's.

The Corporation provides the premises and all the facilities for those transacting business within its jurisdiction, together with the regulatory controls. The actual business is not transacted by the Corporation of Lloyd's but by underwriting members on the one hand and Lloyd's insurance brokers on the other.

Underwriting members are individuals and their liability is unlimited. However, it would be impossible for all those who are underwriting members of Lloyd's to transact the business individually and thus they are formed into syndicates in the charge of the person who is responsible for the transaction of the business on their behalf. This person has complete power of attorney on behalf of the members of the syndicate: naturally, an underwriter with power of attorney needs to have assistance and this is provided by his accredited deputies. Those persons actually accepting insurance have of course to comply with rules and regulations and submit themselves to the disciplines of the Corporation.

The Lloyd's insurance broker is the other part of the market and is also subject to rules and disciplines. He has to be accredited and membership is not granted freely. Only a Lloyd's broker can enter the Underwriting Room and transact business therein. The 'Room', as it is called, is that place where the underwriters sit at 'boxes' and transact the business.

It is normal for Lloyd's brokers to be either limited companies or partnerships rather than individuals, and the chief executive of such a company or partnership is the broking member. The staff of the company with broking powers are known as 'substitutes'. There is in addition a category entitled 'messengers' who are allowed to take messages into the Room to give the broker but who are not empowered to conduct any insurance broking.

Lloyd's broking offices range from the giant companies, through medium-sized operations, to the very smallest broking firms. Many large and medium-sized offices employ specialists and operate a number of separate departments.

Small firms may specialise in one class of business or another. For instance, one broking house concentrates on professional indemnity business, many others on reinsurance, yet others on the hotel and catering trade, and so on. Some small firms, however, operate a general business.

PROCEDURE AT LLOYD'S

If a risk is to be offered to Lloyd's underwriters it can be done only through a Lloyd's broker. In most cases the business will be obtained by the same firm whose brokers will place the business, but it is possible for what are called 'outside brokers' to obtain business and pass the details to a Lloyd's broker, who will then endeavour to place it with a Lloyd's underwriter. When this happens there is usually a shared commission arrangement.

Business is submitted to the underwriting officials by means of a slip in which details, albeit brief, of the risk to be placed are recorded. The slip may be supported by other documents such as contracts, survey reports, correspondence, etc. If an underwriter wishes to accept the business he will see that the terms are set out clearly, stamp the slip with his syndicate's rubber stamp and initial for that portion of the risk which he has accepted. It may require several underwriters to perform this function before the risk is totally placed. Once this is done, the broker's placing task is completed, and the slip together with the necessary documents is passed back to the broker's office for the policy drafter to produce the policy and calculate the premium. It is the Lloyd's broker's responsibility to produce the documentation and submit this in an approved form to the Lloyd's Policy Signing Office to check the details, extract the necessary accounting information (which is produced in a standard form), sign the policy and return it to the insurance broker. A unique feature of the Lloyd's operation is that the Corporation (under whose control the Signing Office operates) provides the necessary accounting functions for both the broker and the underwriters. There is no 'double accounting'.

When claims occur, similar procedures are adopted – that is, the claim is notified to the Lloyd's broker, who in turn notifies the underwriter or underwriters and sets in motion a claims collection procedure. The underwriters might wish to instruct loss adjusters, or others, to investigate the claim on their behalf and ultimately when the claim is agreed it is the broker who carries out the administrative work involved in collection.

There are a number of ancillary services attached either to the Corporation or to the underwriters, for instance a Claims Bureau and the Underwriters' Syndicate Survey Department.

THE PRACTICE OF BROKING AT LLOYD'S

In an ideal operation no person would be allowed to work as a broker at Lloyd's before first learning a great deal about the law and practice of insurance. This would normally involve working in the office with those whose duty it is to prepare information and slips for the executive who goes to see the underwriter.

The first step after this type of experience may be to become a messenger. This position allows entry into the Underwriting

Room and a good deal can be learned about the geographical position of the boxes, who occupies them and what class of business they will transact or are best at; a general feel and working knowledge of the Room and its occupants will soon be obtained. Standards of behaviour and ethics and the formalities are equally well learned at this stage. After such experience the individual progresses to become a substitute. A substitute may start as a junior broker, who none the less is empowered to approach underwriters and transact business. For difficult insurances, however, the terms may be obtained by someone more senior, and the junior broker will then be required to complete the slip following the stated lead.

A market such as Lloyd's cannot exist without both written and unwritten rules. There is much information that is exchanged only orally, and so great care, ethical behaviour and trustworthiness are particularly important. The most crucial factor is utmost good faith. A recent Chairman of Lloyd's has stated: 'Lloyd's has got to be different. Standards of conduct are not, despite what is frequently said or written, matters of fashion. They are part of the eternal verities, and deviation from the path of the utmost of good faith is something that we cannot allow.'

The Council of Lloyd's takes care of the probity, honour and solvency of Lloyd's broking firms. The checks and balances of the market take care of the individuals. While there are innumerable approaches to presenting a risk, the strand of integrity must never become frayed. Deviation can result in a dreaded note written to the head broker which would read: 'Mr A, underwriter for B, C, D and others, would prefer not to do business in future with Mr Z, who is one of your substitutes.' A stricture such as this can ruin a person's career.

The following comments, though they should not be taken as comprising the contents of a detailed instruction manual, are intended to acquaint the reader with some salient features of broking at Lloyd's.

The slip

The slip has to be correctly compiled. This document is now in a standard format which is intended to assist not only the underwriter giving consideration to the risk but also the policy drafter and those responsible for checking and accounting for the premium.

Information

The slip provides a précis of the risk, but the broker needs to be well briefed with additional facts and figures and to have available all relevant material such as survey reports, maps, plans, detailed claim records and any other documents or information which may have a bearing on the risk. The broker is required to assemble a balanced and accurate representation of the risk and should anticipate as far as possible questions which are likely to arise. If, however, a question is asked to which the broker does not know the answer, it is his duty to say so and refer back for further information. The need to disclose every material fact must always be borne in mind.

The lead underwriter

Where it is necessary that a risk be spread among a number of syndicates, for a rate to be agreed that is likely to prove acceptable to other subscribing underwriters the lead underwriter, or 'leader', must have the confidence of other underwriters. To know which leader to approach first is an important part of the Lloyd's broker's expertise, though it does not follow that the first underwriter approached will necessarily lead the slip. Clearly where high amounts are required to be insured, and a large number of syndicates have to be involved, there is less opportunity for competition. For smaller risks the broker may find a keener rate or better terms by shopping around. The lead underwriter is not necessarily the one who can write the biggest line, though normally he will write a substantial line.

Negotiating methods

A good broker needs to be a good negotiator. Tenacity is required but not to such a point as will prevent conclusion of the business. The aim is to bring the discussion to such a successful conclusion that both the underwriter and the broker together with his client are reasonably satisfied that the best possible arrangements have been made. There are times when a Lloyd's broker needs to obtain almost unfairly competitive terms. A co-operative underwriter may provide these, so long as there is a bulk of business which has been concluded at sensible rates.

Completing the insurance

After obtaining a lead (which may be for only a small percentage), the broker needs to complete the placement. It may be that the risk can be placed using only Lloyd's underwriters, but sometimes the size of the exposure may necessitate the use of insurance companies in London or even overseas.

Binding authorities and line slips

A binding authority or a 'cover' provides the cover holder with authority to accept risks within the limits and terms set out. The broking operation here is to negotiate the binding authority, the limits and the terms agreed. No reference is required to the underwriters once the arrangement has been set up though the binding authority will need to be renewed annually.

Line slips, on the other hand, do not give full authority to the cover holder. If a risk is to be placed under a line slip, it is normal that the two or three lead underwriters have to be seen, and they have to accept the risk and its terms and conditions. The remaining underwriters, however, abide by their agreement under the line slip for their stated proportion.

Completion of the risk

Once an underwriter has signed as accepting the risk from a given date, then the insurance is effective from that date. As soon as the placement is completed, the client will be advised and the slip and its documents will go through the policy issuing and accounting process.

Claims

The Lloyd's broker who has placed the risk may sometimes be required to negotiate with the underwriter regarding a claim. However, except for the very smallest broking companies, it is more usual for a special claims broker to be appointed whose sole responsibility is to deal with these items. If loss adjusters or other assessing and negotiating parties are employed by the underwriter, then it may be the broker's duty to negotiate with them as well.

DIRECT DEALING

While there is a principle that transactions have to be carried out in the Room itself there are a few exceptions to this. It would be totally impractical for Lloyd's to transact motor insurance business, particularly for individual policyholders, in this way.

Certain motor insurance syndicates have overcome this problem by allowing provincial insurance-broking firms to deal direct with them but requiring that the premium is guaranteed by a Lloyd's broking firm. Some of these syndicates have actually set up offices in provincial cities and the local insurance brokers deal direct with these offices. This method enables syndicates to compete with insurance companies having local branches.

EDUCATION AND TRAINING

There is an obvious need for care in selecting those who are authorised to conduct the actual negotiations in the Room at Lloyd's and in practice it is mainly the substitutes who carry out these negotiations. A sound knowledge of insurance law and practice is essential, and this can be obtained by working in an insurance broker's office. However, the level of knowledge and experience among substitutes often varies considerably. Lloyd's therefore requires proof of this knowledge before a substitute's ticket can be granted and a person is allowed to practise. New substitutes and principals, authorised for the first time after 1 January 1986, must now pass the Lloyd's Introductory Test (which can be prepared for by a course of formal instruction) before being granted their 'ticket'.

CONCLUSION

In a chapter of this length one can do little more than outline some of the factors that enter into insurance broking in the Room at Lloyd's. Lloyd's broking is a particularly practical matter, and to be effective in this role one requires a good basic knowledge of the insurance business, complete integrity, a pleasant manner, a perceptive approach so as to learn how to conduct oneself in the unique institution of Lloyd's, and above all a great deal of experience.

FURTHER READING

Bondi, Andrea H. and Hudson, Colin A. (eds.): *Textbook for the Lloyd's Introductory Test* (Witherby & Co. Ltd, 1986).

Carter, R. L. (ed.): *Handbook of Insurance* (with updating service), (Kluwer Publishing).

Gibb, D. E. W.: *Lloyd's of London: A study of individualism* (Corporation of Lloyd's, 1957).

CHAPTER 5

The elements and principles of insurance

P. V. SAXTON, FCII, FITD

Secretary-General, The Chartered Insurance Institute

The very words 'elements' and 'principles' sound rudimentary and simple, and do not encourage the feeling that they are worthy of any great depth of study. It is important to state at the outset of this chapter, therefore, that this is an extremely complex subject, full of pitfalls for the unwary, as many brokers down the years have found to their cost. The principles that guide the conduct of insurance have been built up over several centuries of development, by custom of trade, by statute and by case law. They are not immutable but constantly evolve to meet the perceived needs of the day.

In a single chapter it is possible only to take a superficial view of all the facets of the subject. Much further study would be necessary to comprehend it to the extent required by the professional broker. It is hoped that this will serve as an introduction for those who wish to know more and as a useful summary of the important issues which form the foundation of our business.

THE NATURE OF INSURANCE

The need for insurance arises out of the risks we all run in the course of living. Our lives are constantly in danger through accident or illness; our property may be subject to loss or damage, while losses incurred by others may affect us in some way or another. We also run the risk of causing injury or damage to other people or their property at a subsequent heavy cost to ourselves.

There is thus a constant striving for security, for some means of eliminating a risk, reducing it or transferring it to someone or something better able to bear it. This becomes a matter of growing importance as economic life develops because of the increasingly onerous burden of risk.

In ancient times, individual possessions were meagre, trade was by simple barter, and life, being 'nasty, brutish and short', was not held to be of any great value. The growth of commerce and industry, plus the introduction of money as a means of exchange, led over the centuries to a more complicated society in which losses not only were more severe in their impact but also became measurable and capable of evaluation. The early merchants could attempt to protect their property by guarding it against robbers, while ships could hug the coastline to avoid the greater perils of the sea, but it was impossible to provide complete protection and so some method of replacing lost goods at least in financial terms was sought.

Of course, traders could build up reserve funds for that purpose, but that would tie up capital which could be used more productively in the business itself, while the sums required might be enormous in the case of a major catastrophe. Again, it would be essential to have several years of successful and trouble-free trading to build up sufficient reserves, so that new entrants to business would be at a disadvantage and initiative would be stifled.

The answer was for merchants to pool their resources to provide central funds out of which losses could be met without disastrous effects upon any one contributor. In time some merchants became particularly interested and skilled in this new area of business and dropped their other occupations to become professional acceptors of risks. Gradually they acquired an understanding of classes of trade and the hazards involved so that they were able to assess the risks inherent in a particular venture and decide what contribution it should make on an equitable basis to the central fund.

There was, as there still is, plenty of scope for individual opinion, expertise and portfolio development in risk assessment. It was not long, therefore, before intermediaries appeared to act as a link between merchants and insurers.

From this it will be clearly seen that the introduction of insurance was absolutely vital in the development of trade as a means of transferring risk. Over the years the insurance industry has also played its part in risk reduction and elimination. By increasing premium rates, imposing excesses or asking an insured to carry a part of a risk himself, it has encouraged the improvement of 'poor' risks. The use of trained surveyors to inspect properties proposed for insurance has also resulted in many recommendations for increased security provisions and better fire protection systems. The inspection services provided by engineering offices reduce the chances of loss or damage. In a more general sense, leaflets and films produced on a range of topics by the insurance associations help to educate the public to be aware of the existence of hazards, especially in the home. A Swiss company even sponsors keep-fit facilities as an encouragement to better health. Insurance-financed research, such as at the Motor Vehicle Research and Repair Centre at Thatcham, sponsored by the Association of British Insurers, affects the design and the repair of cars.

Risk management forms the subject of Chapter 11, but it is worth pointing out here that some insurers and brokers have created risk management organisations to assist clients in reducing and preventing hazards.

Although the development of insurance was furthered mainly by the desire to cover property lost at sea, in time fire insurance, life assurance and a whole range of other classes were introduced to meet the needs of the day. These, as they exist now, are dealt with extensively in Chapters 6 to 10 so that it is necessary here only to state that the insurance market has always been ready to meet and provide cover for new risks. In recent times, much greater insurance capacity has had to be found owing to the introduction of huge values for such symbols of modern technology as the jumbo jet and the supertanker, the phenomenal growth in liability risks through, for instance, nuclear power stations or pharmaceutical manufacture, and the effects of natural disasters such as earthquakes and typhoons on developed communities. This has greatly accelerated the development of the reinsurance market as a back-up to direct insurers as has the increasing nationalism of countries which see insurance funds as a prime national asset and restrict their exportation by foreign insurers. It has also led to a need for highly qualified brokers to deal between clients and insurers, and insurers and reinsurers. The modern worldwide insurance market is thus an immense and complex industry, without which modern life would hardly be possible. Its value to the community can be summed up as follows:

1. It spreads the cost of losses over all those exposed to risk, rather than those who actually suffer loss, thus providing security for minimal cost.
2. It reduces the need for individual reserve funds, thus freeing capital for productive use.
3. From its own accumulated funds it provides investment capital for governments and industry.
4. It encourages loss-prevention activities, thus helping to create a safer society.
5. The UK insurance market, in particular, gains about 70 per cent of its non-life business from abroad so that it is a valuable 'invisible' exporter.

RESERVES AND PROVISIONS

The accumulation of reserves is necessary in insurance to provide for future claims, especially catastrophes. In life assurance, under the level premium system, reserves are built up in the early years to meet the accrued liabilities in later years. In addition, as many life contracts include an investment element, reserves need to be invested wisely to secure a good return on policyholders' money. In marine insurance a three-year account basis is operated and the balance of premiums is put into reserve in each of the first two years.

Over the years, insurers accumulate hidden reserves, which do not appear in their balance sheets, usually created by the cautious valuation of assets, such as property.

A provision is an amount set aside to meet a known commitment or liability such as outstanding claims, which can be estimated, or unexpired risk where the end of the accounting year does not accord with a policy year.

All these reserves and provisions are invested to increase income at as high a yield as is compatible with maximum security over a wide spread of government stocks, equities and property.

INSURANCE AND THE STATE

Not everyone sees insurance purely as a factor for good. Failures of insurers over the years have, in particular, suggested to many people that individual clients need protection *against* insurers, or rather, against unscrupulous people who might be using insurance for their own ends. In addition, because insurance policies are complicated documents with a quota of 'small print', it has been felt that lay people need help in maintaining their rights under insurance contracts.

Most countries in the world have, therefore, made strict regulations about the control and conduct of insurance business, covering essentially the qualifications of people operating the business, its continuing solvency, the investment of funds, the publication and authorisation of its accounts, and provisions for action by government agencies if the business fails in any of these respects.

In the past the United Kingdom has been fairly relaxed in its controls, but these were tightened up considerably in the Companies Act 1967 and later Acts leading to the Insurance Companies Act 1982, which consolidated previous legislation, while the insurance directives of the European Community are importing new controls. The Insurance Brokers (Registration) Act 1977 was another part of the continuing effect of governmental actions upon commercial life. However, most other countries still have much stricter controls, particularly in terms of ownership of companies, separation of classes of business, investment regulations and inspection procedures.

The State is often, too, a direct competitor with the commercial insurance market. In many countries the only insurer is the State-owned company, while in others the State has majority shareholdings in at least the leading insurers. Some classes of insurance may have been taken over by governments, such as employer's liability or motor insurance, on the basis that injured persons must be recompensed. An alternative solution to that problem is the imposition of strict liability for some forms of accidents. Most governments are sole providers of social security benefits and, increasingly, of pensions. The industry can in most cases operate quite well in tandem with governments. But it must be free to transfer funds over national borders if it is to deal with international catastrophes, and this is often resisted. It must also have some freedom of investment or policyholders' security might be endangered.

'Protection' of the public takes other forms, such as the insurance ombudsman, who deals with complaints against insurers, and the attitude of some courts that they must lean towards policyholders in making decisions because they are opposed by the might of great financial institutions. Other aspects of this subject will be discussed later, but it will be seen from this that as the holder of funds in trust to meet claims the insurance industry must be scrupulously honest and fair in its dealings with the public. Whether it should be generous is open to question as a generous settlement in one case might be said to reduce the funds available in others. On the other hand, it might maintain or increase business to the benefit of all. The treatment of claims has therefore become a fruitful source of argument between brokers and insurers.

In any event most qualified observers see governments playing an ever stronger role in insurance in the future. The old UK maxim was 'Freedom with publicity'. In future it is likely to be less and less freedom with more and more publicity.

THE MARKET

The UK insurance market consists of buyers, sellers and intermediaries. The public are the buyers and may be individuals or corporations across the spectrum of human endeavour. The insurers, as sellers, and the intermediaries fall into narrower categories and can be catalogued as follows.

Insurers

Lloyd's
Lloyd's professional underwriters operate as individuals, writing business on behalf of their fellow non-professional underwriters in syndicates. Most syndicates specialise in one class of business, e.g. marine or motor, though they often combine allied classes. The Corporation of Lloyd's provides the physical facilities and back-up services, together with the regulations by which business is conducted. Some special features to be particularly noted about Lloyd's are the following:
1. The liability of underwriters is personal and unlimited.
2. The public cannot deal directly with underwriters but only through accredited Lloyd's brokers.
3. Underwriters cannot write long-term business so that no life business other than term assurance can be placed at Lloyd's.

Lloyd's is a unique insurance institution providing enormous flexibility and capacity. It has been a major factor in the development of London as the international centre of insurance. Its success has prompted the establishment of rivals such as the New York Insurance Exchange, formed in 1979, and others in America.

Companies

Companies may be divided firstly into proprietary (i.e. owned by shareholders) and mutual (usually owned by the policyholders). Most are incorporated with limited liability under the Companies Acts, but a few older offices were established by Royal Charter or by special Acts of Parliament. They may be further divided into the following categories:

1. *Composite offices.* A composite office is a company that transacts more than one major class of business. The great UK insurance companies are all composites and transact all the major classes. This differs from some other countries where regulations forbid, for example, the acceptance of long-term business by a company that also deals in short-term insurances. This view largely prevails in Europe and has been carried into European Community insurance directives, so that, although existing UK composites may continue to exist in future with stringent rules as to the internal separation of certain classes of business, it is unlikely that the formation of new composites covering all classes will be permitted. The position so far as the EEC is concerned will become clear when the provisions of the Life Establishment Directive of March 1979 are reviewed, which is scheduled for 1989.

2. *Specialist offices.* These concentrate on one major class, such as life, marine, aviation, engineering, credit or contract guarantee. Outside the life field, in which there are a number of large independent companies, most specialist companies are owned by composites.

3. *Mutual indemnity associations.* Such associations have been formed by specific trades to cover their special risks, such as the protection and indemnity clubs set up on a mutual basis by shipowners to cover risks excluded from, or only partially covered by, standard marine policies.

4. *Friendly societies.* These are mutual companies set up to transact industrial life (often called 'home service') assurance.

Intermediaries

Many companies deal directly with the public through their own selling force, who may be variously called 'inspectors', 'agents', 'collectors' or 'representatives'. Only a few refuse to deal with outside intermediaries, and these are always specialist offices.

Insurance brokers

The brokers are the full-time specialists in arranging insurance business. Under registration provisions the name 'insurance broker' is reserved for those with the competence, financial solidity and ethical standards to be registered by the Insurance Brokers Registration Council. They may be very large international companies or tiny firms, but they must be qualified to give advice to clients and place business on an independent basis.

Lloyd's brokers

These are insurance brokers who have been accredited by the Committee of Lloyd's to place business with Lloyd's underwriters.

Consultants

In the past it was fashionable among some intermediaries, particularly in the life field, to describe themselves as insurance consultants in the belief that this gave them a higher standing with the public than brokers. Now the term is more widely used by those independent intermediaries who do not wish to, or may not be able to, register under the Act as brokers.

Agents

In the main, these are people with a full-time occupation outside insurance, such as solicitors, accountants, estate agents or garage owners, who are in a position to influence the placing of insurance business by their clients or customers. They usually introduce business to one or more companies with whom they have agency agreements. Unlike brokers they do not normally possess particular insurance expertise.

Sometimes an agent may be concerned only with the insurances of his own organisation, in which case he is referred to as an 'own-case agent'. This is in fact merely a form of rebated commission to a client, and though it is allowed in the United Kingdom it is an illegal practice in some other countries.

Market associations

It is impossible to describe all the associations in the insurance market in this chapter. Some of the more important bodies are the following:

The Association of British Insurers

The ABI exists for the protection, promotion and advancement of the common interests of member companies. It acts as a channel of communication between them and the government or any other bodies; engages in general public relations work; deals with complaints against members by the public; liaises between insurance and education bodies; compiles central statistics; and conducts research.

The Association was established in July 1985 to combine the functions of the old British Insurance Association, the Life Offices, Industrial Life Offices and Accident Offices Associations and some functions of the old Fire Offices Committee. This rationalisation enables general features of the work of the previously separate bodies to be handled centrally, while specialist committees deal with technical matters in the various fields of insurance.

The Loss Prevention Council

This body was also established in July 1985 to combine the work of the Fire Protection Association, the technical department of the Fire Offices Committee, the Insurance Technical Bureau and the Fire Insurance Research Technical Organisation, all in the cause of reducing loss of life and property by fire.

The Reinsurance Offices Association

The ROA performs functions similar to those of the ABI for its members, having regard to the special needs of reinsurers. Because of the nature of reinsurance, it has an international membership.

The Motor Insurers' Bureau

The MIB is an association of all motor insurers, formed to provide compensation for victims of road accidents in cases where motor insurance does not cover the loss. As a member of the European Council of Bureaux it issues the international motor insurance cards, known as 'green cards', which allow the passage of vehicles from one country to another. Although not so vital nowadays for travel in the EEC, they are still useful as evidence of cover.

The Institute of London Underwriters

The ILU promotes and protects the interests of company marine underwriters. It also provides the secretariat for the joint commit-

tee with Lloyd's Underwriters' Association. It has produced hull
and cargo clauses which are used by the whole marine market. Its
policy department arranges for the signing of combined policies
on behalf of members and checks additional premiums and returns.

The British Insurance Brokers' Association

The BIBA brought together the former four main broking bodies
into one professional organisation for insurance brokers. It
operates a central negotiating service with government, companies and other agencies and provides a focal point for broker
training, information and other services. Its regional committees
cover all the United Kingdom.

The Chartered Insurance Institute

The CII is the main educational and professional body for
insurance. Its qualifying examinations lead to the diplomas of
ACII and FCII. It has an extensive library, produces its own
publications and conducts careers work on behalf of the industry
in schools, colleges and universities. Its College of Insurance
conducts training courses for trainees sponsored by insurance
employers, while its Tuition Service provides a full correspondence course system of study for its examinations.

Local Institutes exist in most towns and cities in the United
Kingdom. The benevolent work of the CII is achieved through
the insurance charities.

THE PRINCIPLES OF INSURANCE

The general law of contract applies to a contract between an
insurer and the insured, and this can be summarised as follows:

1. *Offer and acceptance*. There must be an offer which is unequivo-
   cally accepted by the other party. In insurance the proposer
   makes an offer to the insurer which the latter either accepts or
   rejects. The parties must be in agreement as to the intention of
   the contract.
2. *Intention*. There must be an intention to enter into a legal
   relationship under which both parties have a legal obligation
   to perform the contract.
3. *Consideration*. There must be some payment, right or benefit
   granted by the parties to a contract. The premium forms the
   policyholder's consideration in return for the insurer's
   promise to pay according to the terms of the policy.

4. *Capacity*. The parties must be legally capable of entering into a contract.
5. *Legality*. The object of the contract must be lawful.

In addition there are special principles which relate to contracts of insurance, namely, utmost good faith, insurable interest, indemnity, subrogation and contribution. The principle of proximate cause applies when claims are made.

Utmost good faith

An insurance contract is founded on trust and is therefore subject to the rule of 'utmost good faith' as distinct from the normal contract rule of 'let the buyer beware'. Both of these rules have been criticised from time to time as it is felt that they are unfair to the consumer. Hence the protection given to the purchaser of goods under the Misrepresentation Act 1967 and other legislation.

Utmost good faith applies to insurance because the proposer is deemed to know all the facts about the risk being proposed whereas the insurer may have only general or statistical knowledge on which to base his acceptance or rejection. The rule therefore puts the onus on the proposer to declare all the material facts known to him about the risk before the contract is concluded. This duty exists not only at inception but also at each renewal except in the case of life assurance.

What is material has been defined as 'every circumstance . . . which would influence the judgement of a prudent insurer in fixing the premium, or determining whether he will take the risk' (Marine Insurance Act 1906). Facts that need not be disclosed are those that:

(a) lessen the risk;
(b) are inferred by insurers, usually because they are normally associated with the type of risk proposed;
(c) are public knowledge or should be known by the insurer in the ordinary course of business;
(d) are matters of law;
(e) are possible of discovery where the insurer has been put on enquiry;
(f) insurers have waived information about;
(g) are unnecessary because of a warranty;
(h) are offences which are 'spent' by virtue of the Rehabilitation of Offenders Act 1974.

Where a proposal form has been completed, the proposer cannot rely upon a question not having been asked to render it immaterial. The position of an intermediary in relation to information supplied to an insurer is complex, but he is usually reckoned to be the agent of the insured in this respect. Brokers have been found liable to their clients for unpaid claims arising from non-disclosure because they failed to ask specific questions relating to the insurance cover required.

A proposer may therefore be in breach of the duty of utmost good faith by:

(a) *concealment*: i.e. deliberately concealing a material fact;
(b) *non-disclosure*: failing to disclose a material fact either inadvertently or because it was not thought to be material;
(c) *fraudulent misrepresentation*: making a statement known to be false with the intention of deceiving an insurer;
(d) *innocent misrepresentation*: making an inaccurate statement of fact but without fraudulent intent because it was believed to be true.

In all these cases, if the contract has been effected, the insurer can avoid the policy and repudiate liability from inception.

In most cases, of course, insurers would take this extreme step only if they had good reasons to suspect fraud or a deliberate attempt to mislead. However, a report (No. 104) published in 1980 by the Law Commission suggested that the law was in need of reform and that the proposer should have to disclose only those facts which 'a reasonable man in his circumstances' would consider to be material. Where there is a proposal form he should have to answer only the questions on the form, provided that he does not deliberately conceal facts which he knows to be material although they are outside the scope of the questions asked.

A draft EEC directive on the co-ordination of insurance law proposes less fundamental changes to the proposer's duty of disclosure but suggests that the insurer's remedy to its breach should lie in the 'proportional' rule used by some other European countries, whereby for example in the case of a claim the insurer pays only a proportion based on the premium he actually received compared with what he would have charged had he known all the facts.

The Law Commission report also criticised insurers' rights to repudiate liability based upon breaches of all warranties. A warranty is a further duty accepted by the insured in connection with the policy which may be 'expressed' in writing or 'implied' if it is implicit in the contract. The breach of a warranty should in the Commission's view lead to repudiation only if it is material to the risk.

Naturally, the insurance market strongly defended the present system, especially as the associations have produced statements of practice relating to insurers' rights of repudiating liability which showed that this would never be done unreasonably. The BIBA, however, supported some of the Commission's arguments in relation to the need for reforming proposal forms, the need for renewal notices to contain a warning about the duty of disclosure and the materiality of warranties. The government, having made some progress towards drafting a bill, has now dropped the idea in favour of more stringent statements of practice which were issued by the insurers' Associations in January 1986.

Insurable interest

Insurance contracts are enforceable at law because the insured must have an insurable interest in the subject matter of the insurance. For this to exist there must be:
(a) property, rights, interest, life or limb or potential liability capable of being insured and which is in fact the subject matter of the insurance;
(b) a legally recognisable relationship between the insured and the subject matter from which he gains benefit or might suffer loss;
(c) a monetary value to the relationship;
(d) a real interest and not merely an expectation.
The rule differs according to the type of insurance effected. In fire and accident insurance, policies cannot be assigned and so the interest must exist at inception and at the time of loss. In life assurance insurable interest is necessary only at inception, whereas in marine insurance the interest need exist only at the time of loss.

The basic statutes establishing the rule of insurable interest are the Life Assurance Act 1774, the Gaming Act 1845 (for goods and merchandise) and the Marine Insurance Act 1906, although there are a number of other statutes which create insurable interest in specific circumstances.

It is important to distinguish between the subject matter of the insurance, which is the property or the event at risk, and the subject matter of the contract, which is the interest the insured has, since insurance cannot protect property but only the insured's interest by providing money, repair, replacement or reinstatement.

Indemnity

An insurer promises to make good an insured's losses within the limit of the sum insured, thus placing the insured as nearly as possible in the same position financially after the loss as he was before. This principle does not apply to life assurance or personal accident insurance as loss of life or limb cannot be assessed in such monetary terms. The principle was originally established to avoid the temptation to the insured of bringing about the event insured against in the hope of securing a financial gain. It has, however, been relaxed in modern inflationary times by 'new for old' clauses in some household and motor policies whereby insurers will replace objects up to a certain age by new items without asking for a contribution towards the cost from the insured.

Indemnity may be provided by a cash payment or by repair (usual in motor claims), replacement (of goods or glass) or reinstatement (especially of buildings or equipment).

Insurers often face under-insurance by policyholders and to maintain the principle of indemnity insert an 'average' clause into their policies. This simply provides that in the event of loss the amount paid will be in the same proportion as the sum insured is to the full value of the property covered.

Subrogation

As a corollary of the principle of indemnity, insurers have a common law right, after payment of a loss, to assume all the rights and remedies of the insured in order to reduce or extinguish their loss. The subrogation condition in most fire and accident policies extends this right to insurers before the claim is paid.

Contribution

Contribution operates in contracts of indemnity where two or more policies are in force at the time of loss, covering the same subject matter, the same insurable interest and the same perils. In these circumstances the insured may recover his loss from one insurer who then has to call upon the others for their proportions. The contribution condition in policies varies this position by forcing the insured to claim from all the insurers involved their rateable proportion of the loss.

Proximate cause

Not all losses sustained by an insured are covered by his insurance policy. Some are outside the scope of the wording, while others may be specifically excluded or 'excepted', such as war risks. In some cases there may be doubt as to whether the loss was caused by an insured peril or not and in these cases the insurer must be satisfied that the dominant effective cause comes within the terms of the policy.

The principle of proximate cause is, in effect, that the loss must arise directly from an insured peril, or be the result of a direct chain of events begun by an insured peril. It is the 'chain of events' that sometimes causes problems, as the intervention of new factors into the chain may give rise to doubts as to the actual eventual cause of loss. A fire in a ship may not have caused it to sink except for a subsequent storm, for example. If the first or intervening factor is not an insured peril, it may be that insurers may avoid liability or have only partial liability according to the facts, which may ultimately have to be decided by the courts.

The proposal and policy

Most personal business and much commercial business is underwritten on the basis of information supplied on a proposal form. The information forms the basis of the contract and is often incorporated into it by specific reference in the recital clause of a policy. The completed form is useful as a record of the risk and as a basis for statistics. Invariably it contains a declaration to be signed by the proposer warranting that all the answers given are true. The use of 'slips' instead of proposal forms is of course common in marine, aviation and transport business and other large risks but they give only abbreviated information which must be supported by all the material facts.

The policy is evidence of the insurance contract, although, as an insurance contract can be based on oral agreement (with certain exceptions – guarantee, marine and motor vehicle – by statutes), it is not the contract itself. However, as the policy describes the parties, the subject matter, the consideration, the events leading to compensation, and any special regulations and conditions applying to the contract, it is vitally important. In the case of disagreement, the terms of the policy may be subject to interpretation by the courts. The terms used to distinguish the sections of a policy are as follows:

1. *Recital clause*: setting out the parties, the period of cover and other details.
2. *Operative clause*: setting out the scope of the cover and specific exceptions. This may be divided into sections if more than one type of cover is included.
3. *Attestation clause*: authorising the policy by the signature of the underwriter or other senior official.
4. *General exceptions*: setting out the general exceptions to the cover provided.
5. *Conditions*: listing express conditions in order to define or limit the contract (such as the procedure to be followed in making a claim or altering the contract).

Policy wordings are often complex and difficult for the layman to comprehend. Insurers often issue with the policy a statement of cover in plain language to assist policyholders to understand the insurance protection provided, but these summaries do not cover everything in the policy. Some insurers have, therefore, tried to simplify the wordings themselves. There are dangers in this area since the traditional wordings have been tried and tested in the courts, whereas simplified translations are unproved and may import areas of uncertainty as to the cover provided. Nevertheless, the experiments are a welcome sign that insurance is not wedded to the past, but that in both principle and practice it is constantly developing to serve the community more effectively. This is part of the fascination of the business for all who work in it.

FURTHER READING

Cockerell, H. A. L.: *Teach Yourself Insurance*, fourth edition (Hodder & Stoughton, 1980).

Hansell, D. S.: *Elements of Insurance*, fifth edition (Macdonald & Evans, 1985).

Steele, John T.: *Principles and Practice of Insurance* (CII, 1984).

CHAPTER 6

Insurances of the person

JOHN H. S. CHALMERS, BSc, FCII, FLIA
Principal, Chalmers Insurance Brokers

Revised by Leslie J. Goman
Life & Pensions Director, Wadmans Insurance Ltd

and Brian R. Booth, MA, FCII
Director, Brookhouse Insurance Brokers Ltd

From the broker's point of view, insurances of the person require a totally different approach to clients from that adopted in respect of general insurances. The latter are partly compulsory by law and when not compulsory are readily recognised by clients as a necessary part of private and business life. This is not so with insurances of the person. People do not readily admit the important part played in financial planning by life assurance. Many individuals are initially reluctant to consider the possibility of their early death. The broker is in a unique position to be able to cater for his clients, for as an agent of several insurance companies he can offer an extensive range of contracts.

In the space of one chapter it is impossible to do more than indicate the importance of this subject. It should be stressed that this is not a technical exposition and is not intended to do more than provide basic information. The chapter will outline the main types of life assurance contract and suggest some uses for them and the opportunities that they present to the broker. There is in addition reference to personal pensions, permanent health insurance and accident insurance.

TYPES OF CONTRACT

Outlined below are the basic types of contract. Space does not allow for more than brief comment.

Term assurances

Level term assurance
Details of the contract are as follows:

Cover	For a fixed term, e.g. 1 year, 10 years, 15 years
Premium	Payable throughout the term; amount of premium depends on the length of the term: the *longer* the term the *higher* the premium
Sum assured	Payable on death within the specified term
Surrender value	Not available
Paid-up policy	Not available

In general this contract is used to meet very specific requirements, whenever cover is needed for a known term and whenever all that is required is pure life cover. The following instances may serve to demonstrate:

1. *Covering a life for the duration of a loan.* It is normal for lending institutions to insist on life cover during the currency of a loan. The requirement here is normally for the cheapest form of cover available. Level term assurance is usually the solution.
2. *Key man insurance.* This cover is often effected by a company or firm which relies heavily on the skill and services of certain individuals. If the company stands to suffer financial hardship on the death of such people, it can effect a life assurance policy on their lives. The proceeds of such a policy will alleviate the hardship. Again the least expensive policy is ordinary term.

It should be noted that many offices have special rates of premium on sums assured in excess of £50,000.

Convertible term assurance
This is a much commoner contract than level term. The contract is basically the same but has a built-in option to convert part or all of the amount payable to other types of assurance contract (e.g. whole life or endowment assurance), and in some cases to a new term assurance policy, without medical evidence, during the currency of the contract.

This option has two important implications for the broker:

1. The underwriting will be more stringent than for ordinary term – the company has to be prepared for a considerable extension of the original term. This increases the possibility of medical examination and hence extra administration.
2. On the credit side it produces a future further sale for the

broker. It is imperative that a broker keeps track of his clients who effect convertible term, because in theory at least these contracts will be converted in the future. On conversion the broker will of course earn further commission.

Renewable convertible term
This is generally a five- or ten-year convertible term policy with the option to renew at the end of the term for a further five- or ten-year term plus an option to convert the policy at any time to a whole life, endownment or term assurance.

Increasing term assurance
This type of policy is a useful hedge against inflation. It provides an increasing death benefit which is chosen by the assured when the policy is arranged. The premium which is fixed at the commencement of the policy is naturally higher than for level term assurance. The plan can include an option to renew or convert all or part of the policy to a whole life, endowment or term assurance, and this type of policy is becoming increasingly popular.

There are many occasions when convertible term assurance can be sold either on its own or as an additional rider to another policy. In general the inexpensive nature of the cover provided, coupled with the right to convert during the term without medical evidence, makes it an ideal contract for everyone who needs protection.

The broker should always be alert to occasions on which to sell this inexpensive cover. There are very few clients who would not benefit from such a contract. In small brokerages, which perhaps gain the majority of their earnings from motor and small general risks such as shops and small businesses, it would be prudent to approach such clients with a view to effecting this cover. It is ideal for young persons who need protection and yet cannot afford too high a premium, but who will require whole life or endowment assurance at a later date. This policy guarantees future assurability regardless of state of health. Further, it is prudent to sell convertible term on top of other contracts which may be for a specific use, as in house purchase.

Family income benefit
Details of the contract are as follows:

Cover	For a fixed term, e.g. 10 years, 15 years
Premium	Payable throughout the term
Benefit	Payable only on death within the fixed term; the income continues until the end of the term; when the term expires so does the income
Surrender value	Not available
Paid-up policy	Not available
Conversion	With certain companies this temporary assurance is convertible in the same way as convertible term; policies may also include an increasable benefit
Tax	According to present Inland Revenue practice the income would be regarded as instalments of capital and would not be taxable

As the name implies, the purpose of this policy is to provide an *income* for the family on the death of the breadwinner, although they are also issued on a joint life basis. It is normal to set the level of benefit and term to correspond with:

(a) income required for the family to live;

(b) the number of years required for the youngest child to be independent of the remaining parent.

It is often assumed that this policy should be written only on a father's life, but it should be kept in mind as an ideal vehicle for providing extra income to the father on the early death of the mother. This income could help a father to provide housekeeping and child-minding help until the children were old enough to no longer require such close care.

There are very few occasions when family income benefit cannot be justified as part of a personal insurance portfolio.

Decreasing term
This is a type of term assurance where the sum assured decreases at intervals – normally annually. It is ideal for protecting a mortgage where the debt outstanding decreases every year.

Joint lives
Term assurance policies may be effected on two lives with the sum assured payable on the first or second death.

Non-smokers
In recognition of the lower mortality experienced generally by the non-smoker, a discount is given by many assurers. To be a

non-smoker the proposer(s) must not have smoked any cigarettes in the past 12 months and have no intention of smoking cigarettes in the future.

Term assurance policies effected under s.226a of the ICTA 1970
These policies are available to individuals who are not members of a pension arrangement, or whose arrangement does not include a lump-sum death-in-service benefit. The premium for these policies must not exceed 5 per cent of earnings.

Trust policies
To write term assurance policies under trust is a practical way to mitigate inheritance tax.

Waiver of premium
This benefit provides that in the event of the life assured being disabled for a continuous period exceeding six months, any premium falling due after that six months will be waived while disablement continues.

With-profits assurances

Life assurance companies periodically value their life funds with a view to calculating how much surplus can be distributed to the with-profits policyholders. The surplus is usually allocated in the form of bonuses expressed as a percentage of the sum assured. Once applied these bonuses are guaranteed. For example, a bonus rate of 4 per cent means that the holder of a £10,000 with-profits policy can expect an addition of £400 profits to his policy in the first year. If the bonus rate is simple, the second year will produce a further £400 and so on. If the bonus rate is compound, the bonus rate per cent applies to sum assured plus profits. In the example quoted the second year's profits would be 4 per cent of £10,400 = £416.

In addition to the bonuses described above – the reversionary bonus – many companies now pay terminal bonuses. This arises because the reversionary bonus system does not really reflect investment performance directly but rather the amount of surplus which the actuary feels can be safely distributed. In the face of competition from unit-linked companies the traditional companies have introduced a terminal bonus which is applied as a once-only payment on maturation.

Unlike reversionary bonuses, the rate of which does not vary greatly (in fact historically it has been rising gradually over the years), the terminal bonus is usually an annual declaration which can fluctuate widely from one year to another depending on investment conditions.

Unit-linked assurances

Life assurance policies can be linked to unitised funds. These funds may or may not be authorised unit trusts. As each premium is paid, part of the premium buys life cover (decreasing term), part buys units in the fund and part is taken to meet company expenses. As the years go on, the policyholder amasses a large number of units.

The value of these units fluctuates in accordance with the values of the underlying securities. When unit price is low, more units can be purchased for a given premium than when it is high. When the unit price rises, so does the value of the units purchased previously. Thus the unit-linked policy can reflect directly the value of the client's investment.

The biggest disadvantage of this type of policy lies in the fact that if the value of the securities underlying the fund is low at maturity, then the benefit could be substantially reduced. This is overcome by leaving the maturity date 'open', which allows the investor to choose the date of maturity to coincide with a high unit price.

Permanent insurances

Whole life assurance
Details of the contract are as follows:

Cover	For the whole of one's life; this is a permanent protection policy
Premium	Payable for the whole of one's life *or* for a restricted number of years
Benefit	Payable only on death; the policy may be with or without profits or unit-linked
Surrender value	Available subject to conditions laid down by particular company, usually applicable after one or two years.
Paid-up policy	Normally available subject to conditions laid down by particular company after one or two years

Whole life assurance is a contract which should be effected by every person. It is primarily a protection policy. As seen above, it has an advantage over other types of protection policy: the protection lasts throughout life. This means that the benefit is always paid on death.

Whole life assurance lends itself to certain situations, such as the following:

1. *Mitigation of inheritance tax.* Where inheritance tax will become payable on death it is prudent for a broker to advise his client to effect a whole life policy to meet, wholly or partly, the likely tax liability. There are many possible variations depending on the client's wishes and intentions regarding the disposal of his estate. It is common for whole life policies to be written on a joint life basis, on either first death or last survivor basis depending on the individual requirement.

2. *Partnership assurance and share purchase assurance.* In partnerships and private limited companies a serious problem can arise on the premature death of a partner or shareholder. Life assurance arrangements can obviously alleviate this situation by providing money to allow the remaining partners or shareholders to purchase the holding of their deceased colleague. Whole life assurance provides the answer.

By way of cautionary advice, these two subjects are highly technical and it is imperative that great care is taken when advising clients in these cases.

Flexible whole life assurance

This is a unit-linked assurance policy which gives the proposer the freedom to select any level of guaranteed death benefit to suit his/her personal circumstances. Naturally the higher the level of guaranteed death benefit the higher will be the monthly deduction from the unit holding necessary to cover the risk. The plan normally includes options to increase the guaranteed death benefit without further medical evidence.

Endowment assurances

Details of the contract are as follows:

Cover	Normally for a fixed term (except for flexible endowments)
Premium	(a) Payable for the whole of the term
	(b) More expensive than whole life or term per £1,000 sum assured
	(c) The size of the premium depends on the length of the term. The *longer* the term the *smaller* the premium payable for any given sum assured

Benefit	Payable on death or expiry of term; the policy may be with or without profits or unit-linked
Surrender value	Available subject to conditions laid down by particular company, usually after one or two years
Paid-up policy	Normally available subject to conditions laid down by particular company, usually after one or two years

Endowment assurances are really savings plans. The basic contract is outlined above, but there are many variations too numerous to describe in this section. Endowment assurances can be unit-linked or with-profits. Numerous arguments rage – and the reader is encouraged to acquaint himself with these arguments – as to the relative merits of unit-linked and with-profits plans.

One thing is clear, however. The introduction of unit-linked endowments with their open-ended choice of maturity date (after ten years) and relatively high surrender values has forced the 'traditional' offices to introduce flexible endowments. These are contracts which can be matured any time after ten years and will produce a benefit very similar to what would have been gained by initially effecting a fixed-term endowment.

Some offices reluctant to introduce the flexible endowment do offer, for a very small extra premium, early maturity options, normally operable after two-thirds of the term.

From the broker's point of view, the flexible endowment and the unit-linked endowment will often be the best recommendation to the average client rather than fixed-term policies. This is notwithstanding particular situations where fixed-term policies are essential.

Two uses of endowment assurances are as follows:

1. *House purchase.* Endowment assurance policies can be used as security against a building society loan. Endowment mortgages of this type present certain advantages. This is not the place to enlarge on the technical aspects of the subject but rather to indicate the importance of this use of endowment policies. It should, however, be noted that when compared with other methods of house purchase, the endowment method can be the most expensive. This has prompted the assurance companies to market a policy referred to as a low-cost endowment, a combination of endowment and reducing term assurance. This plan compares very favourably with the building society repayment method, incorporating a mortgage protection policy, and is the plan most favoured.

At some time or other a large number of brokers' clients will consider house purchase. This presents the alert broker with an invaluable opportunity to sell life assurance. Where larger mortgages are required, it is often necessary to arrange a 'top-up' mortgage facility in addition to that offered by a building society. There are several life assurance companies that are willing to lend money for this purpose and the broker should acquaint himself with the various schemes available.

This is one occasion where little difficulty is experienced in convincing clients of the need for life assurance. It has been this writer's experience that the broker who successfully negotiates a client's mortgage has a client for life and consequently handles all that client's insurances. There are of course many brokers who specialise in this aspect of insurance.

2. *Provision of school fees*. The endowment assurance contract lends itself admirably to the provision of future school fees. There are many variations which can be employed and it is essential to know the market.

Personal pensions (s. 226 policy)

The personal pension contract is very important to the broker. It is relatively easy to interest a client in the benefits. Apart from the obvious benefit of a pension at retirement, the premiums qualify for tax relief and thus the personal pension forms an important part of tax planning.

The 1978 Finance Act allowed life offices to offer an open market option as part of the contract. This effectively means that the investment performance of the life office pension fund is the single most important consideration when choosing a company. Personal pension contracts can, like life policies, be with or without profits or be unit-linked. In addition many offices are now offering certain forms of 'guaranteed' performance.

The broker should acquaint himself fully with the various contracts on offer. Many brokers advise their clients to split their personal pension investment between with-profits policies and unit-linked policies. This provides the stability of the traditional policy with the possible high return from the unit-linked policy. It avoids the potential situation where the unit price might be depressed at retirement date and allows the pensioner to delay taking his unit-linked pension until the market has recovered.

Many unit-linked offices now allow the client to switch his investment to a cash fund a few years before retirement is planned; this obviously can overcome the eventuality of a drop in unit value. It is now very common to incorporate a waiver of premium in personal pension policies.

The contract can be marketed in tandem with general insurance business. A broker who holds the general and motor insurances for self-employed clients should consider broaching the subject of pensions with these individuals. The annual renewal nature of general insurance provides the broker with the ideal opportunity to arrange his client's pension. It is important for the broker to ascertain his client's accounting date; this will be readily available where the broker already holds liability insurances. Most clients make their contributions when they are fully aware of their earnings for the year.

In many cases this contract is the bridge between general insurances and life assurance. Once a broker is catering for his client's personal pension needs it is usually a short step to his business and personal life assurance needs.

Accident and sickness insurances and permanent health insurance

As the name implies, accident and sickness policies provide money in the event of accident or sickness. These are annual policies which can be cancelled by the insurer in the event of adverse experience. Permanent health insurance on the other hand is a non-cancellable contract which normally runs to age 60 or 65. The details of these contracts are best gained from company prospectus leaflets and technical handbooks.

The importance to the broker lies in the fact that these policies can often be sold along with and complementary to other policies. For the private individual who effects a mortgage-related endowment, for example, the permanent health policy would, in the event of permanent disablement, mean that his mortgage would be paid and he could remain in his home.

There are opportunities for group schemes since many employers recognise the goodwill they will inherit from the establishment of accident and permanent health schemes for employees.

In general there are many opportunities for brokers – if they remain alert to them – to sell this class of business.

CHOOSING THE COMPANY

There is no substitute for the broker's own experience. Before placing a risk a broker will usually obtain several quotations and proffer advice based upon these and his knowledge of the market. He will interpret the quotations, taking into account the various different ways in which they are produced.

Since 1 November 1986 the life assurance industry has had a Code of Practice covering future projections for with-profits policies. This means that the choice of product or company will be dependent upon:
(a) past performance records;
(b) financial strength of the office;
(c) expenses;
(d) service;
(e) mutuality.
The Code of Practice lays down a consistent basis for projecting future benefits based on a maximum rate of return on premiums invested of 13 per cent per annum for pension contracts and 10¾ per cent per annum for life policies.

Term assurances

Premium rate is the most crucial factor. If the client's requirement is for ordinary term assurance, then the least expensive premium available for his age will dictate the choice of company.

Medical underwriting can also be very important. If the client has an adverse medical history or current medical problems it may be necessary for the broker to effect simultaneous proposals with several companies in order to ascertain the best terms that can be obtained. Experience will tell the broker which companies are likely to give the most favourable terms.

It should be noted that acceptance terms can vary considerably from life company to life company. It has been the writer's own personal experience that certain medical conditions can lead to non-acceptance by one life office and acceptance at normal terms by another.

It is better to effect simultaneous rather than consecutive proposals as a result of a non-acceptance or imposition of special terms. This is because:
(a) it can cut down on the broker's administration;
(b) often the same doctor can simultaneously give a medical

examination to the client for all of the offices proposed;
(c) it will result in a speedier conclusion of the business;
(d) from a public relations point of view it allows the broker to impress the client with his knowledge and professionalism.

Convertible term, whole life and endowment assurances

In all of the above there are normally additional factors to consider when advising on the office with which to effect life assurance. Where the contract will always remain a non-profit contract then the same criteria which apply to the selection of an office for term assurances apply here also.

Convertible term assurance is a special case: where the insurance is being effected on its own it is essential that it is taken with an office which offers conversion into as large a variety of policies as possible. There are many offices which offer a wide range of traditional and unit-linked policies. Often, however, this does not apply as the convertible term assurance will be effected simultaneously with another contract and with the same underwriting office.

The basic criterion has to be ultimate profitability. The broker has to select the office which will eventually give his client (or his client's heirs) the best return for his money. Of course, where there is a medical problem there may be a very limited choice of company available.

'Traditional' with-profits policies

With these policies it is of the utmost importance that great care is taken when comparing life assurance companies.

Bonus rate is not a particularly good guide because of the variation in basic sum assured. In fact a company with a lower bonus rate but a higher basic sum assured could produce the better maturity value. The only acceptable comparison is one based on premium, i.e. which office gives the best value for a given amount. This is the basis of comparisons such as are found in *Planned Savings, The Economist* and *Money Management*.

In the case of with-profits policies, the very nature of the method of distributing surplus means that past performance is a fair guide to future performance (although not an infallible one). A quick glance at comparisons of past performances will show the enormous differences that exist between companies. The broker would be well advised to acquaint himself with these comparisons.

Unit-linked policies

The performance of the fund combined with an educated guess as to likely future performance is the best guide. These policies provide the choice of many funds, including with-profits, and allows switching between funds. Now that life assurance premium relief no longer applies, regular savings plans are less attractive. Many major life offices are becoming more active in the unit trust field.

The prudent broker will select an office whose management charges are lower than its competitors'. Such comparisons are available updated on an annual basis. The effect of pound-cost averaging means that variation in performance can be as important as steady growth.

Insurance for expatriates

There are several assurers which have established separate companies overseas, principally in the Isle of Man and the Channel Islands, and which market policies for expatriates. Policies are issued in several currencies and are not subject to UK tax, but are also not covered by the Policyholders Protection Act. On return to the United Kingdom the policies may be converted into sterling UK policies.

Personal pensions

This contract is one in which there are considerable variations from company to company. The broker has to be able to compare the benefits offered. Otherwise much the same criteria apply as for life assurance.

Accident and sickness insurances and permanent health insurance

Apart from premium rates there are three very important additional factors to be considered with these contracts:
1. *The definition of disablement.* Sufficient differences exist in the definitions offered by insurers that the broker must be careful

to choose the one most appropriate to his client's situation and wishes.

2. *Occupations.* It should be noted that differences do exist in the way in which insurers regard occupations. The broker should carefully select the office which offers the best terms for a given occupation or a possible future change in occupation.

3. *Geographical limits.* This could be important if a client travels extensively. Some companies place little or no restriction.

A broker can serve his clients better than any single company. No insurance company will claim to be best at all contracts and as in other areas of insurance there are 'horses for courses'. It is therefore essential that the broker understands 'form' and keeps up with the ever-changing range of contracts on offer. Wide and constant reading of the insurance press is an essential for the broker who wishes to succeed.

FURTHER READING

Three study course books issued by the Chartered Insurance Institute and updated periodically are:
Insurance of the Person.
Legal and Economic Aspects of Life Assurance.
Life Assurance Application and Underwriting.

Other useful publications are:
Gilchrist, Christopher: *How to Plan your Life Assurance* (Martin Books/ Woodhead-Faulkner, 1979).
Sell Tech (updated biannually), IETC Ltd, 246 Upper Street, London N1 1RU.

Periodicals that should be consulted regularly are:
Money Management (Fundex).
Planned Savings (Wootten Publications).
Post Magazine and Insurance Monitor (Buckley Press).
Prospect (the journal of the Life Insurance Association).

CHAPTER 7

Property and interruption insurance

GORDON J. R. HICKMOTT, MBE, FCII, FCIArb
Chairman, Trinity Insurance Co. Ltd and specialist consultant

To a modern broker the old terms 'fire insurance' and 'consequential loss insurance' are outdated. He has to face current business needs and undertake the efficient and adequate placing of covers for his client.

PROPERTY INSURANCE

The initial subdivisions of property insurance are as follows:
1. Domestic insurances.
2. Traders' and small business insurances.
3. Commercial and industrial insurances.

These are discussed in the following paragraphs.

Domestic insurances

With the non-application of a tariff to domestic insurances and the introduction of 'comprehensive' schemes by all insurers, the broker is faced with a multiplicity of slightly different policy forms with variations of words not always clearly showing the actual intention of comparative protection *vis-à-vis* more normal, traditional wordings.

Generally cost is indicative of the extent of the cover, most of which nowadays includes some 'all-risks' type of protection to some property, and the application of the 'excesses' is likely to vary also. Naturally the smaller insurance offices and Lloyd's syndicates tend to draft their schemes to the particular markets to which they have access.

Thus a broker is faced with the decision of choosing a selected few of the covers to provide adequate alternatives to his clients with their various needs, and so build up a reasonable portfolio with each to achieve a satisfactory administrative and claims association.

The problem of sufficiency of sum insured still remains a constant difficulty; indexing schemes give a crude but generally adequate solution.

Traders' and small business insurances

Today insurers provide a range of 'inclusive' or 'package' covers for the small business risks which are of sufficient number or which can be easily grouped to enable a designed form of broad coverage to be given (including liability and other classes of business).

The range of cover is wide, but with some variation between insurers. Methods of treating the interruption cover are likely to be on a formula basis in some cases (i.e. up to 20 per cent of the contents figure, although the form of indemnity wording will be traditional).

The cost will vary as a result of particular insurers' views on the desirability of the business in the context of fire, theft and other insured perils, and of the pressure from the competition for good business in this field which produces a reasonable premium per policy and thus provides a worthwhile contribution to 'overhead' costs.

A broker is thus again faced with choices, which administrative costs and the near-impossibility of matching individual cases to covers reduce to the selection of two or three insurers' schemes considered best suited for the clients he handles. The matter must also be considered in the light of the other classes of business included in or omitted from the package cover, the extent of the protection offered and costing.

The schemes usually are separately designed for the following: retail shopkeepers (with some special schemes for specific trades); motor garage businesses; launderettes; hoteliers; boarding houses and the like; professional men (often with special schemes for specific professions such as doctors, dentists, architects, surveyors, estate agents and so on); and office-type risks designed to cope with the wide variety of activities so embraced.

The problems of maintaining adequate sums insured are ever

present and indexing is not usually available on a permanent basis. The inclusion of buildings in the cover adds to this problem since the increase in value of these may well be at a different level to that of the fixtures and fittings, etc., and stock. Provision for automatic increase in value of stock in suitable cases for seasonal periods is desirable. It is also necessary to see that provision is made under these covers to deal with the following:

1. Debris removal.
2. Stock declarations if stock values are high.
3. Professional fees of architects, etc.
4. Protection of stock in transit (especially delivery risks).
5. 'Reinstatement' or 'indemnity' basis.
6. Local authority requirements after loss protection.
7. Inflation protection during the renewal period and the reconstruction time thereafter.

At one time warranties covering oils, waste, and storage measures regarding water damage exposure, hands employed, etc., were common. Generally they should be avoided as likely to cause difficulties by inadvertent breach.

Commercial and industrial insurances

This is the area where the larger cases are involved and the premiums justify individual treatment to a greater extent.

Property and interruption insurance policies for industrial risks are in common form in the United Kingdom (the arbitration condition varies in Eire), with the exception that there is a slightly wider explosion cover given under a Lloyd's policy when it does not form a coinsurance cover with an insurance company policy. The Lloyd's policy conditions also vary slightly and no arbitration condition is included. A 'collective' policy is one where several insurers express their cover in a single document issued by the leading office (usually the underwriter with the largest share). Lloyd's underwriters do not join a company collective policy, but in accordance with their usual practice their document on behalf of all participating insurers will be issued by the Lloyd's policy issuing and signing office, or a broker may issue a certificate on Lloyd's behalf. Where the Lloyd's interest is part of the whole, being a percentage of a common specification, it is usually endorsed with what is called a 'warranty to follow' clause – i.e. it follows the 'leading office' on claims settlements. There may be, in addition, other certificates or policies for certain of the smaller insurance companies (frequently referred to as the 'fringe' market).

The basic protection by insurance of a business is of its capital assets, i.e. buildings, plant and machinery, etc., and stock. Buildings and plant and machinery can be insured either on an indemnity basis (i.e. current values) or on a reinstatement basis (cost of restoring new for old). Stock in trade can be insured for its value at the time of loss (by agreement the immediate replacement value) and is usually covered on a monthly declaration basis, the premium being adjusted at the end of the period and the sum insured being fixed to exceed any likely declaration. Occasionally limited replacement covers are available.

Except for most private insurances, virtually all other policies incorporate the 'average' provision. This is an attempt by insurers to produce rates which are based on a simple equitable level of comparison between one insured and another. Some 'first-loss', i.e. non-average, policies are issued in respect of water damage-type perils and in a few other special cases.

In a period of somewhat unpredictable inflation the broker's advice on the various methods of dealing with this problem for property insurance is probably of most importance. Numerous schemes are available to deal with inflation during the currency of the policy and during the period of reconstruction after the loss, and all have their merits. It is always important to remember the effect of taxation on capital gains, i.e. the difference in value of the insurance payment and the tax written-down value of that asset and the new depreciation allowance levels.

The selection of perils needs careful assessment, not only of the potential hazard involvement and the financial risk relating thereto, but of political risks such as riot, etc., against the likelihood of the market withdrawing the availability of such cover if conditions deteriorate. The Northern Ireland position is an example of a long period elapsing before the extra cover was withdrawn. The new situation regarding insurance cover must be advised to the insured by their brokers, especially those for whom the cover in this area is an occasional feature (transit risks, etc.).

It is now possible throughout the whole market to insure on an industrial all-risks basis, i.e. the exclusion to the cover will be set down as such. It must be remembered that the contract is still one of insurance and thus the perils are still against a fortuitous event. This form of cover usually has certain optional items (collapse, etc.), and compulsory deductibles for the non-traditional perils, the level of which will be a matter of premium. It is unusual for engineering type perils to be included because that form of cover is more appropriate to selected items of plant, etc., rather than the blanket approach to the cover under an industrial all-risks policy.

Following the introduction of the Theft Act 1977, the term 'theft cover' replaced 'burglary', and the insurance is usually restricted to 'following violent forcible entry'. In larger cases such covers are often on a first-loss basis, with an excess for any one loss.

In arranging covers the broker needs to deal with the following ancillary aspects:
1. Architect's and/or other experts' fees.
2. Debris removal.
3. Local authority requirements after damage.
4. Temporary removal of machinery for repairs, etc.
5. The basis of cover for deeds, documents, records, computer and electronic machine production material, goods in transit, employees' effects and the like.

In the event of a loss of any significance (say over £2,500) it is normal for the insurers to appoint a loss adjuster to resolve the matter on their behalf. It is usual for such experts to act in a neutral manner, to assess the loss in accordance with the policy terms and to clear the amount in discussion with the insured's technical advisers, i.e. financial director, works manager, secretary, etc. The broker's services in this field vary in practice but usually extend to give broad advice on the manner in which to present the claim and any points regarding the extent of the policy cover. Loss assessors are available if so desired by an insured at a fee which is best negotiated in advance if their services are considered worth while. In the majority of cases losses are happily concluded directly with the loss adjuster.

If a loss occurs, unless there is provision to the contrary, the sum insured is reduced immediately by the amount to be subsequently determined in accordance with the normal laws of contract. It is advisable therefore to reinstate the sum if the property is restored or replaced prior to the next renewal date, and clauses allowing for automatic reinstatement of the sum insured in such circumstances are often found in policies.

The cover on plant fixtures and fittings comprises all other property except stock, and care is needed to see that an insured includes provision in the sum insured accordingly. Packing cases and packing materials may be worth a considerable amount and their value, together with other often non-capital items such as stationery, must be included in the assessment of the sum to be insured.

Stock is usually insured on a declaration basis and prompt returns are essential to avoid inadequate amounts being insured in times of inflation. The valuation of stock by an insured is frequently on a historic basis, which is inadequate in fixing the cover.

With many UK insurances being arranged for non-UK companies, care is needed to avoid using British insurance practice terms without ensuring that they are understood by the client. For example: (a) the term 'fire' in US insurance practice includes that event arising from explosion or earthquake, whereas this is not so in the standard UK forms; (b) the term 'coinsurance' in the United States means a form of participation in the cover by the insured, which can be on an agreed basis.

INTERRUPTION INSURANCE

In addition to the physical loss, the financial loss to the business stemming therefrom needs to be dealt with by an interruption policy. Formerly called 'consequential loss', 'loss of profits' and/or 'profits insurance', which can be misleading terms, the protection granted is in accordance with a policy formula, i.e. rate of gross profit applied to the reduction in turnover of the business in consequence of an insured peril, together with the increased costs to minimise an aggravated loss (but not exceeding the loss so saved) arising within the maximum indemnity period (as selected to be insured). Provision is made for the accountancy definitions and the business, the premises and the insured to be defined. In any claim, adjustment can be made to the previous financial account figures so that the loss is in respect of the 'would have been' results that would have applied if the damage had not occurred.

The perils insured (for which there must normally be counterpart physical damage cover) can extend to include those normal to property insurances and such special perils as failure of public electricity or gas supply, loss from infectious disease for hotel and similar trades, or electrocution of cattle in farming risks. Machinery breakdown covers can usually be arranged on selected plant. Advance profits covers can be arranged for new ventures and these may include marine transit risks.

Provision can be made, with first-loss limitations applying, to extend interruption insurance to protect the financial trading of the business following damage to other people's premises (those of suppliers, subcontractors, customers, etc.) and in transit.

It is normal, in current conditions, to insure 100 per cent of the remuneration of all employees at a reduced-rate level, but more limited cover can be arranged in this respect in suitable cases. This employee cover is largely a 'social' protection to staff and their retention after a loss is thus safeguarded. While savings can be made by non-replacement where employees leave, the cover is not on the basis of the insured having to minimise the loss by dismissals.

The indemnity period, usually at least 12 months, is the limit up to which the recompense under the policy continues. It needs to be sufficient not only to restore the physical equipment and buildings but to allow turnover to reach the 'would have been' level. The sum insured is the forecast amount (including a margin to avoid under-insurance) that might be at risk for the 12 months from the end of the renewal period of the policy. Where the maximum indemnity period insured exceeds 12 months the figure is then proportionately increased. The premium is adjustable normally only to the extent of over-insurance.

For the small and medium-sized cases, it is now possible to insure on what is termed a declaration basis. The cover may or may not include a maximum sum as a limit, but there will be no reduction applicable in the event of under-insurance (or a high sum insured limit is applied to avoid this); the premium is adjustable on the annual declaration, which must be received in a limited period from the end of the insured's financial year.

The cover automatically provides for the cost of auditors in preparing financial details from the accounts, but not for the preparation of the claim itself.

It is often found that consequential losses will arise such as liquidated damages, above-economic increases in cost of working, deterioration or wastage of undamaged stock, etc. Special items can be added to deal with these exposures. This section has indicated the need for individual review when arranging an interruption insurance and for the policy accountancy definitions to be suitable to the system of accounting adopted.

A further form of special cover called 'book debts insurance' provides for the loss flowing from the unrecovered monies from trading *prior* to the damage through the destruction of the account records and the inability to collect the outstanding debts. The essence of the insurance is the monthly declaration of outstanding book debts, which serves as a datum against which after damage the shortfall in recovery of book debts can be measured. A low rate is involved and the degree of duplication, protection of the records and sum insured determines further reduction to it.

It is in the field of interruption insurance that the importance of the assistance from loss adjusters and others arises, since much can be done in emergency conditions to minimise the potential loss.

WORLDWIDE COVERS

With large organisations that operate on an international basis, it is not unusual for a worldwide basis cover to be arranged so that uniformity of protection is secured and the interruption cover is properly interlinked.

This arrangement may involve a single cover in one territory or separate policies in some or all the territories involved, with what is called a master policy providing the overall linkage. The variations stem from the requirements of local governments, the insurance market regulations, the insured's own preferences, matters relating to payment of premiums and losses, and the surcharge payable on non-locally placed insurances.

Care also has to be taken because of the variation in the cover under an American type business interruption policy with that of the British type form, which directly affects the extent of the cover from external events, the calculation of the loss, the period of indemnity and the association with the stock material damage assessment.

FURTHER READING

Carter, R. L. (ed.): *Handbook of Insurance* (with updating service) (Kluwer Publishing).

Carter, R. L., and Doherty, N. A. (eds.): *Handbook of Risk Management* (with updating service) (Kluwer Publishing).

Carter R. L.: *Reinsurance*, second edition (Kluwer Publishing, 1983).

Colinvaux, R.: *The Law of Insurance*, fifth edition (Sweet & Maxwell, 1984).

Hickmott, G. J. R.: *Principles and Practice of Interruption Insurance* (Witherby, 1982).

Ivamy, E. R. Hardy: *General Principles of Insurance Law*, fifth edition (Butterworth, 1986).

Kiln, R. J.: *Reinsurance in Practice*, second edition (Witherby, 1986).

McGillivray, E. J. and Partington, M.: *Insurance Law*, seventh edition (Sweet & Maxwell, 1981).

Peverett, E. J. D.: *Fire Insurance Law and Claims* (Chartered Institute of Loss Adjusters, 1982).

Riley, D. (David Cloughton, revision editor): *Consequential Loss Insurance and Claims*, sixth edition (Sweet & Maxwell, 1985).

CHAPTER 8

Credit insurance

R. G. BLASZKOWSKI, BA

Information Manager, Hogg Robinson (Credit & Political) Ltd

INTRODUCTION

Companies supplying goods or services to other organisations on credit terms risk non-payment due to a customer's insolvency or, where the customer is based overseas, the occurrence of political or economic events. Credit insurance provides protection against losses arising from such trading risks. Although variations have been developed, this description covers the majority of business placed in the credit and political risk insurance market.

Because of the magnitude of the political and economic risks to which exporters may be exposed, export credit insurance has in the past tended to be underwritten by government organisations. In the United Kingdom, for example, the Export Credits Guarantee Department (ECGD) provides a package of risk protection covering insolvency, buyer default and the political and economic risks. In some other countries, insolvency and default are covered by private-sector insurers, with reinsurance for political and economic risks being provided by their governments.

In recent years, however, the private sector has expanded its activities substantially, and now provides both insolvency and political risks insurance for exporters. The major developments have taken place in the London market, but the clients are international. The underwriting market for 'domestic' (that is, inter-UK trade) credit insurance has also expanded considerably in the last decade.

Credit insurance does not apply to pure financial credits such as bank loans, although it does play a significant role in trade finance; nor does credit insurance apply to consumer credit.

Insurable risks

Cover against the following principal causes of non-payment is available:

Commercial risks
1. Insolvency of a private buyer.
2. Protracted default by a private buyer.

Political risks
1. Non-payment or repudiation of the contract by a recognised government buyer.
2. Export/import licence cancellation/embargo.
3. Exchange transfer delays where the buyer has paid locally, but the country has a shortage of the currency of contract.
4. War, civil war, insurrection and revolution.
5. Government action such as the enactment or enforcement of a law, order, decree or regulation.

Depending on the underwriter, cover may apply to losses before shipment, or post-shipment, or a combination of both.

THE BROKER'S ROLE

The UK credit insurance underwriting market has widened substantially since 1980. In the past, there were two underwriters dominating credit insurance to the exclusion of almost all others. Trade Indemnity, a publicly quoted company formed in 1918, has provided insurance for principally inter-UK trade against insolvency risks. ECGD, a division of the Department of Trade and Industry formed in 1919, has provided cover for UK exporters against commercial and political risks. The broker's role was restricted by virtue of having only one option each for domestic and export clients.

There are now some ten underwriters active in this field of insurance. Particularly with the growth of political risk insurance at Lloyd's, specialist insurance brokers have played a significant part in developing the present market. The number of underwriters and their different approaches to credit and political risk insurance enable the broker to offer a range of options to his clients.

In this respect, the credit insurance broker now plays a similar role to his counterpart in other fields of insurance. He is able to negotiate the most appropriate cover for his client from the most appropriate underwriter, but he may also offer alternatives at different costs, with a different range of insured risks, or at different levels of indemnity or with excesses.

The credit insurance broker also has a part to play in a client's overall risk management strategy and in this he works in concert with his counterpart advising on the client's other insurances. Credit insurance is, after all, concerned with the protection of an asset – a company's debtors. Statistics show that for most companies the debtor item comprises some 25 per cent of the total assets shown on the balance sheet, and 40 per cent of current assets. The prudent businessman insures his fixed assets – such as the buildings in which he carries on his business and the machinery he uses; he insures his raw materials, work-in-progress and stock; he may also be responsible for insuring his goods in transit to his customers. To complete his risk management strategy, it is logical to consider credit insurance since it protects not only what is his most liquid asset – after cash – but an asset which is in the hands of his customers and out of his control.

SOME GENERAL PRINCIPLES

Cuthbert Heath was actively involved in the early development of the credit insurance market and was the first chairman of Trade Indemnity. He established a number of ground rules which have been the basis of credit insurance underwriting throughout the world, and some of which remain valid today.

Perhaps the most fundamental principle is that the client must retain an interest in his exposure. This is usually established by limiting the insurance to a proportion of the loss (i.e. 'compulsory co-insurance'). Indemnities may range between 75 per cent and 95 per cent of the loss. Alternatively, an excess or deductible is applied and the insured must bear this himself, claiming for the balance.

The thinking behind this rule leads to another fundamental principle of credit insurance: that it is not intended as a substitute for sound credit management or for clear contract drafting. Retaining an interest in his exposure emphasises the need for the insured to exercise good credit control and to draft clear contracts which specify the buyers' obligations to pay. All underwriters look for evidence of the insured's skills in these areas, and for some underwriters satisfaction with the credit control systems or the strength of the contract dictates whether cover may be offered.

Credit insurance does not guarantee payment on the contractual due date and all policies incorporate waiting periods for claims. Again this basic rule emphasises the need for the insured to take steps to obtain prompt settlement from his customers where possible: after all, it is preferable to receive payment in full from the buyer at or near the due date rather than wait for a claim to be admissible under the insurance. The length of waiting periods varies according to underwriter, nature of risk and location of risk, but tends to vary from 30 days to 180 days for commercial risks and 120 days to 360 days for political risks, although longer periods may be required.

Underwriters also exclude from cover disputed debts and will not consider a claim until a dispute has been settled or it can be proved that the customer has raised a frivolous dispute to disguise his inability to pay.

TYPES OF COVER

The following comments apply at the time of writing. New concepts may emerge and the range of underwriters may alter in the future.

Whole turnover

For both domestic and export credit insurance, the majority of underwriting by Trade Indemnity and the ECGD is on the basis of whole turnover cover. The client declares all his insurable sales, which gives the underwriters a spread of both good and less than blue-chip customers, and pays a flat premium rate on turnover. Cover is provided by credit limits established on each individual buyer. Up to a certain level, called the discretionary limit, the insured is responsible for setting the limits; above this level, the underwriter approves credit limits.

Trade Indemnity offers this type of policy for both domestic and export policyholders, with cover against insolvency and private buyer default. It can also offer selective political risk cover by endorsement to the export policy. The level of indemnity is normally 80 per cent, although it may vary both below and above this level. It is also usual for the policies to have an excess to exclude smaller losses.

ECGD's policy insures exporters against commercial and political risks and offers standard indemnities of 90 per cent for the first category of risk, and 95 per cent for the second. There is no standard form of excess, although ECGD has now begun to offer variations along these lines to meet competition.

Insurances of Credit Company, a UK branch of a Belgian credit insurer, offers whole turnover cover for UK debtors and a certain amount of export business, but there are no other insurers providing cover in the whole turnover format.

Catastrophe insurance

Catastrophe insurance is a relatively new concept in credit insurance. It was first offered in 1981 when British National Insurance Company formed a credit insurance division to write cover solely on this basis. The division was later taken over by PanFinancial Insurance Company and provides its main source of business.

The PanFinancial approach involves the insured taking for his own account the aggregate of all losses up to an agreed level. The policy then pays 100 per cent of subsequent losses up to an agreed maximum liability. Premium is a fixed sum, based largely on the amount of cover bought. There is no system of underwriter-approved credit limits. Instead cover is offered only to those companies that satisfy PanFinancial's criteria for sound credit management controls. The cover tends to be attractive to larger organisations which invest in sophisticated credit control systems, and which are prepared to take substantial losses for their own account and seek protection only against catastrophe losses.

PanFinancial's policy provides protection against insolvency only, but can apply to both UK and export debts where customers are in Western-style economies. It can also be offered to insureds based in certain Western countries.

Other insurers offer variations to this form of credit insurance. American International Underwriters (UK) Ltd (AIU) – a subsidiary of AIG, the large US insurance group – provides a comprehensive export credit insurance policy covering both commercial and political risks where the insured must stand a substantial deductible and must demonstrate first-class credit management. However, a credit limit system applies, although AIU considers only a small number of major customers, leaving the insured to set the majority of limits under a substantial discretionary limit. AIU charges premium as a percentage rate on outstanding receivables balances. Policy and country limits are set, but do not directly affect the premium. AIU offers 90 per cent indemnity over the deductible. Again, this cover is appropriate to larger companies.

CIGNA provides cover on a basis similar to that of AIU both for export and domestic policyholders. However, it is limited in the degree of cover it can offer for political risks.

Both Trade Indemnity and ECGD have responded to these facilities offered by competitors. Trade Indemnity offers an aggregate first-loss policy which is underwritten much on the basis of its standard whole turnover cover, but with the insured taking a significant level of aggregated losses for his own account. Credit limits are set by Trade Indemnity for major buyers, the insured having a substantial discretionary limit. Indemnity may be set at different levels, including 100 per cent. Premium may be charged as a fixed amount or as a rate on declared turnover. There is no maximum liability figure. This policy may be offered for both export and domestic insureds.

Trade Indemnity also offers an excess of loss catastrophe policy along similar lines to PanFinancial's cover but there remains a requirement for the underwriter to set credit limits on major customers.

ECGD also offers an aggregate first-loss policy which, apart from the substantial level of losses the insured must take for his own account, is very similar to its standard whole turnover policy.

Specific account and single contract insurance

Specific account cover is available for both domestic and export risks, although for export risks it is more accurate to describe the cover as single contract insurance, since the policy would normally be designed to protect a specific contract rather than a series of transactions with a regular customer. All cover on this basis is subject to the underwriter's approval.

Specific account cover is available where a client has one or a number of major customers or has an exceptional contract. Because indemnities do not receive a spread of risk, premium rates tend to be higher. Premium is either a fixed amount, a rate on declarable turnover or a rate on a limit of liability. Levels of indemnity vary from 75 per cent to 95 per cent, but lower levels may be selected by insureds or offered by underwriters.

Trade Indemnity offers specific account cover for both domestic and export commercial risks, but not for political risks.

Credit and Guarantee Insurance Company specialises in specific account and single contract cover for insolvency risks only. It insures principally UK risks but also covers buyers in some other European countries.

CIGNA offers specific account cover for both domestic and export commercial risks.

ECGD offers specific insurance for single contracts. These are normally project-type contracts, inappropriate to the standard form of cover. Commercial and political risks are covered, the level of indemnity is 90 per cent and premium is charged as a rate on the contract value.

AIU offers two types of specific account cover. Where the customer is a private company rather than a government organisation, both commercial and political risk cover is available. Where commercial risk cover is inappropriate or not required, then solely political risk cover is available. As with ECGD, this type of cover is more appropriate to single contracts.

This is true of the rest of the political risk underwriters. Lloyd's, which with AIU dominates the political risk market, is unable to write cover against insolvency risks. It does, however, insure contracts with private companies against political risks. PanFinancial also offers specific political risk insurance but does not cover single buyers or contracts against losses from insolvency.

Black Sea and Baltic General Insurance Company, the UK subsidiary of the USSR international insurance organisation, also offers specific political risk insurance but is limited to covering contracts with customers in Eastern bloc countries.

Other types of cover

There are various other types of cover available in the credit insurance market for risks run by companies in their trading activities.

A substantial amount of export business is contracted on terms of payment secured by irrevocable letters of credit. Insurance is available against the inability of the bank opening the letter of credit to effect payment due to political risks.

In export contracts again, it is quite common for exporters to be asked to provide on-demand bank guarantees as security for advance payment or for good performance. Insurance is available against the calling of these guarantees due to political events or to an unfair call by a government buyer.

Many companies have goods held in stock with overseas agents for marketing and ease of delivery purposes. In addition, many companies have investments overseas, either in fixed assets such as plants or in equity holdings. Such assets may be confiscated or nationalised, events or regulations may prevent the re-export of stock, and dividends and earnings from investments may be withheld or subject to currency transfer delays. These risks are all insurable in the private market.

Insurance is available for other risks such as countertrade, non-performance of suppliers due to insolvency or political events, the insolvency of buyers of companies, and losses in equipment leases.

Banking solutions

One development which has had a significant effect on this field of insurance is the ability of some banks and finance companies to buy companies' credit risks. This removes the exposure from the client and thus may be an appropriate alternative to credit insurance.

For insolvency risks in the United Kingdom, London Bridge Finance Company, a subsidiary of Hill Samuel Bank, offers a discount purchase facility. London Bridge Finance sets credit limits on a company's major customers. It then guarantees to purchase at any time – even when a customer has become insolvent – invoices at normally 85 per cent of their value up to the amount of the credit limit. In return for this guarantee, the company pays London Bridge Finance a commitment fee, calculated as a rate on sales to the approved customers. The facility is the equivalent of specific account credit insurance, but London Bridge may consider a large number of customers.

For export contracts, the growth of forfeiting as a form of export finance gives exporters a viable alternative to credit insurance. A bank or specialist forfeiter purchases bills of exchange accepted by an overseas customer and guaranteed by a reputable bank; often this is a State-owned bank. The exporter is paid normally 100 per cent of the guaranteed bills by the forfeiter, less a commission. The forfeiter collects the interest payable on the bills by the buyer. The forfeiter accepts the credit risk and has no recourse to the exporter in the event of non-payment.

UNITED KINGDOM CREDIT INSURANCE BROKERS' COMMITTEE

If guidance is required, a letter or telephone call to the BIBA is suggested.

FURTHER READING

A History of ECGD 1919-1979 (Export Credits Guarantee Department, 1979).

ECGD Services (Export Credits Guarantee Department/Central Office of Information, revised edition 1986).

CHAPTER 9

Insurance of liabilities

PETER MADGE, LLM, ACII, FCIArb
Director, Willis, Faber & Dumas Ltd

INTRODUCTION

The liability insurance market operates against a background of constant change. The business is not subject to tariffs, and therefore the broker has no guide to give him a feeling as to what the rate should be. There are no standard wordings. Indeed, wordings differ enormously and even the same wordings may receive different interpretations from insurers.

In an age of consumerism there has been much legal reform, with more pending. Legislation is becoming more complex and difficult to understand. The Unfair Contract Terms Act 1977 and the Latent Damage Act 1986 are good illustrations. Developments elsewhere in the world add international dimensions to the UK broker's role. Exports to the United States are one example of the UK broker having to familiarise himself with another country's legal systems and the problems that have arisen. The United Kingdom's membership of the European Community has meant that the UK broker has had to keep an eye on EEC developments and proposed changes in insurance law. Important legislation in recent years includes the Convention on Jurisdiction and the Enforcement of Judgments in Civil and Commercial Matters, which came into force on 1 January 1987 and the directive on liability for defective products, which is being implemented in the United Kingdom at the time of writing by the Consumer Protection Bill.

Perhaps in no other sector of insurance have these developments created demands for broker expertise in an area where generally the insured himself lacks it. Traditionally the insured has been shielded by his insurers from many of the developments that have taken place in legal reform. If employees were injured, or third parties sustained injury to their person or property, the matter was passed over to insurers to deal with. Liability was denied or the claim settled as the case may be, and usually that was the last the insured knew about it. Generally there was no need for him to know the law involved. Consequently it is fair to say that in industry itself, although many organisations employed their own legal experts or had legal departments, such departments had no great expertise in those areas of risk which were normally covered by insurance. Why should they? It was the insurers' problem. That is why they paid their premiums.

But now the rising cost of liability premiums and proposed areas of law reform are causing management to ask questions. Nowhere is there a better illustration of this than in the proposed developments towards strict liability for defective products. What does it mean? What will it involve? How much will it cost? Very often there is nobody within the insured's own organisation who can supply the answers. Increasingly, the insured is having to turn to his broker for advice.

These days the modern broker cannot hope to discuss liability insurance arrangements with his client without having some understanding of legal developments both past and present.

KNOWING THE LAW AND KEEPING ABREAST OF CHANGE

Court decisions are reported in the national press. The insurance journals cover those of interest to insurers, often expanding those of major importance with expert commentary. Law reports and legal journals cover cases in greater detail.

The UK broker is not expected to be a lawyer but he cannot hope to service existing accounts or gain new ones unless he is able to speak intelligently to his client about legal developments and keep abreast of change. Brokers should subscribe to relevant journals and delegate to some employee the responsibility of trying to keep in touch with legal innovations.

KNOWING THE RISK TO WHICH THE CLIENT IS EXPOSED

It is necessary to visit the client's premises and probe into his business to understand what he does. Only by understanding the business is the broker able to advise on the risks involved and the type of insurance required.

For example, the client may be storing valuable property belonging to customers. Where is his cover if it is damaged? Most public liability policies exclude damage to property in the insured's custody or control. The client may offer advice to customers for a fee. Is there a professional negligence exposure?

Merely to sell the client the basic off-the-peg policy with no attempt to adapt it to his individual needs has no future.

ESTABLISHING A PHILOSOPHY

Many clients have a major overall philosophy in their approach to insurance buying. For those who do not it is part of the broker's role to advise on one. Liability insurance protection is part of that overall philosophy. Thus the insured may consider himself big enough to self-insure large areas of risk or conversely may be so insurance-minded that he wishes to insure most risks from the first pound upwards, subject to cost.

Some insureds may decide that they are able to carry only a certain amount of risk in any one year and thereafter require insurance protection. Assume a client decides that he can carry the first £250,000 of risk in any one year. In which areas will he carry those risks? It may be by accepting deductibles under his fire or business interruption policies, or by self-insuring the damage risk under his motor fleet. Or it may be by taking deductibles under his products liability cover. Which is the best approach? Which is most cost-effective? Until this is known the individual risks themselves cannot receive their correct treatment.

Part of this philosophy is to understand the client's overall approach towards insurance. There are those who are prepared to play the market with constant change of insurers every time there is an increase in premium – in effect to recover their premiums in claims. Others take a different approach. Insurers are in business to make a profit. Thus in the long term normally (subject to catastrophe claims) the insured will pay more in premium than is paid out in claims. Long-term relationships with insurers have much to commend them. Even in today's competitive world commercial good-will still counts for something.

Subject to cover, competitiveness of premium and efficient claims handling, there is much to be gained by having a long-term relationship with insurers rather than shopping around each year.

LIMITS OF INDEMNITY: CATASTROPHE PROTECTION

Essentially liability insurance is about catastrophe protection. The business which is faced with a small claim can deal with that claim whether it is insured or not. The business which is faced with a catastrophe claim will fail or run into difficulties if not adequately insured. What is a catastrophe depends upon the size of the business. A £100,000 product claim may bankrupt the small business and is therefore a catastrophe. To a multinational it is a drop in the ocean. In establishing a philosophy therefore it should be the aim of the client to insure for adequate limits. Often this can be achieved by self-insuring the first part of the risk and using the premium so saved to buy higher limits of indemnity to cover the catastrophe.

We hear much these days about under-insurance in terms of property values. The same can also be said about limits of indemnity. Many UK firms are under-insured, having limits of indemnity of £1,000,000 or less: £1,000,000 ought to be regarded as the *minimum* limit of indemnity. Serious claims take a long time to settle. This is particularly the case with injury claims. The plaintiff's lawyers will not allow the claim to be settled unless and until a complete recovery has been made. What the broker has to bear in mind is the adequacy of the limit of indemnity at the time of the settlement of the claim, not at the time that the cover is arranged. Since very serious claims may not be settled for upwards of five years after the date of the accident, what effect will inflation have had? A limit of £1,000,000 arranged in 1987 effectively may have been reduced by over 50 per cent when settlement is negotiated five years later.

While personal injury claims may have a long delay factor in settlement, it is normally property damage claims which present the catastrophe exposure. Not only may the physical damage to property be expensive, but so too may the consequential losses flowing from that damage. Fire and explosion are usually the major sources of catastrophe claims. Where the insured's premises are close to others the spreading fire risk may be heavy.

The risk may also be heavy where there is the use of blow-torches and the like on other people's premises. Where the insured discharges chemicals or waste products into the atmosphere, on to land or into water there may again be a heavy exposure. It is not easy to advise on the maximum limit of indemnity required. Since there is no financial limit to the amount of compensation a plaintiff may claim in law, ideally policies should be without limit. But that is not possible. At the end of the day the indemnity selected will be based on the cost involved. Where there is a products liability exposure it must be remembered that the limit is an *aggregate* one.

Very high limits of indemnity are arranged either by coinsurance or by means of excess-of-loss policies. Since the early 1970s there has been an expansion of the excess-of-loss market, but newcomers do not always have the expertise. Correctly arranged, the excess-of-loss policy will cover exactly the same liabilities as are covered by the primary policy, with no gaps in cover. Thus there will be no difference between the insured having one policy with insurers A for a limit of £5 million and his having the policy with insurers A for £1 million and excess-of-loss cover with insurers B, C and D for £4 million. But in practice different wordings may be used for the excess-of-loss cover so that a gap may appear between the primary and the excess cover. It is the responsibility of the broker to see that this does not happen.

The introduction of 'claims made' policies presents many problems and the broker should understand the reasons why they are being used by insurers and the implications to the insured.

CLAIMS

Part of any broker's role is to analyse the previous claims experience if there is one. If there is a run of small claims it may be worth the client's time in considering the application of an excess to cut these out. There is no future in continuing to make small claims on insurers if the effect is a premium increase at each renewal date. That is simply the swapping of bank notes. If an excess is to apply, it is important to decide who will handle the claims under the excess. Sometimes the insured will wish to do this himself since it involves his relationship with third parties and there is thus a public relations exercise involved. Sometimes the insured will prefer insurers to do it on his behalf.

There is a growing internationalism about liability claims. This is particularly true of product claims. Goods exported from the United Kingdom may cause injury or damage anywhere in the world. The insured may be sued in foreign courts. The parent company may find its overseas subsidiaries are drawn into litigation. Particularly in the products liability area there is a growing need to think in terms of worldwide covers protecting the *group* as a whole rather than to allow each individual company in the group to arrange its own cover – often with a multiplicity of insurers.

CHOICE OF INSURERS

This is one of the major areas where the broker is employed to exercise his professional skill. The choice is not always easy because no one insurer provides the answers to all the problems.

Many factors will affect the choice:

1. The financial stability of the insurer.
2. The extent of cover afforded and the flexibility of the insurer in being prepared to cater for the special needs of the client.
3. Services offered, e.g. liability survey, risk management advice.
4. The level of premium.
5. The position of the insurer in the market-place – he may be a newcomer anxious to expand premium income with no deep knowledge of the subject, or he may be an established insurer adopting either a conservative approach or an expansionist approach, underwriting for premium income and investment income purposes rather than underwriting profit. Some insurers are keen to underwrite employer's liability risks but not public liability. The reverse applies, too.
6. The insurer's attitude to claims.
7. The relationship between insurer, broker and client – many risks remain with the insurer because of the goodwill which arises out of liability insurance surveys and recommendations.
8. A risk producing a good premium will be regarded more as a prize to be retained by the small to medium-sized insurer than by the larger insurer to whom it may simply be one of many.

In any choice of insurers, premium is important but is not necessarily the determining factor. The extent of cover, the attitude of the insurers towards claims and the provision of other services are all relevant. You cannot compare one without looking at the other.

Moreover, the intelligent broker will establish a professional relationship with his client, a relationship which of necessity involves forward thinking. The broker who obtains a particularly competitive quotation which he knows is unlikely to hold good in future years should tell his client at the time he puts the quotation forward. This way he forewarns his client that, if the quotation is accepted, an increase is likely in the future and he thus paves the way for the time when the increase arises.

Until the beginning of the 1970s it was considered sound practice to place the employer's liability risk and the public liability risks with the same insurer. This was on the basis that sometimes grey areas could arise in which it was not always possible to define the status of an injured person and both the employer's liability and the public liability insurers may have argued that the claim was not covered. Often the public liability exclusion dealing with injury to employees was worded differently. Nowadays most public liability policies have an exclusion of injury to employees which dovetails with the operative clause under the employer's liability policy. Although some borderline cases may arise, the need for having both insurances with the same insurer is no longer as strong as it used to be.

Because so much interest arises in the liability area these days – particularly products liability – the broker ought to have a specimen of the policy available in his files so that he can answer clients' questions as and when they arise.

Very often it is necessary to reach certain agreements and understandings with insurers over the interpretation to be attached to particular phrases and aspects of cover. Not only is it important for these understandings to be established in writing, but it is equally important that these understandings are kept on the file so that they may be referred to at a later stage when a claim arises.

THE BROKER'S CONTINUING RELATIONSHIP WITH THE CLIENT

Not many risks remain static. Changes occur. The business expands, new product ranges are introduced or other changes are afoot. Part of the broker's relationship with his client is to keep abreast of these changes and where necessary to notify them to insurers. If the insured issues a house journal then the broker should be on the mailing list, as this is one useful way of keeping up to date. The trade or business description of the insured stated in the policy should always be kept under review. A system will have to be established for dealing with claims. Many brokers insist that all claims are routed via themselves to the insurers including correspondence ensuing therefrom. Many brokers see this as an essential part of their job.

Some brokers agree with their clients that all claims are reported direct to the insurers and negotiations are handled direct between insurer and client with the broker being called in when some problem arises – for example, a dispute on policy cover. Yet others adopt a half-way house, with employer's liability claims being reported direct to the insurer but with public liability and product claims being routed via the broker.

The choice is essentially one for the broker to make. The channelling of claims direct to the insurers does release the broker from much routine administrative work. It is also true that in some areas of claim, particularly employer's liability, the broker has but a limited role to play. As against that, just as the insurer has a lot to learn from claims, so has the broker. It is one way of keeping abreast of the client's affairs.

PROFESSIONAL NEGLIGENCE

Where the risk relates to that of a professional man, e.g. accountant, surveyor, architect or estate agent, established markets exist to provide the cover. Most brokers are aware of these markets and the extent of cover available.

Where some brokers face difficulties is in dealing with a professional negligence exposure where the client is not a professional firm but is a commercial firm, employing professionals who make professional judgements or give professional opinions or advice. Often the broker will be asked whether the professional negligence exposure is covered.

If the client's public and products liability contains no exclusion relating to professional negligence, then such exposure is covered to the extent that it causes injury to persons or damage to property within the meaning of the liability policies. But the exposure may not stop there. There may be an exposure to financial or economic loss claims not dependent upon injury to persons or damage to property. Such exposure will not be covered by the normal type of public or products liability policy.

EMPLOYER'S LIABILITY

This form of insurance protects the employer against his legal liability for accident, injury or disease to his employees which arises out of and in the course of their employment. In the United Kingdom it is compulsory by virtue of the Employers Liability (Compulsory Insurance) Act 1969. Although the Act calls for a minimum limit of indemnity of £2 million on any one occurrence, most insurers issue policies with indemnities unlimited in amount. Unlike public and products liability insurance (where cover differs from insurer to insurer), most of the cover given by insurers is very similar. The major role of the broker, therefore, is to obtain competitive premiums, preferably with an insurer who understands this class of business.

The underwriting of this form of insurance is governed by underwriting trade endorsements, e.g. the policy may exclude work at heights or depths, the use of explosives and similar hazardous work unless the appropriate premium is paid. The broker's duty is to make sure that the client understands the limitations.

The Employers Liability (Compulsory Insurance) Act 1969 requires an employer to display at each place of business a certificate from his insurers that he is insured against such risks. The following information must be shown on the certificate:

1. The name of the policyholder.
2. The policy number.
3. The date of commencement and expiry of policy.
4. Certificate that the policy satisfies the terms of the Act.
5. The name of the insurer and the signature of the authorised official.

This information is required for two reasons. It gives evidence to employees or their representatives that their employer is complying with the legal requirements of the Act, thus protecting them in case of bankruptcy or liquidation. And it means that employees or their representatives are able to satisfy themselves that the insurers are sound and thus able to meet any claim arising out of an industrial injury or disease to any member of the workforce.

DIRECTORS' AND OFFICERS' LIABILITY IN THE UNITED KINGDOM

Directors can be sued and they frequently are. Directors owe a duty to *the company* and to third parties, a breach of which may give rise to liability. Most directors are employed by their companies under service contracts and a director is liable under this contract, whether by implication or expressly, to exercise a reasonable standard of care commensurate with his recognised attributes and qualifications in the carrying out of his duties.

The following are the five main grounds that could lead to a director being sued:
1. Breach of fiduciary duty, not necessarily involving dishonesty.
2. Breach of authority.
3. Negligence.
4. Fraud or dishonesty.
5. Breach of statute.

A company may indemnify a director, but Section 310 of the Companies Act 1985 makes void any provision indemnifying him against liability arising from 'any negligence, breach of duty or breach of trust'. It does, however, provide that in proceedings in which judgment is passed in his favour, indemnities may be given. Section 727 of the Act provides that the director may be reimbursed his costs *if* the court finds that he acted honestly, reasonably and that he ought to be fairly excused. It is highly unlikely that the court will answer in the affirmative to these three tests and therefore reimburse part or all of a director's costs if the director has benefited from his breach of duty.

A Directors' and Officers' Liability policy is in two parts. The first grants an indemnity to the directors and officers in their *personal* capacity in circumstances where they are not entitled to be indemnified by the company under common law or under the memorandum or articles of association of the company. The second part indemnifies the company against costs incurred by it in indemnifying directors or officers of the company pursuant to the common law or under the memorandum or articles of association of the company. It is in effect a reimbursement of the amounts incurred by the company in indemnifying their directors or officers, hence it is known as the Reimbursable Policy.

Policy exclusions normally include libel or slander, bodily injury or damage to property and claims based upon directors gaining any personal profit or advantage to which they were not legally entitled, among others. Premiums depend upon the size of the firm, the location of any overseas subsidiaries abroad (particularly in the United States), the number of directors and officers to be insured and several other factors. Each case depends upon its own facts, but broadly 90 per cent of the premium relates to the protection of the company and 10 per cent to the protection of the directors, who must pay the premium out of their own pockets.

FURTHER READING

Carter, R. L. (ed.): *Handbook of Insurance* (with updating service) (Kluwer Publishing).

Directors' and Officers' Liability Insurance (Advanced Study Group No. 226 of the Insurance Institute of London, 1986).

Heppel, E. A.: *Products Liability Insurance* (Pitman, 1967).

Madge, Peter: *Professional Indemnity Insurance* (Butterworth, 1968).

Madge, Peter: *Liability Policy Wordings and Cover* (Buckley Press, 1972).

The Insurance of UK Products Liability Risks on a Worldwide Basis (Advanced Study Group No. 207 of the Insurance Institute of London, 1979).

Owles, Derrick, and Cockerell, Hugh: *Liability for Defective Services* (1985).

CHAPTER 10

Insurances of transportation

DUDLEY F. HAWKINS
Director, City Training

Marine Section revised by Len Wilkins
Senior Tutor, London Centre, CII College of Insurance

AVIATION INSURANCE

In the aviation insurance market the broker travels widely and keeps very much up to date with the new needs of the operators. Aircraft values are still increasing, court awards are still rapidly rising in many countries, and developing nations are expanding their aviation operations; all these factors must be taken into consideration and the broker may often influence the introduction of new forms of cover.

Types of cover

The aviation department of a broking house deals with a wide range of risks and this section aims to consider the broking aspects of each. The main risks in aviation insurance are hull, third-party legal liability, passenger legal liability, airport owner's and operator's liability, products legal liability and refuelling liability, profit commission cover and deductible cover. The aviation broker may find he must also negotiate business in respect of personal accident cover, passenger personal accident cover and loss of licence cover. These areas are usually dealt with in a specialised market.

Hull cover
The Lloyd's policy wording AVN1A indicates the basic hull cover. The individual broker develops his placing slip with this wording in mind.

The cover states that the underwriters will at their option pay for, replace or repair accidental loss of or damage to the aircraft described in the schedule arising from the risks covered, including disappearance if the aircraft is unreported for 60 days after commencement of flight. The broker will summarise this on his slip as: *'Interest* – the original assured's aircraft against flight, taxiing and ground risks'.

The option that the underwriters will pay for or replace is a negotiating point for brokers in that they may require an 'agreed value' rather than an insured value; thus the option to replace in the event of a total loss does not have any validity. Technically an agreed value may carry a higher rate, as gradual deterioration or 'value at time of loss' would not be taken into consideration in the event of total loss, because the agreed value is carried until renewal or lapse of policy. In the event of an agreed value being applied the cover should be subject to an agreed value clause AVN 61 25.4.86 to ensure deletion of all references to replacement in respect of claims adjusted on the basis of a total loss.

Other hull cover included in a standard policy would be 10 per cent emergency expenses incurred due to forced landing and certain repairs and transport of labour and materials.

When placing a risk, the broker has to take into account a number of considerations. The main areas are deductibles, pilots and uses.

Deductibles are an important aspect of negotiation and can vary considerably, but the broker must always bear in mind the client's best interests and be aware of his attitudes. For instance, he may be willing to carry a high deductible to obtain a keen rate or he may prefer to take a low deductible and accept a higher rate. As deductibles have increased over recent years a limited market has developed for deductible insurance.

Pilots are again a major area for negotiation. It is vital that the broker obtains full details of the pilot(s) as their experience can carry considerable influence on the rating. This becomes obvious when the pilot information seen on slips ranges from 'AB Crown 20,000 hours 5,000 on type' to 'As approved by assured'.

It does not need very much imagination to realise that *use* is a vital negotiating factor from a broking point of view. It is important that the broker elicits as much information as he can from the client concerning the uses. The standard uses are 'private pleasure', 'business', 'commercial' and 'rental for private pleasure and business only'.* If the broker can elaborate on the standard use it can be a 'rate reducer'.

*Standard uses on US form Aviation 16 are 'business and pleasure', 'industrial aid', 'limited commercial' and 'commercial'.

Aviation hull war risks have traditionally been placed in the marine market but have been dealt with by the aviation department of the broking house.

It is most important that the broker dealing with war risks is absolutely certain of the cover offered by the London market. A detailed study of the cover is not practical in this chapter but the summaries on pages 114 to 117 will give a broad picture of the overall position.

From a broking point of view, careful consideration must be given to the client's needs – for example a writeback under the open market placing AVN51 gives limited cover only, particularly since exclusions *(a)*, *(b)*, *(d)* and *(f)* are still in force.

In 1977 a new war wording appeared in the London market, 'Aviation Hull Political Risk Policy RJM Airline One 1.1.77'. This wording is sometimes referred to as the 'mirror wording', because it covers the majority of the sections excluded by the war exclusion clause. It is therefore considerably broader than the September 1970 wording, with cover given in respect of extortion and hijack expenses.

Breach of warranty cover is an extension of the hull cover and can be included subject to an additional premium. It is therefore a useful way of giving one's client a service regarding any lien he may have with respect to the purchase of aircraft.

The cover offered is that the insurance afforded by the policy shall not be invalidated as regards the interest of the lienholder by any act or neglect. In other words, in the event of a loss of any kind the lienholder's investment is protected.

Third-party legal liability and passenger legal liability cover
The cover offered in the aviation market is substantial and from a broker's point of view the capacity of the London market is very high.

The coverage can be summarised as 'to indemnify the insured for all sums which the insured shall be legally liable to pay as compensatory damages in respect of accidental bodily injury (fatal or otherwise) and accidental damage to property. Also accidental bodily injury (fatal or otherwise) to passengers, and accidental damage or loss of baggage and personal articles.'

The particular aspects which are negotiating factors are *limits*. It is, to a large extent, the broker's responsibility to advise his client concerning his third-party legal liability limit and passenger limits. Territorial limits, uses, pilots and brokerage all have a negotiating importance.

Other liability cover

The aviation broker needs to have a reasonably detailed knowledge of several other aspects of liability cover.

Airport owner's and operator's legal liability is the liability arising from use by third parties of premises owned by the airport authority or operator, and hangarkeeper's liability arises from damage to aircraft and equipment stored in hangars. Products legal liability is liability arising from any products sold or repairs carried out on the airport precincts. This is a specialised area and can be satisfactorily studied by analysis of the 'Ariel Airport Owner's and Operator's Liability Insurance' wording.

Refuelling liability is once again a specialised area which can be further studied by analysis of a suitable wording.

Profit commission cover and deductible cover

From the broker's point of view this cover can be a very good negotiating factor with his client. If a profit commission is included in the placing, the client will be pleased with the service if it can be protected. That is to say he can insure against the loss of his profit commission or the deductible being applied to a loss.

Aviation claims

The claims broker's job entails the need for an in-depth knowledge of the aviation policy wording. Initial advice of a claim is notified to the broker and a great deal of time and effort can be saved if his knowledge is sufficient to take the correct action at this stage. On large risks, for instance, the broker may have set up a special procedure which enables funds to be available to the client within hours of the loss. Quick and efficient arrangements for settlement of claims are a vital part of the service given to the client by brokers. Failure to act quickly can mean lost business to the broker and perhaps the London market.

In aviation insurance the broker plays a strong intermediary role in that he may deal with surveyors and adjusters on behalf of underwriters, although the actual appointment of surveyors and adjusters is by underwriters.

MOTOR INSURANCE

Perhaps a major difference, from a broker's point of view, between the motor market and other non-marine markets is that

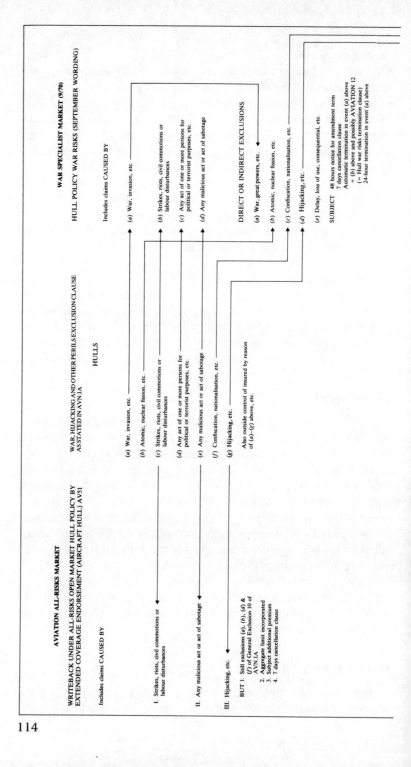

SCHEDULE SUMMARISING MARKET PRACTICE FOR WAR AND KINDRED RISKS

HIJACKING ENDORSEMENT TO ADD TO HULL WAR RISKS POLICY AVN50 DIRECTLY OR INDIRECTLY

(a) Hijacking, etc.

(b) Loss subsequent and because of (a) (i.e. indirect cause)

SUBJECT   15 days cancellation clause

CONFISCATION ENDORSEMENT DIRECTLY CAUSED

Confiscation, nationalisation, etc.
Except by government and/or public authorisation as named (i.e. country of registration or owner)

CONFISCATED AIRCRAFT ALL-RISKS CONTINUATION (RJM)

Cover extended to include loss or damage occurring subsequent to confiscation which would have been covered had the confiscation not taken place (i.e. indirect)

SUBJECT   15 days termination clause

Note: All sections of AV48B can be covered except Part (a) in part, i.e. between great powers, and Part (b) in no circumstances at all.

AVIATION WAR RISKS – APPENDIX II

AVIATION ALL-RISKS MARKET HULL POLICY BY
EXTENDED COVERAGE ENDORSEMENT (AIRCRAFT HULL) AVN51

Includes claims CAUSED BY

I. Strikes, riots, civil commotions or labour disturbances

II. Any malicious act or act of sabotage

III. Hijacking, etc.

BUT 1. Still exclusions (a), (b), (d) & (f) of General Exclusion 10 of AVN.1A
2. Aggregate limit incorporated
3. Subject additional premium
4. 7 days cancellation clause

WAR, HIJACKING AND OTHER PERILS EXCLUSION CLAUSE AS STATED IN AVN.1A

HULLS

(a) War, invasions, etc.

(b) Atomic, nuclear fission, etc.

(c) Strikes, riots, civil commotions or labour disturbances

(d) Any act of one or more persons for political or terrorist purposes, etc.

(e) Any malicious act or act of sabotage

(f) Confiscation, nationalisation, etc.

(g) Hijacking, etc.

Also outside control of insured by reason of (a)–(g) above, etc.

WAR SPECIALIST MARKET

AVIATION HULL POLITICAL RISK POLICY RJM AIRLINE ONE 1.1.77

COVER

(a) War, invasions, etc.

(b) Strikes, riots, civil commotions or labour disturbances

(c) Any act of one or more persons for political or terrorist purposes, etc.

(d) Any malicious act or act of sabotage

(e) Confiscation, etc. except by governments as specified in schedule

(f) Extortion and hijack expenses, etc. 90% excluding any country where not lawful

EXCLUSIONS

(a) War, great powers, etc.

(b) Atomic, nuclear fission, etc.

(c) Debt failure to provide bond or security, etc.

(d) Repossession, etc.

(e) Delay, loss of use consequential, etc.

SUBJECT 7 days notice for amendment of terms
7 days cancellation clause
Automatic terminations in event (a) above

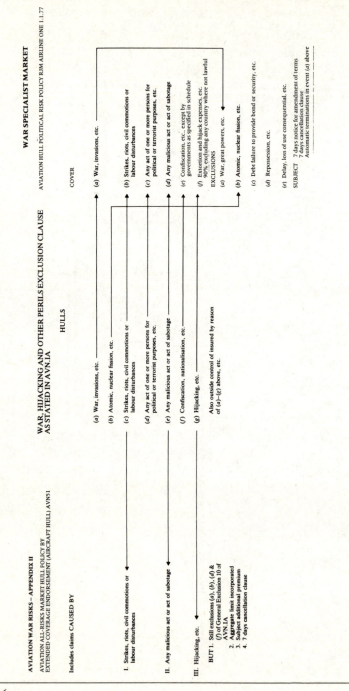

SCHEDULE SUMMARISING MARKET PRACTICE FOR WAR AND KINDRED RISKS

Note: An important clause was instituted in October 1983; it was the 50/50 provisional claims settlement clause. This was produced in an endeavour to alleviate the difficulty of identifying the actual cause of loss, i.e. a war loss or an all-risk loss. As the time delay in identifying the exact cause could be considerable, the clause was produced to ensure the claim was paid half by the open market and half by the war market, final settlement being made when the cause was confirmed. However, this clause has had only very limited success.

the spread of risk is smaller. This is because a very high proportion of motor business is placed on the basis of 'one risk, one
underwriter' – that is to say, a Lloyd's underwriter or company.

It is not the intention in this section to deal with the detailed
cover offered as this is the province of the appropriate textbooks.
It should, however, be noted by the potential motor broker that it
is absolutely vital that he is fully aware of *(a)* the cover offered in
a standard motor policy and a commercial policy and *(b)* the
differences in cover offered by the various underwriters with
which his department does business. He should also be aware of
the statutory insurance requirements of the Road Traffic Acts.
These provide for compulsory insurance against liability for
injury or death of third parties. At the same time of writing, legislation
is under consideration in compliance with the EEC Second Motor ·
Directive to extend the statutory requirement of the Road Traffic
Act to make provision for compulsory insurance against liability
for third-party property damage.

The two main areas dealt with by the broker are the private
individual's motor policy and the commercial fleet motor policy.
A marked tendency in the large broking house during recent
years has been to concentrate more and more on the fleet
placings, and less and less on the private sector of the market.
Many large brokers feel private car business is uneconomic, and
so sub-brokers or provincial brokers are dealing with a greater
proportion of this class of motor business.

The commission available in the motor market varies somewhat. It may range from 7½ per cent to 10 per cent although
with large fleet business, brokerage may be agreed on a fee basis
which is often charged over the whole portfolio for that particular
client.

In the past a standard rate or tariff which was agreed and
reviewed by a professional body was used in this market. This is
no longer the case, but this approach still influences underwriters
in some areas. In recent years, however, many larger brokers have
developed what is known as a 'direct dealing account'. This is
where the broker introduces a sub-broker to underwriters and
then permits him to deal directly with them under a fronting
agreement. The accounts, however, will still pass through the
main broker. The commission is split between the main broker
and the sub-broker, with the sub-broker usually commanding
the higher percentage. An important restriction applied to the
sub-broker within the fronting agreement is that he must pass ⁄

the premium on to the main broker within 30 days of inception of the risk.

An area which has possibly given rise to some concern to the motor broker is the development of quotation systems such as 'Quotel'. These are computer-based quotation systems which have been used successfully by some brokers. The benefits are a very quick service, although it may still be advantageous to 'shop around' for the best deal for one's client.

Lloyd's motor market tends to give a greater variation in approach and rates than the company market, although it tends to put greater restrictions on high-powered vehicles.

An area of direct competition which may affect brokers in the future is the tendency towards self-insurance. This is where a large company sets up its own insurance branch to deal with the physical damage losses but still requires the open market to accept third-party and passenger legal liability risks. The effect of this is to make for an imbalance of premium allocation. In a motor premium for comprehensive cover there has been a tendency for the liability proportion of the overall premium to rise steeply whereas the vehicle premium has increased less dramatically.

Another area of direct competition to the motor broker is where large insurance companies set up their own provincial offices and the public go direct to them. The disadvantage to the individual is that he does not see the broad spectrum of cover offered in this field.

As can be seen from the above, there are a number of routes which can be taken by a proposer to obtain his insurance. It is important for the broker to understand these routes fully.

The main routes to completion of cover by Lloyd's or companies for a private individual are via a large garage, the Automobile Association, a Lloyd's broker or a bank, or from a provincial broker via a fronting agreement with a Lloyd's broker. For a commercial fleet (which is more than ten vehicles but may be thousands) the placing can be from a provincial broker to a Lloyd's broker or direct to a Lloyd's broker. Of course, for both private and commercial business the client may deal with most insurance companies direct.

It might be of interest to consider how an enquiry regarding a motor insurance may be processed in the London market. When a Lloyd's broker receives an enquiry he will prepare a slip; a quote is then obtained and the client informed. If the client accepts the quote, a temporary certificate of insurance is issued by the broker and the risk is placed with a company or with Lloyd's. Next a debit note is sent to the client, the premium is collected and passed to the company accepting the risk (or Lloyd's as the case may be) less the broker's commission. The company prepares the full certificate of insurance, which is dispatched to the broker, who finally forwards it to the client.

In connection with the issue of temporary certificates of insurance the broker has an agreement with the underwriter in which the main cover note books are safeguarded. Obviously misuse of blank certificates could cause enormous problems.

The broker must also agree to issue certificates in accordance with legal requirements. For example, it is illegal to backdate cover notes or temporary certificates of insurance and it is also illegal to issue a cover note and hold it in the office until the premium is received. The layout of cover notes and temporary certificates varies: some merely state legal requirements, while others contain a considerable amount of detail in respect of the extent of cover offered.

An important area from a broking aspect is the broker's advice to his client in connection with the 'green card'. Until the EEC agreement came into force the position was straightforward, the green card being required for temporary driving abroad to ensure full cover. Now a motorist is not required to produce a green card in the majority of Common Market countries. Insurers, however, have to deal with claims which fall under a particular country's compulsory requirements, which can vary from those specified by the UK Traffic Act. Some underwriters reserve the right to recover against the policyholder in these circumstances. The broker must therefore ensure that his client is fully aware of a possible gap in cover and that he is advised to effect a 'green card extension' and so have full cover.

One area of insurance which gives rise to the greatest number of problems with the insurance public is the handling of motor insurance claims. It is very important that these are dealt with promptly by brokers within the guidelines and requirements of the holding insurer. For detailed reference, see *Bingham's Motor Claims Cases*.

MARINE INSURANCE

The marine market is very large and has a complex and fascinating history. The main areas of this market are hull cover (i.e. loss of or damage to the ship itself), liability of the shipowner, liability of the charterer, liability of the ship repairer, liability of the mortgagee, loss of or damage to cargo (may include over land as well as water), liability of cargo owners and carriers, freight and marine war risks.

In addition the broker needs to have knowledge of specialised classes such as tugs, dredgers, drilling rigs, heavy lifting vessels, barges, salvage cranes and yachts (from weekend dinghies to 5,000-ton motor yachts). The conditions of insurance for these are similar in many respects and they are dealt with as a class of their own by the broking house.

Historically and unlike most other branches, marine insurance is mainly governed by one Act – the Marine Insurance Act 1906 – to which a great deal of case law has been grafted on. This Act must be borne in mind when considering marine risks.

Types of cover

The special aspects of each cover offered are considered below.

Hull cover
This is usually subject to the Institute Time Clause, which is written in modern-day language and is relatively easy to interpret. Both Lloyd's and company underwriters use the Institute forms, which are drafted by the Institute's Technical and Clauses Committee (whose members are from both the Lloyd's and company marine markets). The clause is attached to a plain policy which contains no conditions of cover but which sets out details of the specific risk to be covered and the underwriters' proportion of that risk. It is of great importance that the broker and/or technician and/or claims person has a complete understanding of the clause. The cover consists of both physical damage and collision liability. The insured ship is covered for loss caused by maritime perils, which are called perils of the sea, plus fire, explosion, violent theft, jettison, piracy, earthquake and volcanic eruption. Damage caused to the ship by the following is also covered: land/dock equipment, aircraft, accidents in loading/ unloading cargo, barratry, latent defect and negligence of the officers and crew. In addition, cover is given for three-quarters of any collision liability that the insured ship might incur by colliding with another vessel. Traditionally the marine market

gives three-quarters cover with the remaining quarter insured with the owner's P & I club (see Shipowner's Liability).

Voluntary losses made in time of peril are governed by the principle of *general average* (GA). This means that when a loss is incurred voluntarily for the safety of the common adventure, this loss will be borne proportionally by all the interested parties. The principle is entirely independent of marine insurance.

Although the basic idea of general average would appear to be quite simple, in practice it becomes very involved. The broker should continually develop his knowledge in the area and endeavour to keep up with the numerous case laws dealing with it.

As far as *salvage charges* are concerned, there is no sacrifice or expenditure incurred on behalf of others. In this case therefore the salvors have a separate lien on the property so that they can negotiate separate terms with the owners. This is the basic difference between salvage charges and general average.

Sue and labour charges are incurred by the insured or his agents in attempting to avert or minimise a loss covered by the insurance. It should be noted, however, that legal charges incurred by the insured in resisting a claim which would fall under the policy are not sue and labour charges.

There are other Institute clauses which must be studied and understood by the broker. Some give more limited cover than the Time Clause, while others give the same cover but for just one voyage rather than the 12-month cover usually given under the Time Clause. In addition, there are special clauses which are used to give cover while a vessel is under construction or is laid up in port. It is important that broking staff fully understand these. An excellent summary of them is contained in Robert H. Brown, *Summary of the Institute Time Clauses* (Witherby).

Shipowner's liability cover
Shipowners usually insure their liability in mutual insurance associations known as P & I clubs (P & I standing for 'Protection and Indemnity'). These clubs give a very wide form of cover and operate differently from the marine insurance market. They also cover the shipowner for the one-quarter collision liability that is not given under the Institute Time Clause. Shipowners have the option to place any or all of their liability cover in the marine market. (See also page 125).

Charterer's liability cover

When a person or company charters a vessel they will require charterer's liability cover if this is not included under the owner's policy. The cover will be in respect of liabilities to others than owners of the chartered vessel by way of reimbursement for claims brought against them by third parties as stipulated in clauses CL345 NE or E(1/74). These clauses should be studied and understood by the marine broker.

Ship repairer's liability cover

The cover is for loss of or damage to any vessel or craft in the care, custody or control of the ship repairer or any vessel or craft upon which the repairer is working. The cover will also include damage to machinery or equipment of any vessel or craft which is in the repairer's care, custody or control. Other liability cover provided may be loss of life or bodily injury to third parties arising out of the insured's operations as ship repairers. An important exclusion to be aware of concerns faulty design: any liability arising from this would not be covered. The broker should study this clause carefully to ensure his understanding of the conditions and exclusions.

Mortgagee's liability cover

Mortgagees who have a financial interest in a vessel or craft may require a form of security to cover them if the lienholder's policy, after a final court judgment or average adjustment, does not uphold a claim and the lienholder is therefore unable to recover from the vessel's hull underwriters. If this happens, the mortgagee may lose his money and so cover to protect him from this loss must be arranged.

Cargo cover

Like hull insurance, the cargo policy is a plain form which gives details of the specific risk to be covered and the underwriters' proportion of that risk. There are three main Institute cargo clauses and a number of special 'trade' clauses where the extent and period of cover has been agreed between the Institute's Technical and Clauses Committee and trade associations. A broker needs to have a full understanding of these clauses.

The main cargo clauses are known as 'A', 'B' and 'C'. 'A' covers all risks of physical loss or damage and the others cover named perils only, with the 'B' clause giving wider cover than the 'A' clause.

Generally speaking, the contract of sale will be free on board (FOB), which means the seller is responsible for the cargo until it is on board ship; or cost, insurance and freight (CIF), which places the responsibility for arranging marine insurance to destination on the buyer.

The broker should be aware of the many people interested in the insurance of cargo. These include the manufacturer, merchant, shipping agent and forwarding agent, haulier, shipping company, customs, intermediary consignee, selling agent, and of course the insurance broker and market underwriters.

The *type of cargo* being carried is obviously a vital aspect to consider when broking a cargo risk. The range of cargo carried around the world is enormous and the range of risk involved therein extremely broad. A broker must therefore be fully conversant with the properties of the cargo being carried and the hazards involved together with the method of packing. He must discuss any peculiarities with his client, who may not be readily aware of the risk exposure.

Other covers

The broker should endeavour to develop a sound technical knowledge regarding the more important peripheral covers such as the following:

1. *Rejection insurance.* This covers rejection of imported foodstuffs by government health departments.
2. *Consequential loss.* As in other branches of insurance a consequential loss can arise due to loss of business arising directly from the original claim.
3. *Seller's contingency.* This occurs where a UK seller sells on FOB or similar terms and hence does not insure for the marine voyage. However, he may be worried about the existence and quality of cover arranged by the buyer. In certain areas of the world a country may insist by legislation that goods in transit either to or from it are insured locally.
4. *Confiscation.* This means confiscation by any government or government agency through whose territory the goods may be passing *en route* to their destination.

As well as being aware of the normal areas of procedures within the marine market, it is vital that the marine broker is able to deal with those enquiries from clients which do not conform to the normal requirements.

The 'line slip' is a relatively new development in the marine market when seen in the context of 300 years of Lloyd's history, having been in general use for 15 to 20 years. It is an agreement whereby the broking house has the authority to accept risks on behalf of underwriters without the need to see all participants in the line slip. Each acceptance is a declaration off the line slip and each declaration is within the terms and conditions of the line slip agreement.

Protection and indemnity associations

Protection and indemnity associations – traditionally known as P & I clubs – were originally formed to combat the monopoly in the marine insurance market. When in the mid 1880s the liabilities of shipowners to third parties increased, the P & I clubs started taking these risks.

The scope of the cover given by a P & I club is quite wide and can embrace the following:
1. Loss of life and personal injury claims.
2. Hospital, medical and funeral expenses.
3. Wages payable to crew after shipwreck.
4. Loss of personal effects.
5. Damage to property of third parties.
6. Liability arising from collisions.
7. Tug owners' claims.
8. Raising and demolition of wreck.
9. Fires.

From a broking aspect there tends to be a direct link between the shipowners and the P & I clubs because the owners mutually contribute to the club funds. Nevertheless a broker can, and often does, get involved. Premium is not charged as such but 'calls' are made which are 'net' to the club. If a broker is involved, he may charge a fee to his client.

The marine broker's flow of work

In order to see how each aspect of the broker's work fits into the overall picture, we can consider the flow of work from the client's enquiry by telex, letter or telephone until the successful placing of the risk and final settlement of accounts.

The broking house seeks business and with the support of a competent team of service staff endeavours to keep it. On receipt of an enquiry the broker or technician considers and assesses the risk involved, clarifying his own view of the rates and conditions applicable. The broker then prepares a slip and searches the marine market to obtain satisfactory quotes. Often there is a high proportion of unsuccessful quotes to orders secured. The broker then advises the client of the quotes and if one is acceptable the order is received and 100 per cent cover is obtained, often in small amounts. Sometimes risks or parts of risks are placed in overseas markets.

When the risks are placed, the transaction is confirmed with the client, the cover note is sent off, and the signing slip is prepared and initialled by the leading market. The debit note is then sent to the client and copies sent to accounts and the computer data-processing department. Finally the policies are prepared and forwarded to the underwriters for signature and then dispatched to the client. The final actions are the reconciling and settlement of accounts.

Marine claims

The marine claims broker must, of course, have a detailed knowledge of the policy forms and classes. He must also have a working knowledge of other aspects of business which affect the settlement of claims.

Hull claims

When the notification of a loss is received by the broker, it is vital that this information is passed on to the underwriters immediately. The main reason is that the underwriters can then appoint a surveyor. Any delay can cause problems concerning the possibility of further damage, the incurring of unnecessary expenses and delay in actual payment.

The broker must then advise the client that he has lodged the claim with the underwriters and that a surveyor is on his way to inspect the damage. The broker should advise the client to appoint an 'average adjuster' to act on the client's behalf. The average adjuster will then work in collaboration with the surveyor.

In the case of almost any hull loss there are at least five interested parties – the insured, the average adjuster, the claims broker, the surveyor and the insurer. The broker's job is to link all the parties together. The final report and recommendations are usually submitted to the broker, who will then negotiate settlement with the underwriters.

In certain cases the insured may request 'payment on account'. In this situation the broker must negotiate the payment with the underwriters. The broker arranges this in conjunction with the average adjuster. When considering a collision claim the broker must advise the client to instruct a solicitor to act on his behalf and advise the hull insurers when this action has been taken. It may not be necessary if it is a very straightforward case such as collision with a moored ship or fixed object.

Cargo claims

From a broking point of view, cargo claims can be looked at under two headings: (1) imports, and (2) exports.

1. *Imports*. The first thing that will happen is that the consignee will receive goods in a damaged condition or find that some goods are missing. Notification of the loss will be sent to the broker, who must *immediately* advise the underwriters.

   The underwriters may accept the claim at this stage or appoint a surveyor. The broker will then instruct the surveyor accordingly. At the same time it is vital that the broker instructs the client to advise all other parties involved that they are being held liable for the loss or damage or part thereof.

   The surveyor and consignee will agree how to approach the claim and the surveyor's report and recommendations will be sent to the broker so that settlement can be negotiated with the underwriters. In controversial cases the report may go directly to the underwriters.

   Subrogation action differs from marine hull claims in that Lloyd's Recoveries Department will deal with any subrogation which might arise.

2. *Exports*. In the event of a loss a consignee does not want long, protracted negotiations with London, and so the broker will set up a 'claims payable abroad system'. This system gives the local Lloyd's agent the right to act as surveyor and adjuster, and in many cases actually to pay the claim. In these circumstances there is very little action for the London broker to take other than to mark up his records when final details are sent to London.

   A broker may have to become substantially involved when the local Lloyd's agent is not authorised actually to pay the claim. If a dispute arises, the broker will be involved because the subsequent discussion, negotiations and arbitration will usually take place in London. Where a very large loss occurs overseas, the underwriters will appoint a specialist surveyor to inspect the damaged cargo and report back.

This completes this necessarily brief summary of the main features of the aviation, motor and marine markets. It is hoped that the chapter has succeeded in its aim of acquainting the reader with the main types of cover encountered in each market and the negotiating factors that the broker constantly has to take into account.

FURTHER READING

Aviation Claims (CII Tuition Service Study Course No. 76b).
Aviation Underwriting (CII Tuition Service Study Course No. 75b).
Batlen, A. G. M., and Dinsdale, W. A.: *Motor Insurance* (Stone & Cox, 1965).
Brown, R. H.: *A Dictionary of Marine Insurance Terms* (Witherby, 1975).
Brown, R. H.: *Principles of Marine Insurance* (Witherby, 1975).
Brown, R. H.: *A Summary of the Institute Time Clauses – Hull (1/10/70)* (Witherby, 1972).
Din, Salah el: *Aviation Insurance, Practice, Law and Reinsurance* (distributed by Sweet & Maxwell).
Hudson, N. G.: *Marine Claims Handbook* (Lloyd's of London Press, 1977).
Motor Insurance Practice (CII Tuition Service Study Course No. 63).
Taylor, T. A. (ed.). *Bingham's Motor Claims Cases*, ninth edition (Butterworths, 1986).

CHAPTER 11

Risk management

P. A. BAWCUTT

Managing Director, Risk and Insurance Research Group Ltd

INTRODUCTION

The term 'risk management' was probably first used in the United States in the early 1950s. It developed out of the dissatisfaction of US insurance managers with the lack of premium credit they were being given by the insurance industry for the loss-prevention methods that were being introduced for property risks and the desire to retain more risk within large US corporations. In parallel with this activity, the universities in the United States extended their insurance curricula to include risk and especially mathematical and statistical methods of calculating loss probabilities.

The development for many years was slow, but gradually the concepts of risk analysis, loss prevention and self-insurance spread throughout North America and through multinational company activity in Europe. More sophisticated methods were introduced to calculate maximum possible losses (MPL) and estimated maximum losses (EML), and increasing expenditure was devoted to sophisticated fire protection systems and the use of highly protected risk (HPR) standards for new properties.

These activities were primarily related to more effective insurance buying linked with the introduction of much greater self-insurance, in the form of deductibles and the establishment of captive insurance companies. This meant that there was a tendency for risk management to become part of the insurance function. As the insurance-buying portion of the insurance manager's job reduced and he became more active in managing self-insurance programmes and loss control budgets, the term 'risk manager' became more common and today is used by the majority of those who would have been called 'insurance manager' in previous years.

The approach to risk management in the United States has until recent times been somewhat dogmatic in that the risk manager has been regarded as the man who manages pure or static risk within the company. In Europe the approach has always been that the risk manager acts in an advisory capacity to line management and coordinates insurance and risk management activity. The European view, which is certainly more practical and less onerous for the risk manager, is currently gaining much ground in the United States and is now probably the more common approach both there and throughout the world.

Many larger firms have their own risk management departments, whose senior staff are usually members of AIRMIC, which is the professional body for risk managers.

DEFINITIONS

Definitions abound on the nature of risk and the role of risk management. The following has been developed over many years of practical consultancy work by my ex-colleague Jim Bannister:

'The identification, measurement and *economic* control of risks that threaten the assets or earnings of a business or other enterprise.'

Where a non-profit-making body is involved, the definition can be amended to read:

'. . . risks that threaten the continued provision of essential services or supplies.'

The emphasis of the definition is on economic control. There is no point in spending more on controlling risk than can be justified by the losses that are being prevented or the reduction in possibility of a major loss. This 'trade-off' is a major factor in risk management and needs to take account of social, political and environmental cost factors, as well as the physical cost of loss.

RISK MANAGEMENT TECHNIQUES

The essence of risk management is a systematic approach that contains the following factors:

1. Awareness of the threats facing the company.
2. Preparation and planning for events that could occur.
3. Recording of decisions and data on which plans have been developed.
4. Ongoing monitoring of the results of the decisions and subsequent events.

The ultimate objective of risk management is to make this approach an integral part of the day-to-day activity of all management, so that it becomes one of their responsibilities and is a factor in judging performance.

There are three main techniques used in the risk management process:

1. Risk evaluation (which includes risk identification and measurement).
2. Risk control.
3. Risk financing.

These are discussed in the following paragraphs.

Risk evaluation

Identification of risk

This is inherently difficult owing to the uncertainties that exist about the future. It is usual to separate 'pure' risk into property. earnings and liability threats. Using available information sources, physical inspections and verification by interview and discussion, it should be possible to work with management and others to produce a list of the assets and earnings that are at risk in the company.

Property risk can be relatively easily identified by inspection and records analysis but needs to include non-physical factors such as goodwill.

Earnings exposures can be isolated by the use of flow-charts which indicate the key areas at risk, bottlenecks, loss of market possibilities and opportunities for easing loss situations by system improvement or proper contingency planning.

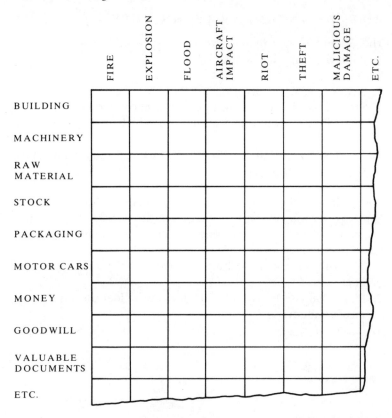

Fig 11.1 Property risk identification chart

Liability can best be identified by careful analysis of the activities of the company and consideration of the possible consequences, including a breakdown of the threats to which the company is exposed, how the threats arise and how they are increased or reduced.

Identification is often recorded on charts. Examples of charts which can be used for property, earnings and liability work are shown in Figs. 11.1–11.3.

Measurement of risk

For property and earnings exposure, risk measurement is fairly easy. There is access to historical loss data in relation to the company, its industry and the country of operation. This information needs to be used as a guide to which changing factors,

	EARNINGS EXPOSED	CIRCUMSTANCES	ALTERNATIVE PLANS, ETC.
RAIL SUPPLY			
LOCAL SUPPLY			
DESIGN			
FORMING			
PACKAGING			
STORAGE			
KEY CUSTOMER			
ETC.			

Fig. 11.2 Earnings exposure chart

	BOTTLING	FILLING	DELIVERY	SHOPS
NATURE OF EXPOSURE				
CIRCUMSTANCES				
OTHERS' PROPERTY EXPOSED				
OTHER PEOPLE EXPOSED				
LOSS CONTROL MEASURES				

Fig. 11.3 Liability exposure chart

such as inflation, change in structure of the business, alterations to the spread of risk and so on, are built in. It is also important to consider the exposure change that may occur on a day-to-day or hour-by-hour basis.

Property measurement will take account of the total value of risk adding to the likely cost of rebuilding and additional expenses. The total exposure will be reduced by the effectiveness of factors that will limit risk such as separation of buildings and fire protection. However, in evaluating a maximum foreseeable loss figure it should be assumed that the worst will happen and that the protection hardware will not function. An example of recording measurement data for property loss is shown in Fig. 11.4.

Earnings can be measured by utilising the flow-charts developed in the identification process and applying values at risk in particular bottleneck situations. If machinery is involved, replacement time, availability of spare parts and capability to manufacture in-house are some of the factors that need consideration. Such studies can involve analysis of the company's reliance on key suppliers or customers whose own loss could seriously affect the company's earnings.

The increasing cost of liability awards, the impact of consumerism and changes in legal attitudes make liability measurement extremely hard. The potential in many products liability cases can be astronomic and the effect of pollution on major cities beyond comprehension. It is necessary for management in these situations to recognise that the potential at risk is the total assets of the company and that the only practical solution is to buy as much liability insurance as can be afforded while introducing liability loss control measures. It is becoming normal for most large UK companies to have at least £10 million liability cover and in some cases this is as much as £50 million. For airline operators limits of £250 million are normal.

Risk control

Risk control has often been regarded as synonymous with risk management, but it is in fact one of the techniques used as part of the overall process. Work on risk evaluation enables a company to assess the circumstances that are involved in risk situations and determine the control needed. As an example a fire requires a source of ignition, flammable materials and a source of oxygen if it is to grow without containment.

RISK	CIRCUMSTANCES	VALUES EXPOSED	LIMITING FACTORS	AGGRAVATING FACTORS
FIRE	ACCIDENTAL Electrical Process Smoking	All of main building £25.3 million	INCEPTION Electrical installation modern & checked Process flames enclosed No smoking SPREAD Fire walls between blocks (primary processing is biggest value, £9.3 million) Sprinkler system Works fire brigade Local fire brigade at 2 minutes' call time 24 hour working	Difficult to enforce rule 100% All fire walls have self-closing doors which might jam or be wedged open Fire brigade strike Annual shut-down for 3 weeks
	DELIBERATE	As above	As above Security guard	Sprinkler system: (1) could be disabled; (2) designed to deal with single ignition source. False alarm could increase attendance time to 7 minutes

Fig. 11.4 Sample chart for recording risk measurement data

A company can help to control the fire situation by a pre-loss action which would very often involve separation of the fire risk and control of the ignition sources by limiting the availability of flammable materials and oxygen. The control activity can be continued during the loss by use of fire protection devices such as sprinklers and fire extinguishers.

In the post-loss situation measures can be available to salvage materials, stock and property which have been subject to fire and any contingency plan can also be implemented.

The process of control involves the analysis of the loss potential, the implementation of prevention methods and, very importantly, training and motivation of staff to ensure that in the event of an incident action is taken to limit its spread.

It is important to recognise that decisions affecting the introduction of loss control are trade-off decisions. The intention is to spend a specific amount of money now to reap benefits later. Therefore the benefits that can be expected from loss control action need to be calculated both in terms of reducing the probability and the size of loss and by asking what it is worth to the company to reduce the expected possibility of loss when viewed against the cost of the risk control measures that have been recommended.

Risk control work will often involve a risk factor analysis which is similar to the work carried out in the evaluation process but is extended to consider methods of risk control, including changes in design, introduction of protection systems, and training, motivation and monitoring systems for employees and outside people. A specimen chart is given in Fig. 11.5.

The use of loss experience is also valuable as an aid to loss control: it can enable the company to analyse losses to discover multiple factors that could have made such losses more serious and help it to develop means of controlling loss in an economic way.

In assessing the cost of losses and the cost of loss control measures the estimates for the former can very easily be underestimated. The main factors in the property loss can include not only the replacement and repair of the property but also any earnings lost by the non-availability of the item of property, the loss of management and other time both when the loss occurs and in subsequent investigation, reporting and replacement, and the loss of sales through non-availability of equipment.

Where one is involved in a major loss the delay factors can be

RISK FACTOR ANALYSIS		SITE:		DATE:
ACTIVITY	EQUIPMENT INVOLVED	OPERATIONS INVOLVED	HAZARDS	COMMENTS

ANALYSIS CARRIED THROUGH BY: (risk management adviser)

CHECKED BY: (line management)

Fig. 11.5 Sample chart for risk factor analysis

excessive due not only to rebuilding time but also to changes in the social and political scene which may involve the company in complying with new regulations and standards which did not exist when the property was originally built.

In trying to calculate the cost of losses one needs to look at these direct and indirect factors, estimate the future cost and then calculate the cost of each loss control measure that is being considered. By balancing these costs against the estimated future benefits in the form of losses avoided and losses reduced, the company can begin to come to conclusions on whether the measures are economic and will therefore give it a good economic pay-off in both the short and the long term.

Risk financing and insurance

The last process in the risk management activity is the financing of the residual risks that have not been dealt with by risk control measures. Although one can do a certain amount to eliminate uncertainty it is not possible to eliminate loss and the company therefore needs to be able to cope with the financial consequences.

Financial methods available involve meeting losses out of normal budget operations, the creation of special funds to pay for losses as they occur, the use of insurance, and the use of credit and government grants. In determining the methods of particular situations the overall cost needs to be calculated, taking full account of the time value of the money that is involved.

In considering the insurance methods the options generally open to the company involve the direct regular market, the reinsurance market and the establishment of an insurance company, often called a 'captive' (see below). The risk-financing objective is to be able to meet after-loss expenses by replacing assets lost, replacing earnings that would have otherwise been achieved and paying for any additional special expenses.

In developing a risk-financing and particularly a self-insurance strategy it is important for the company to decide how much loss it can afford to retain within its own operations. It is useful to approach this problem by firstly calculating the total amount of losses that are not insured and retained within the company and then applying the company's risk-taking approach to the potential amount of risk. For a normal company which is neither conservative nor a risk-taker a starting-point could be 1 per cent of pre-tax profit plus any insurance premium saved by a self-insurance programme. It is, however, important to ensure that the company does have available funds in the event of losses occurring, particularly as there is a significant difference in the timing of funding for types of claim. For example, a small property claim would involve a very prompt payment, but a large liability claim would involve a payment which could be spread over seven, eight or ten years.

In considering methods of self-insurance the most attractive method where small losses are involved is the inclusion of such losses in operating budgets, which enables the company to pay for the losses as they occur rather than in advance if an insurance premium is involved and also eliminates the additional cost of insurance, which always includes the insurance company's overheads, expenses and profits.

The use of funds to pay for losses is theoretically a useful method of self-insurance but has a major disadvantage if the fund is to be carried forward from one accounting year to another as it would then be subject to normal corporation tax.

Common methods used for self-insurance involve the use of participative insurance including excesses or loss deductibles, the use of aggregate deductibles in order to protect the company's position in the event of accumulation of losses within the primary excess excepted and also the use of franchise and co-insurance schemes. Other rating methods introduced in recent years include retrospective rating plans and cost-stabilisation plans which enable the buyer of insurance to share in the investment income earned by the insurance company through its retention of premiums while waiting for claims to be settled, which as already mentioned can in the case of some liability claims spread over a decade.

One fairly recent innovation in the United Kingdom has been the establishment of captive insurance companies, which are insurance companies formed by an industrial buyer primarily to handle his own insurances. Although the captive is old as an idea, the innovations in recent years have been linked to the establishment of such companies offshore, primarily in Guernsey for UK companies, in order to obtain additional tax benefits, which provide the ability to build up reserves rapidly and avoid the tax disadvantage of internal funds within a normal operating situation.

The particular advantage of the captive insurance company is that it enables the insurance buyer to gain access to the reinsurance market, which operates more economically than the direct insurance market because of its lower overheads and organisational structure. In addition, in any environment where the direct insurance industry is unwilling to give enough credit to the insurance buyer with a good record in the form of either reduced premiums or good discounts for deductibles or excesses, the captive provides a mechanism where these benefits can be achieved. There has been a significant growth in such companies in recent years and it is almost certainly the case that the majority of the top 100 companies in the United Kingdom have a captive insurance company located in an offshore environment.

THE ROLE OF THE INSURANCE BROKER IN RISK MANAGEMENT

As risk management has developed, the insurance-broking industry has recognised that additional technical services are needed by its clients as well as more innovative solutions to insurance buying. Brokers have responded to this need by the establishment of risk control departments specialising in technical engineering skills, the establishment of management companies that can look after the captive insurance companies of their major clients, and the transition from the conventional commission-earning basis to a fee basis which reflects much more accurately the work and professional advice supplied by the broker rather than relating directly to the amount of insurance that is being sold.

The insurance buyer in looking for the broker that can help him with his risk management will require one who is prepared to spend a considerable amount of time becoming familiar with the client's operations and risk exposures, who can help to plan a programme for handling such exposures including the buying of insurance, and who can offer advice on the creation of risk retention levels and the implementation of loss-prevention schemes.

The broker's general role in this context is therefore to ensure that the client's risk exposures are properly handled, and in the financial area this means by insurance and non-insurance measures. In addition the broker should, through his skilful negotiating, volume of profitable account and innovation, produce more effective insurance-buying programmes and, last but by no means least, help the client to reduce losses.

The overall objective is therefore to improve the company's financial performance by helping to reduce expenditure and avoid potential loss situations.

FURTHER READING

Baglini, Norman: *Risk Management in International Corporations* (Risk Studies Foundation, New York, 1976).

Bannister, J. E., and Bawcutt, P. A.: *Practical Risk Management*, second edition (Witherby, 1986).

Bawcutt, Paul: *Captive Insurance Companies*, second edition (Woodhead-Faulkner, 1987).

Captive Insurance Companies 1979 (Risk Research Group, June 1979).

Carter, R. L., and Doherty, N. A.: *Handbook of Risk Management* (with updating service) (Kluwer Publishing).

Crockford, Neil: *An Introduction to Risk Management*, second edition (Woodhead-Faulkner, 1986).

Foresight – Europe's only specialist risk management journal, available monthly on subscription from Risk and Insurance Research Group Ltd, 4 Henrietta Street, Covent Garden, London WC2E 8PS.

How to Manage Computer Risk (Risk Research Group, July 1979).

Mehr, Robert I., and Hedges, B. A.: *Risk Management Concepts and Applications* (Richard D. Irwin, Homewood, Illinois, 1974).

Risk Management – the official monthly publication of the Risk and Insurance Management Society Inc., USA.

Williams, C. Arthur, and Harris, Richard M.: *Risk Management and Insurance* (McGraw-Hill, 1964).

CHAPTER 12

Corporate pension plans

KNEALE J. PHILLIPS, ACII

Pensions Administration Manager, Reed Stenhouse Investment Services Ltd

Revised by James Wigmore

Manager, Newton Trustee Services Ltd

THE INTENTION

The establishment of employee benefit plans over and above statutory schemes is a voluntary act on the part of the employer. In recent times, the principle that such plans are really deferred remuneration has become widely accepted. Legislation providing guaranteed rights to members of these plans has enforced this view.

Although negotiations will normally be initiated with company management, it is as well to remember who are meant to be the beneficiaries. Where larger corporate bodies are concerned, trade union involvement is becoming generally accepted and some employee representation both in the negotiation and the administration of a plan is to be recommended.

The benefit parameters can range from a small lump-sum death-in-service benefit to the maximum allowable under current legislation. Whether we are concerned with the shopfloor worker, administrative or managerial staff, or a senior executive, the parameters and relative costs are paramount.

The reader should note, however, that 1986 saw a fundamental change in the legislation affecting pensions and that the full implications for corporate pension plans cannot yet be fully gauged. After several years of review, the government published its proposals, in the Social Security Act 1986, which will come into force in April 1988. These proposals will change the design and financing of occupational pension schemes by encouraging more individual ownership of pensions. In addition, banks, building societies and unit trust groups will be allowed to compete with insurance societies (and certain friendly societies) for the provision of all pension requirements, though at retirement the pension must be purchased from a life assurance company or friendly society.

THE MEANS

Establishment of corporate pension plans can be arranged in one of the following ways or by a combination of them:
1. Benefits may be paid from current company profits; as such they are treated as remuneration to the recipient and are allowable as a trade expense to the employer for tax purposes.
2. A reserve may be established by the company from which benefits paid will be similarly treated.
3. A separate trust fund may be created for future liabilities.

Method (1), known as 'pay as you go', is used only for isolated individual benefits or for the large national body. Method (2) has tax disadvantages in that the reserve will not be allowable as an offset against tax and is suitable only where a company wishes to make no prior commitment for any benefits. Method (3), the irrevocable trust fund, independent of the company, is that which is in general use in the United Kingdom. These are the types of plan we shall look at.

In considering any benefit package, the plan must be devised taking into account the following factors:
1. Whether it will be suitable for a wholly insured arrangement, managed fund or independently self-invested fund.
2. The benefit structure.
3. The State earnings-related scheme.

THE INVESTMENT

Company management must consider any pension plan as a user of capital and resources and as such it must be compared with other such users within their own organisation. They must consequently achieve the optimum net performance compatible with acceptable investment risks to achieve long-term profits. When dealing with the larger funds, an improvement in profit performance of 2 per cent over a 30-year period can increase the resulting fund by as much as 50 per cent.

The methods of investment available are the insured fund, the managed fund and the self-invested fund, or a combination of these.

The insured fund

In this case the insurer creates one common fund in which contributions from all exempt approved pension arrangements with that insurer are placed. This pooling of resources enables the insurer to provide guarantees of minimum levels of investment return and maximum costs of providing the benefits under a particular plan, dependent on the type of contract being used.

The common fund is valued from time to time in relation to the guarantees provided and any surplus of assets over liabilities is then distributed. The method of distribution adopted by any particular insurer will generally reflect changes in interest yields and in capital appreciation. However, in view of the implicit guarantees and the necessary reserves to cover them, it is unlikely that the insurer will be able to pass on the true investment performance – although in periods of low investment returns the reserves can be used to balance the otherwise fluctuating performance.

Consequently, for plans where the contribution each year is sizeable, say £50,000 or over, a more flexible funding medium is generally preferred. However, particularly in connection with liabilities in respect of guaranteed minimum pensions under plans contracted out of the State earnings-related scheme (mentioned later), the inherent contract guarantees can make the insured plan attractive for that portion of the benefit package.

The managed fund

This type of fund was introduced in the early 1970s to retain the advantages of insurance company investment pooling while allowing a less conservative investment policy to be followed owing to removal of the necessity for reserves.

A wide choice of managed funds is available, ranging from gilt or fixed-interest funds, ordinary share funds and property funds to cash and international funds. The participating employer will generally select a mixed fund, the fund managers deciding on the percentage of each type of fund and the actual investments held. For the very large participating fund, the employer and trustees may generally select their own mixture of funds but not the actual investments held.

Contributions are invested in 'units' of the particular insurer's managed fund. The value of the 'units' is directly based on the value of the investments held. In order to allow for the expenses of the fund managers, 'units' are purchased by contributions at the 'offer' price but can only be cashed to meet liabilities at a lower figure, the 'bid' price. 'Offer' and 'bid' prices are generally determined on a particular day each month and are directly related to the value of the investments held together with reinvested dividends and interest at that moment. Consequently, the value of a particular company plan can be readily monitored and the investment performance assessed, giving the facility for changes in investment philosophy where necessary.

The use of a gilt fund with the underlying security is necessary to cover liabilities in respect of guaranteed minimum pensions under contracted-out plans. This can restrict an active investment policy where such benefits form a large part of the benefit package.

The self-invested fund

This method gives the company and trustees total responsibility for the investment performance of their own individual fund. They may take direct responsibility for the actual investments, which can involve considerable time and a high exposure to risk. Consequently the smaller of such funds tend to follow a conservative investment policy, which can affect the fund performance. Generally, professional portfolio managers, e.g. stockbrokers or merchant banks, will be used for other than the larger public companies. Such portfolio management can be expensive with a resulting effect on performance for the smaller funds. Consequently, a managed fund is generally preferred for such funds where fund management costs are pooled.

THE BENEFITS

The maximum levels of benefits in given circumstances are laid down in the Practice Notes issued under reference IR12 (1979) and various Joint Office Memoranda issued by the Superannuation Funds Office and the Occupational Pensions Board from time to time. As a general rule, these maximum benefits will be as follows:

1. A personal pension at retirement of two-thirds final salary.

2. A widow's/widower's pension on death after retirement of two-thirds the personal pension.
3. Part of the personal pension at retirement may be commuted for a tax-free payment of one and a half times final salary.
4. A lump-sum tax-free death-in-service benefit of four times current salary may be paid to dependants.
5. A widow's/widower's pension on death in service may be provided of two-thirds the expected personal pension at retirement.
6. Additional orphan's or dependant's pension may be provided up to a similar aggregate amount as in (2) and (5).

All pensions may be inflation-proofed up to an amount of 3 per cent per annum compound interest or up to the annual increase in the Retail Prices Indices if greater. However, the Superannuation Funds Office will allow advance funding at the present time only for increases up to 8½ per cent per annum.

The benefits selected for any particular plan are generally governed by the costs involved. The vast majority of pension fund contributions are determined on controlled funding principles which are briefly described in the following section.

The resulting contribution rates recommended by the actuary to the fund are determined by the following factors:

1. The number of employees, their ages, sex, salaries and retirement ages.
2. An assumed percentage increase in individual salaries up to normal retirement age for benefits based on final salaries.
3. An assumed percentage yield on the funds invested.
4. An assumed cost of pensions when they are due to be purchased.
5. An assumed rate of mortality.
6. In some instances an assumption that employees reaching retirement age are to be replaced with persons of specific age and salary.

The actuary will review his recommendations from time to time in the light of actual experience as compared with the assumed experience. This review must be carried out at least every fifth year.

CONTROLLING THE COST

An employer will wish to know the prospective cost for a period ahead, preferably as a fixed percentage of the payroll. From this requirement has developed, since the mid-1950s, the principle of controlled funding until it is now an extremely sophisticated system governed by the actuarial profession.

The concept is to balance input against expenditure while increasing the total fund to cover accrued liabilities. Generally every three years the liabilities of the fund will be assessed, the fund valued and a costing exercise carried out on the assumptions mentioned previously. As a result of this, the actuary will recommend the rate of contribution necessary to maintain the funding balance.

In addition to the contribution for pension benefits, there are the costs incurred in providing the death-in-service benefits. Such benefits are paid for on a yearly physical cost basis, but this cost can be projected over a period, say ten years, on membership and salary assumptions to arrive at an additional fixed contribution rate for such benefits. The recommended contribution will exceed the physical yearly cost in the first few years and the excess payments will benefit the pension fund. In later years the converse will apply.

EMPLOYEES' CONTRIBUTIONS

Under the existing scheme, the level of contributions by both employee and employer to the State pension schemes has generally restricted the ability of both to pay additional substantial contributions to private pension plans. At the time of writing, employees contribute between 5 and 9 per cent of earnings to the State Earnings Related Pension Scheme if they are contracted into that scheme, with employers contributing between 5 and 10.45 per cent. If they are contracted-out, there is a rebate of 2.15 per cent (employee's) and 4.1 per cent (employer's) which may be paid into a contracted-out pension scheme.

Employees will expect the company to contribute at least half of the costs of benefits being provided, and a total contribution by an employee to both State and private pension schemes in excess of 10 per cent of earnings is not generally acceptable. However, it must be mentioned that employees will receive income tax relief on their contributions to an exempt approved private plan at the highest tax rate to which they are liable, with consequent reduction in effective cost. Employees can receive this tax relief on a maximum of 15 per cent of salary as contributions to such a private plan.

Under the Social Security Act 1986 a single tax regime will apply to all, whether employee or self-employed. If the personal pension scheme has as its sole purpose, the provision of retirement or death in service benefits, it will qualify for tax approval. However, entitlement to tax relief on contributions will only arise if those contributions – whether received from the employee alone or jointly from the employee and the employer – do not exceed 17.5 per cent of earnings.

EMPLOYER'S CONTRIBUTION

At the present time, the whole of the employer's ordinary annual contributions to an exempt approved pension plan is allowable as a trade expense against corporation tax.

From time to time employers may wish to make additional special single payments to the fund, either to provide additional benefits for a particular group of members at a single payment cost or because their company profit forecast has exceeded expectations and they desire to use part of the excess profit to accelerate the funding position. The Superannuation Funds Office must be notified of such special payments and will determine whether corporation tax relief can be allowed in the year of payment or whether such relief must be spread over a period of years, generally five years. Normally, if the aggregate of such special payments in any period of five years does not exceed the normal annual contribution for the particular year, or if the contribution is solely to provide additional pension for existing pensioners, then the payment will be wholly allowable for corporation tax relief in the year of payment. In other circumstances the allowance will be spread, normally on the basis of the period equal to the ratio of the special contribution to the normal annual contribution.

The tax-exempt status of occupational pension schemes will continue without change under the 1986 legislation, although both this and the tax relief given to personal pensions is subject to a consultative document from the Inland Revenue and the final rules are expected to be announced during 1987.

STATE EARNINGS-RELATED SCHEME

The Social Security Pensions Act 1975 provides for exempt approved private plans to contract out of this section of the State pension scheme over and above the basic State pension provided they meet certain specified minimum requirements.

However, the scheme proved extremely expensive to operate, and this led the government to seek alternative means of ensuring adequate pension provisions for the majority of the population. The system was also felt to have weaknesses – it provided no lump sum on retirement, no dependants other than widows (and in some circumstances widowers) were provided for and it made no provision for early retirement.

Under the Social Security Act 1986 the State Earnings-Related Pension Scheme (SERPS) will remain but, in order to reduce costs, any individual who chooses a personal pension will not have the right to call upon SERPS when he retires. The government is to spend some of the money it saves in encouraging the growth of the personal pension system. For the period up to April 1993, the government will fund an additional payment of 2 per cent of relevant earnings into every pension plan taken out before that date.

PENSION FUND SURPLUSES

The Finance Act 1986 introduced provisions which aimed to minimise the tax advantages offered to pension scheme funds if those funds are more plentiful than is required to meet the scheme's future liabilities. The government has decided that from 6 April 1987 any scheme which shows more than 105 per cent of assets over liabilities must take steps to reduce those assets to the required level, or lose part of its tax exemptions. There are three routes offered to any firm whose scheme is in surplus:

1. The benefits payable under the scheme may be increased – subject to limits imposed by the Inland Revenue. This increases scheme liabilities.
2. A contribution holiday may be taken by employer, employees or both – effectively reducing assets over a period.
3. The surplus may be removed from the scheme and returned to the employer – but it will be taxed upon removal.

This last option has caused much debate concerning the ownership of pension funds as option (3) assumes that they are an asset of the company. This is one area where debate continues and further developments may arise.

PLAN MANAGEMENT

An area which has been neglected in the past is the day-to-day administration of benefit plans. Computerisation has generally removed most of the laborious aspects, but many functions still entail substantial man-hours.

Plan management must be considered in conjunction with the type of fund most appropriate. Where a wholly insured arrangement is to be utilised, the bulk of the administrative services (i.e. handling death claims, calculation and processing of benefits for members leaving service, transfers of benefits for individuals to and from the plan, retirement benefit calculations and payment of pensions, record-keeping and accounts) are normally provided by the insurer. The cost of these services is generally inclusive of the whole arrangement, possibly with a separate management charge. Where a managed fund is concerned, these services can be provided by the appropriate fund manager or can be sought elsewhere. For the self-invested arrangement, such services can be provided internally or by various outside firms (actuaries, brokers and the like). Additionally, legal services will be required.

The management of pension plans necessitates the services of qualified and experienced personnel. Only the larger corporate body will be able to provide the necessary expertise internally (other than actuarial advice) and even then the costs will be substantial. An appropriate figure would be 4 to 5 per cent of the annual input to the fund for the medium to large plans. Many larger brokers now operate their own total management services for larger clients at a competitive cost compared with the conventional insurer.

COMMUNICATION

It is essential that plan members are provided with adequate information concerning their benefits and rights. Great improvements have been made in this area and illustrative explanatory booklets and annual individual benefit statements are normally provided through external management services. Specially tailored packages are available, usually at additional cost.

For the member approaching retirement, full counselling

services are now available to ease the withdrawal from a full working life. Such services necessitate considerable expertise and at the present time are available only at additional cost.

There also saw legislation in this area in 1986, with the Occupational Pension Schemes (Disclosure of Information) Regulations. Many members of occupational pension schemes were felt to have little understanding of such schemes, despite previous improvements. The regulations came into force in November 1986 and aim to remedy this. A new member must receive full details of the scheme's benefit structure and on request a member must be told his current benefits and transfer value if he were to leave. Finally, the employee may also request an annual report from the trustees of the scheme, together with audited accounts.

EXECUTIVE PLANS

Generally a case can be made for partially or wholly providing executive benefits outside the main corporate plan on the grounds of confidentiality and specific individual requirements. Individual or small group plans are available with a range of investment opportunities and management services similar to that appropriate to the large corporate plan. From management's point of view an individually identified cost as part of an overall remuneration package can be provided, and from the executive's point of view an individual portable pension plan is an obvious asset.

CONCLUSION

From the foregoing it will be realised that it is not possible for there to be such a thing as a ready-made corporate pension plan. The decisions taken concerning investment philosophy, benefit structure and management services will determine the overall package appropriate to a particular organisation.

The mechanics of the establishment and documentation of pension plans seeking approval under the Finance Act 1970 and subsequent legislation have not been covered in this chapter. The appropriate procedures may be determined from reference to the authorities listed at the end of this chapter.

Those employers who offer a pension scheme are facing an unpredictable future. At present all eligible employees of a firm must be members of a pension scheme offered. From April 1988 however, no such restrictions will be placed upon the individual – which could mean any number withdrawing from company pension schemes. Planning on the basis of an unknown income and number of pensioners is, of course, difficult. The Government, however, hopes that the proposals will not adversely affect employers for two reasons. Firstly they are designing the personal pension provisions so they do not impose an administrative burden upon employers – if an individual takes out a personal pension there should be no need for his employer to be involved at all. The employer continues to pay standard rate national insurance contributions – all other transaction will be between the individual, the DHSS and the Occupational Pensions Board – for approval of the pension.

Secondly, it is hoped that, in an effort to retain scheme members, employers will widen benefits offered by their scheme. A wind of change may blow through occupational pensions schemes – to the advantage of continuing members.

LEGISLATION, STATUTORY INSTRUMENTS AND FURTHER READING

The relevant Acts of Parliament are:
Finance Act 1970
Finance Act 1971
Social Security Act 1973
Social Security Pensions Act 1975
Employment Protection Act 1975
Social Security Act 1985
Social Security Act 1986

The statutory instruments are:
The Occupational Pensions Schemes (Contracting-out) Regulations 1975
The Occupational Pensions Schemes (Equal Access to Membership) Regulations 1976
The Occupational Pension Schemes (Disclosure of Information) Regulations 1986

The Joint Office of the Inland Revenue Superannuation Funds Office and the Occupational Pensions Board issues:
Occupational Pensions Schemes IR 12 (1979)
Joint Office Memoranda Nos. 13, 25, 27, 37, 46, 54 and 58 onwards

Useful publications are:
Hymans, Clifford (ed.): *Handbook on Pensions and Employee Benefits* (with updating service) (Kluwer Publishing).
Jackson, James: *Occupational Pensions: The new law* (New Commercial Publishing Company, 1977).

CHAPTER 13

Reinsurance

LEONARD N. MARDEN, FCII
Consultant, Golding Stewart Wrightson Ltd

INTRODUCTION

Since reinsurance is by definition a form of insurance, it has developed in line with direct business, and the principles and practice governing the conduct of both are in many respects identical. In addition, the development of intermediaries specialising in reinsurance has followed a pattern similar to that of the direct brokers, but there the similarity ends.

Reinsurance brokers, unlike any other intermediary in insurance, have to operate as professionals between technicians, and to justify their position, brokers in this field require a very high degree of technical and legal knowledge of all classes of insurance, coupled with a complete understanding of international markets.

The development of modern communications in this century, particularly in the post-war years, has had a greater effect on reinsurance than on any other sector of insurance. If one also takes into account the enormous concentrations of values found in modern industry and commerce, the necessity to spread the risk, which is basic to all reinsurance, has brought together the insurance resources of every continent, and reinsurance brokers have made a major contribution to achieving this. Brokers in this field, whether they be specialist companies or divisions of larger broking groups, now function independently of the direct market; and despite restrictions such as those imposed by legislation and currency controls, it has been found that reinsurance extends over all frontiers, for by its very nature it is an essential element in the structure of the economy of every country, of whatever political persuasion.

It is not the purpose of this chapter to enter into detail as to the function of reinsurance itself, nor for that matter to deal with technical and legal considerations relative to the intermediary for any particular class of business or form of contract, but simply to outline the functions and role of a reinsurance broker within the industry.* Such functions may be grouped under the following headings:

1. Consultation at management level to advise on the design of a reinsurance programme.
2. Marketing of the selected programme, including advice on international distribution.
3. Administration of reinsurance arrangements.
4. Servicing of claims.
5. Continuity of supervision and supply of market information.
6. Other functions.

These are examined in the sections below.

CONSULTATION AT MANAGEMENT LEVEL

It will be appreciated that just as there are many reasons for an individual effecting a particular form of insurance, so, in the case of reinsurance, it is necessary for an insurance company to consider the reasons for the reinsurance it requires, which may range from the limitation of its capital to the protection of shareholders' funds and solvency margins.

Fundamentally, reinsurance should provide a mechanism for 'smoothing out' the effects of a heavy loss or series of losses by spreading the effects thereof among various companies and markets. It is in this field that the broker should not only be well equipped to assist but generally have the expertise to advise the company accordingly. To ensure that the broker is in a position to give the best advice, the management of the ceding company has to be involved in order to obtain as complete an analysis as possible of the portfolios to be protected, coupled with an understanding of the underwriting philosophy of the company.

---

*Specific reference to Lloyd's, which probably provides the largest reinsurance capacity in the world, has been omitted since the procedure for handling reinsurance follows closely that for direct business, while the duties of a reinsurance broker are similar to those applying in the company market (except in the case of administration and accounting, where the procedure is adapted to fit the Lloyd's market).

Bearing in mind the competitive situation of the insurance market, it is essential therefore that this relationship of the principal (ceding company) and the reinsurance broker should be close, based on mutual trust and good faith, since there has to be a complete disclosure of all relevant information (some of which will be confidential) in order to establish the most suitable form of protection.

Information so obtained will then be used by the broker to recommend a complete reinsurance programme to meet what are considered to be the particular needs of the principal. The significance of the comments at the beginning of this chapter concerning the high degree of technical expertise required by the broker will be appreciated. Such are the complexities of the market and the rate of modern development that companies now tend towards using more than one broker for their overall reinsurance programme, in addition to placing certain shares with professional reinsurers direct. This in no way reduces the degree of consultation; it merely ensures that the principal has access to the complete range of specialisation from all potential sources.

MARKETING OF THE SELECTED PROGRAMME

The next stage is to place the various contracts that make up the overall reinsurance programme.

The brokerage is paid by the reinsurer and, as in the case of an insurance contract, this feature should not be a significant factor in the selection of the appropriate market. It is the duty of the reinsurance broker to place business at the best possible terms in a market that will honour its liabilities in the event of a claim.

It should be stressed that the marketing policy must be the responsibility of management, and the broker, having given his advice, can only accept instructions. This is particularly the case where more than one broker is involved.

Regrettably, in the interests of short-term gain, a broker is sometimes requested to use a market that does not necessarily provide for continuity. It is therefore a feature of modern reinsurance broking that often, particularly where overseas clients are involved, an account may have to be completely restructured annually, including the use of a different market.

ADMINISTRATION OF REINSURANCE ARRANGEMENTS

With such a wide variation in the forms of reinsurance available, it is difficult to generalise as to the broker's function in so far as the administration of reinsurance arrangements is concerned – indeed, this varies even between overseas markets.

Basically, however, the broker, having completed the placing of the order, will as evidence of the terms of the contract send cover notes to the ceding company. This will be followed by negotiations with each party to the contract to achieve agreement of the wording, and subsequently to finalise the transaction by obtaining the signature of both the ceding company and the reinsurer.

The broker then has the responsibility of ensuring that the terms of the contract applying to the payment of premium, adjustments, etc., are adhered to. This would include, *inter alia*, submission of accounts and collection of premiums, which in most cases are on a quarterly basis.

Since the broker's duties under this heading are so varied, depending on the contract itself, it would be impossible to set out all the permutations of the systems applicable thereto. However, to summarise all these duties whether mandatory or by usage, it could be said that the intermediary must ensure that the terms of the contract as expressed in the original placing document or slip are adequately interpreted in the contract wording itself, and that the parties to the contract fulfil their obligations thereunder. And since most reinsurance arrangements are placed on an annual basis, there is a moral responsibility on the broker to ensure continuity of cover where required, irrespective of the fact that the markets used may change from year to year.

The legal position of the reinsurance broker is in practice similar to that of the direct insurance broker and is governed by the law of agency as particularly applying to insurance agents and brokers.

SERVICING OF CLAIMS

The broker should already be aware of the ceding company's organisation from his original contact with management, and this will include an understanding of the policy towards the handling of claims. It goes without saying that the reinsurance claim should be collected in the shortest possible time; in certain cases brokers have been responsible for establishing a market organisation for the centralisation of loss assessment and the availability of funds in the short term, and generally for advising the smaller companies overseas in this field.

With the use of a large number of reinsurers often situated in many countries spread across continents, there could be considerable delays without the organisational backing that the broker is able to supply. This will include the distribution of information, negotiation of difficult claims and arrangement of special settlements.

Frequently brokers are criticised for not financing claims. However, where there is no dispute as to creditworthiness, they are often forced to provide finance by the ceding company. This is despite the fact that the original contract is between the ceding company and its reinsurer, and the most that a broker is legally obliged to do is to expedite settlement within a reasonable period of time. The practice between the marine and non-marine markets differs in this respect, but this is largely a question of the type of claim; the principle of expeditious settlement is the same in all markets.

CONTINUITY OF SUPERVISION

Brokers' responsibilities do not cease when the contract is finalised, for in many cases an after-sales service is expected in the form of monitoring the account, comprising initial advices of loss, changes in portfolio and amendments required consequent upon the introduction of legislation, including taxation legislation in overseas countries.

The broker must also concern himself with the next renewal, more particularly with notices of cancellation. He will also be expected to consult with the ceding company in the event of violent fluctuation in rates of exchange which require even mid-term alterations to limits expressed in other currencies.

OTHER FUNCTIONS

Agency representation

It is an accepted feature of international reinsurance that London is the centre and therefore fulfils the position as an exchange for business. As a result, overseas insurance and reinsurance companies wishing to have contact with the London market, but without the resources to become licensed in conformity with UK legislation, need a limited form of representation not only to keep them advised of developments but also to act as a consultant on business accepted from the market, and in general as a point of contact with UK companies.

While the practice is not as common as in previous years, brokers do undertake these duties on the basis of agency representation without any underwriting authority other than in the case of companies licensed to operate in the United Kingdom. The duties of an agent depend entirely on the terms of appointment with the principal, and certainly over the period of the post-war years, arrangements of this nature have proved invaluable in establishing closer contacts with overseas markets.

Binding authorities and underwriting management agreements

It is a feature of the reinsurance market that for various reasons, principally that of the cost of establishing an office in the United Kingdom, overseas companies seek to obtain a licence to underwrite and grant defined powers to a broker to accept business on their behalf.

This authority can be in the form of either a binding arrangement, which generally implies that the broker has power to bind business for the company subject to definite limits, or a management agreement, which grants full powers of underwriting, again subject to the restrictions of a contract. There is a subtle difference between these two forms of arrangement in that the first is primarily a facility for brokers, whereas in the second case the broker will establish a separate company for the purpose of managing underwriting and in some respects this company will operate on an entirely different basis from the broking organisation as a whole.

Both these arrangements have been criticised on the grounds that there could be a question of conflict of interest in so far as the broker is concerned. However, in practice there is no such conflict in that the binding authority or management agreement has been granted to the broker, who is then the agent of the company providing the security. Therefore any company or broker who makes use of this facility puts himself in the same position as if he were placing the business direct with the reinsurer. In making this point it should be emphasised that the broker concerned should ensure that those using the facility are fully aware of their contractual relationships with their principals.

Education and training

While not directly related to the overall business of reinsurance, the UK broker is in a privileged position in that the international experience he can provide is invaluable to certain overseas companies which inevitably have to restrict their operations to their country of domicile.

This being the case, there is a great demand for brokers in the United Kingdom to assist overseas companies by advising them on the facilities available for education within the field of insurance and reinsurance, and also to accommodate overseas students in their offices in London to give them a certain insight into how international business is conducted in the United Kingdom. This feature tends to emphasise the wide range of services that have to be provided by the international reinsurance broker, all of which helps to consolidate the privileged position of the United Kingdom in international reinsurance.

It will be appreciated that in a short chapter such as this it has not been possible to elaborate in any detail on every function the reinsurance broker has to fulfil. Indeed, this chapter provides just an outline of the overall procedures that have been developed.

Reinsurance brokers now make a major contribution to the invisible earnings of the United Kingdom, since a high proportion of the business they generate emanates from overseas. The wide network of branches and agencies, coupled with the extensive travelling programmes undertaken by brokers, has established facilities for handling overseas business on a scale that has ensured the continuity of British insurance internationally and has upheld the best traditions of insurance as understood in the United Kingdom.

FURTHER READING

Carter, R. L.: *Reinsurance* (Kluwer Publishing 1979).
Miller, Stanford, and Sudekum, Lothar: *The Intermediary in International Reinsurance* (papers presented at the International Reinsurance Seminar of the Reinsurance Officers' Association, 1973).
Study Course IC 302 (CII Tuition Service, London, 1971 edition).

CHAPTER 14

The London market placing operation

MAURICE M. MURPHY, FCII, ABIBA
Director, Stewart Wrightson Ltd

SOURCES OF BUSINESS

It is well known that London has long been a major centre for international insurance business, which is the source of considerable foreign currency earnings for the benefit of the whole community.

This international business comes to London in a variety of ways, either direct or through foreign insurance brokers or agents or other sources. London is used because of its long-standing reputation in the practice of insurance resulting from its expertise, its degree of innovation and the security of its market. Because of the developing technology throughout the world there is a large portfolio of business arriving in London as treaty reinsurance for the protection of the various domestic markets. It is necessary for indigenous insurers to arrange treaties because if certain risks were retained completely within the domestic market, then in the event of a catastrophe such as an earthquake or hurricane the insurers would not be able to take advantage of the basic principle of insurance, which is to spread the risks among many carriers – with possibly disastrous effects on their insurance industry. Prudent insurers will also need reinsurance so that they are not unduly exposed to large losses which are less serious.

The sources of the business coming to London can best be considered in two parts (a) the United States, and (b) the rest of the world.

The United States

Most of the sources of business mentioned above are used in

respect of the United States. However, the occasions when direct business comes to London or to a London broker are relatively few because of the effects of legislation, particularly of tax laws, which make it difficult, if not dangerous, to transact business in this way.

In addition to the large reinsurance portfolio coming to London from the United States, there is a considerable inflow of business by means of the surplus line agencies. Surplus line business is that which cannot be covered in the domestic market for one reason or another. It can be surplus in one of three ways – in terms of capacity, wider cover, or excess protection over primary policies. It is usual in these circumstances for the insured to approach an American broker who may in turn pass the business to a surplus line broker in the United States, often erroneously regarded as an underwriter. The surplus line broker will then pass the business to a London broking house for placement in the London market. In addition to these methods of passing business to London there are facilities whereby London underwriters accept business on binding authorities or covers, which means that they are prepared to accept declarations for particular classes of business with standard policy forms and maybe preset rates. In fact this means that the underwriter is leaving the underwriting decision to the producing agent or broker. In times of adverse underwriting experience the obtaining and approval of binding authorities and covers become extremely difficult, particularly when the influence of the reinsurers to the ceding company granting the cover is taken into account.

Rest of the world

Since we are now considering a much larger area and population, business coming to London from the rest of the world is far more diversified and is affected to a greater degree by local legislation. Basically the source of business remains the same: London brokers are marketing direct to obtain business for the London market, and overseas brokers are marketing on the basis that some of their portfolio will come to London, normally through a London broking house. Again, as in the case of the United States, binding authorities and covers are used. Despite the existence of the huge continental reinsurance companies there is a considerable amount of reinsurance business coming to London, some of which is placed on the Continent with these same companies.

The effects of legislation are much more obvious than in the case of the United States. There are many areas in the world which currently have only nationalised insurance in that there is one State company, possibly augmented by a State reinsurance company. In these circumstances, such companies have a monopolistic position and it is impossible to arrange insurance on any other basis. Nevertheless, there is still business which comes to London from foreign nationalised companies in addition to treaty reinsurance: this is by means of facultative reinsurance when the capacity is such that the treaty cannot cope or where the complexity is such that the local company's decision is to make full use of the expertise available in London. It is also possible in the circumstances of restricted legislation to make use of fronting arrangements whereby, although theoretically the business is exported from the country by means of facultative reinsurance, in practice the local company's control is restricted since it is merely issuing the legal policy, the terms and conditions being set and security provided by the London market. The other important aspect affecting the London broker is the legislation that at the time of writing is under consideration in the European Economic Community whereby free access would be made available on a services basis to all the member countries' insurance industries.

THE BROKER'S RESPONSIBILITIES

The London broker without question deals with the vast majority of the international business coming to London. His activities consist of collating all the information necessary for the preparation of an underwriting submission, placing the business by means of a slip (which is a précis of all the information available and the expression of the intent of the parties involved), the collection and payment of monies, and the servicing of other requirements.

All this has to be done in the framework of the insurance legislation of the country involved, which for example may demand that policies are issued on a predetermined form – in a foreign language sometimes – with no extensions being available to the standard cover. On many of the risks it is considered to be the London broker's responsibility to establish general facts concerning the relevant country, such as climate, appropriate statistics, and the political and economic situation. The London broker, when dealing particularly through Lloyd's on binding authorities and covers, has to convince the Lloyd's syndicates that the broker producing the business from the overseas country has sufficient standing and reputation to ensure that the business will be managed correctly and be of such quality as to avoid unnecessary problems in the London market.

THE MARKET

The market available to the London broker consists of a great many sectors, among which are Lloyd's, the large British composite companies, the fringe market and of course the overseas market, i.e. the underwriting market situated abroad. Additionally, there are various agency arrangements. At the time of writing, work is being undertaken in setting up a London Market Computer Network, which will include Lloyd's, Lloyd's brokers, the Institute of London Underwriters, the Policy Signing and Accounting Centre (PSAC) and London market underwriting companies.

The Lloyd's market has been so well established for such a long time that it is often the first place the London broker will go to obtain support and/or quotations for overseas business. The syndicates involved, supported by their 'names', are in general terms capable of dealing with any class of business other than financial guarantees and long-term business such as whole life, although even in this latter case there are facilities for term assurances.

The large British composite companies which have branches in many countries throughout the world also operate on what is known as a 'home foreign basis', i.e. the underwriting of overseas business in their London offices. It is usual in these circumstances for the company to check with its relevant branch office so as to avoid confusion and the situation where it undercuts the local branch's rates. For areas where they have no local representation these companies operate without restriction, if so permitted by the legislation, and play a major role in the London market for most classes of business.

In addition to the composite companies there are a large number of insurance companies operating in the London market which come under the broad heading of the fringe market. These companies, which have limited liability status, are able to accept business much on the same basis as the Lloyd's underwriters.

Some of the companies have developed specialities which are not normally undertaken by the general insurance market and indeed many of them are foreign owned although registered to transact business under the regulations of the Department of Trade and Industry. There are a number of large American companies operating in London on this basis whose capacity is such that they have an enormous influence on the operations and attitudes of the London brokers.

Quite often in order to avoid the expense of setting up an office and becoming licensed by the Department of Trade and Industry in their own right, overseas companies will accept business in London on an agency basis. This means that an underwriting agent will arrange for a company to subscribe to the portfolio of business which he can obtain by operating in London. It is usual in these circumstances for a number of companies to take a percentage share in the total portfolio retained by such an agent. There has been in recent years a trend for overseas companies to set up contact offices or broking facility offices which are not strictly speaking empowered to underwrite business emanating in the London market. In theory the underwriting decisions are taken at such offices' head office: the service they offer is merely as a contact to gain an entrée into the large international account available in London.

Part of the market available to the London broker is actually situated abroad and because of the ease of communication and modern travel facilities it is not unusual for a risk coming to London from, for example, the Far East to be considered by the London broker and placed with a German company in Germany by the London broker or his correspondent in that country. It is true to say that in recent years international insurance markets have developed in a number of areas, and while a large flow of business into London is maintained there is an ever-growing level of international business passing from London to these overseas underwriting companies, which are located throughout the world as far apart as the United States and Japan.

Another important factor which the broker must be aware of is what is happening in the domestic market where the risk originates so that the negotiations carried out in London are such that there is a reasonable chance of the business being obtained. Obviously, because of the various economic and political conditions throughout the world there is an increasing requirement to cater for the needs of the multinational clients who, whether as manufacturing or marketing concerns, have risks situated in various countries. In these circumstances if there is a master policy it must be recognised that local policies may be necessary if the legislation demands that only registered companies are used and policies are issued on a set format which differs from the master policy. Where such conditions obtain, the master policy issued in London will often act as a 'difference in conditions' cover and may be on an excess basis so that the multinational client obtains the benefit of the cover and limits negotiated by the London broker wherever the particular risk is situated and whatever restrictions are placed on local policies to be issued.

PLACING THE RISK

As already noted, the main duties of a London broker are the collation of information and its presentation to underwriters. Because of the varying legislation and the vast difference in local conditions the London broker over a number of years has had to build up a knowledge of insurance requirements and hazards throughout the world. This is in addition to one of his basic functions of having a knowledge of the market. The success of the London broker lies in knowing which of the various outlets available to him is the best for the particular piece of business he has at the time. It is very important for him to be aware of the information necessary to place the risk and then to collect the information and prepare a submission, including the slip, on a basis which identifies the risks and hazards involved.

The next part of the operation is the actual negotiations with underwriters. Having identified all the risks to his own satisfaction, the broker with his knowledge of the market will decide which underwriter to approach. Usually the underwriter selected will be identified as a 'leader', being one whose reputation in the market is such that any terms and conditions offered by him will be subscribed to by others in the market to enable the broker's slip to be filled 100 per cent. There are of course on occasions a number of probable leaders and thus the broker will see more than one person to obtain a consensus of what is necessary in order to achieve a satisfactory insurance contract. It is here that the knowledge of the market becomes crucial. In difficult market conditions it is essential for the broker to obtain support for the leader's indication since he must be confident that the quotations given to the producing agent or to the clients are such that in the event of a firm order, completion of the risk is possible. Should the occasion arise when the leader's terms are not supported then in the event of a subsequent firm order the broker is placed in a very embarrassing situation even if the premium rates were given as an indication only.

It is unwise to think that cheapest is the best for the client, and the broker has a duty to ensure that the security he uses is of sufficient standing to enable any claims which arise subsequent to inception to be paid without undue delay by a company which is still financially solvent. This is one of the main reasons why certain obligations and responsibilities are placed on people wishing to underwrite insurances in the United Kingdom by the Department of Trade and Industry. In specific terms the broker is trying to achieve a premium commensurate with the risk and the security contained in the policy offered by an underwriter. All too often the cheapest premium is likely to cause problems in dealing with claims settlements, or the policy wording can be so restrictive that it does not meet with the requirements of the client. If the premium terms available vary widely, either the broker can put before his client the alternative covers and relevant premiums and then make his own recommendations, or else he can leave the decision to the client. The approach adopted depends on the broker's commercial attitude and his relationship with his client.

MISCELLANEOUS PROBLEMS

Throughout this chapter attention has been drawn to the effects of legislation directly relating to insurance matters. In addition, other areas of legislation can have quite a dramatic bearing on the placing of business. The most obvious example is where the exchange control regulations of a country are such that it is extremely difficult to obtain permission to remit premiums to London. This of course delays matters considerably for the broker and he can often incur penalties if dealing with Lloyd's, since several of the systems demand payment of the premium within a specified time. Other problems which arise are those concerning shareholdings in local companies which, although normally run by expatriate personnel, are in fact under the control of local shareholders who may be unscrupulous. The servicing of claims can also give rise to problems, especially in those countries where it is extremely difficult to obtain visas. Finally, the London broker has to consider the economy of the area concerned since it is quite possible for the premium to be devalued to a large extent, especially since often countries where this occurs are also those with exchange control regulations. For this reason it is sometimes necessary to transact insurance business in a hard or convertible currency, which is not necessarily the currency of the country involved.

CONCLUSION

This chapter has discussed the sources of business which is dealt with in the London market and has also looked at the considerations, such as legislation, which affect the placing of business whether on a direct surplus line, facultative reinsurance or treaty reinsurance basis. However, one must not lose sight of the fact that there is an extremely large portfolio of business which is recognised as international – particularly marine and aviation business – which to a large extent is not subject to any of the restrictions placed on the types of business transacted in London that have been dealt with in this chapter.

Chapter 15

The marketing of insurance broking

PETER G. MOORMAN, ACII, FBIBA

Managing Director, Whitehouse Moorman & Partners Ltd

A logical starting-point for a discussion of the marketing of insurance broking is the role of the broker. Is he an intermediary or a professional adviser, or both? To his client he tends to be seen in a dual role: firstly, as the skilled buyer of insurance – someone who understands the market and can produce a better deal for the client than he could arrange on his own – and, secondly, as the skilled adviser and interpreter of a complex market and a complex subject. The advice given in this area would be concerned not only with the selection of policies but more usually with which cover is needed and often with managing or controlling the risk.

To the insurer, the broker tends to appear primarily as a producer of business, although this role is almost invariably seen as much wider than selling. The insurer normally relies on the broker to interpret the client's needs and to assist the insurer in underwriting. While complete delegation of underwriting powers is still rare, the underwriting of many risks can involve considerable joint work between broker and insurer.

Perhaps the most meaningful guide to the role of the broker is the method of remuneration. It remains overwhelmingly on a commission basis, and this is unlikely to change substantially for most of the business handled by brokers in the near future.

So far the insurance broker has been talked about as though he were a single clear-cut type. In practice the word 'broker' applies to a wide range of firms from the multinational organisations covering 20 or more countries and providing all classes of insurance, to the smaller specialist brokers and what is popularly known as the 'High Street broker'. For each of these, the marketing will have some common elements and some different elements. Before looking at the segments of marketing for insurance brokers and the need for the different types of broker, it might be helpful to look at the market in which the brokers find themselves.

It is by and large a competitive market, mainly because the rewards can be good and until recently it has been comparatively easy to enter the market. This over-capacity in brokers and the resulting competition lead to considerable innovation as brokers devise new covers and alter the scope of existing ones.

Within this broad pattern, there are two predominant broking approaches. The first is of the essentially conservative broker (who is, however, capable of innovation), who has an acknowledged market position producing a relatively stable income and profit, and whose approach to marketing tends to be to go on doing what he has always done, while being ready always to react to changes in the market and clients' needs. On the other hand, the newcomer is faced with the problem of finding a share of the market he can attack, and in attacking it, while he might not use the word 'marketing', he uses marketing techniques and, in particular, segmentation and the development of a new product or service. This uniqueness may be in terms of a different approach to selling, different types of cover, different types of service, or even concentration on a particular section of the market, in order that he can show a special expertise. These innovatory broking approaches occur in all areas of broking activity. A group of skilled brokers leave a Lloyd's broker and form a new broking firm and in a few years they have established a market position of their own. In the High Street broker market, firms come and go.

In looking at the broker and marketing, a thought should be spared for the customer. One buys in order to guard against a possibility that would otherwise produce discomfort or danger, or to enhance one's position internally or externally. It is often assumed that the motives of those buying insurance are different; this is not in fact the case. Obviously when buying insurance one is as apprehensive as when buying other products, and the marketing approach involves arousing that apprehension while showing how it can be handled.

The client's need for reassurance is met by the broker in many different ways, some relating to the organisation and others to the individual. The prime emphasis might be on high-quality technical service, so removing uncertainty from several aspects of the client's operations. Alternatively, but rarely, it might be on understanding the client's business in detail and using solutions that fit effectively not only the client's technical needs but the actual style and character of his business. Finally, and most important to the majority of clients, is still the personal and social relationship. This has not been analysed publicly but cannot be overestimated. When faced with a difficult and unpleasant subject, the presence of a friendly, understanding, helpful and sociable insurance broker helps reduce the apprehension.

The marketing process for brokers can be considered under five main headings:

1. *The selection of the market position.* Which part of the market does the broker wish to serve and how shall he serve it? His decisions in this area create, if he is successful, the 'unique' position of his business which gives it its particular appeal and share in the market.
2. *The presentation of the broker to his clients and potential clients.* This would include any advertising but, more important, would also include the whole public image of the broker, the aim being to equate the market position selected with the general picture presented to that market by the broker.
3. *The selling process* – involving the selection of individual prospects, the approach to those prospects and the actual sale.
4. *Delivery* or the broking equivalent of delivery of the goods ordered. This can take many forms and might be an analysis of the client's insurance needs, a renewal discussion or the presentation of the insurance policies.
5. *After-sales service* – primarily the provision of technical advice, and the handling of changes and claims.

These five steps have been set forward as though they are a logical, conscious process, but in fact a great deal of insurance broking is a matter-of-fact response to events, with little overall planning or marketing except in some of the major firms. In the author's opinion, the whole character of the insurance market in fact encourages this reaction to events and day-by-day activity rather than longer-term planning. While studies are often carried out by the major brokers preparatory to opening new branches in different parts of the United Kingdom and different overseas countries, in general these marketing surveys do not have the same degree of detail and subsequent accuracy that many industrial market surveys have.

To be fair to the brokers, they do not yet have the quality and quantity of marketing information available to those engaged in selling in the personal and industrial goods markets, although this may merely be a reflection of the fact that as yet there has been no open need for this information. The marketing man faces the task of analysing this market with fairly good general market information and some knowledge of the market shares of different insurers. From the annual reports of brokers some idea of the overall income can be derived and, very occasionally, a breakdown by class or territory.

Similarly, there is quite good scope for deriving data on market size from other information. If one is selling motor-car insurance it is not too difficult to get a view of the number of vehicles in different parts of the country and the number of vehicles which could be approached through membership of various associations. In looking at marine and aviation, precise market information is, of course, available on every fleet and every owner, but moving to the non-marine field, such information is not so precise.

The diligent marketeer could well collect, relatively cheaply, an analysis of the market positions of each of the major brokers among the top 500 or the top 1,000 firms, and some brokers have done this. Market research firms have been retained to produce forecasts of the market size, often with a breakdown by different industrial classifications. Perhaps the weakest point is that there appears to be little evidence of the practical use of such market research in marketing and marketing planning for brokers.

The second broad area is the presentation of the broker to the client and potential client. This again can be broken down into three parts: firstly, the development of the desired image; secondly, the relationship between that image and the real company as it is seen by its clients and potential clients; and, thirdly, the attempts to change that situation by advertising and other means. Most of the major brokers now use advertising and retain advertising agencies who advise on the firm's image. One can deduce some elements of the marketing image from the advertising campaigns of the various brokers. One shows a Lloyd's waiter, linking it with the well-known and highly respected image of Lloyd's. Another focuses on history, perhaps appealing to the need in the buyer for a firm with long experience. Another shows photographs of teams and individuals, perhaps to overcome the widely felt fear of dependence on a single individual to give advice. Yet another focuses on individual, named, prestigious accounts, each technically complex and with considerable standing. Others rely on presentation of the name linked with a claim that it can do everything better than everyone else, everywhere in the world.

What can one deduce from this advertising? A claim to ubiquity, a claim to technical competence, a claim to teamwork, a claim to considerable experience, a claim to have handled particular projects well. Probably the only message that works in relation to interesting potential clients is the case history approach. The other advertising will be helpful in presenting the name, so as to back up the sales efforts of the company. It should be noted, however, that the Financial Services Act may affect the way in which a broker can advertise his services. The Act imposes stringent rules in respect of long-term insurances, which will be stricter than those of the Advertising Standards Authority.

One of the most interesting facts to emerge from market research studies on the standing of individual brokers is the wide disparity of views about the same broker held by different people. Rarely does one find anything approaching unanimity. This probably reflects the fact that broking, particularly for industrial clients, is still very much a personal business. If one gets a skilled account executive and is well served, naturally one tends to think that the broking firm is very good, and, if the reverse is the case, that the broking firm is not much good. Often these attributed characteristics relate only to a particular individual or, at the widest, an individual department. Whatever the disparity of views, however, in the industrial, marine and aviation sectors dependence on brokers is very high indeed and most clients would be reluctant to do without their services, at least in part.

That having been said, there has been a trend in recent years, accelerated by the growing importance of insurance managers in many industrial companies, to reduce the income of brokers and the work handled by brokers on their behalf. Some of these companies have set up their own captive brokers, others have decided to buy insurances direct from insurance companies and others have focused on reducing the broker's income by negotiating commission rebates or fees.

The third part of the marketing process is the actual sales operation. At the personal level, there is a fairly high rate of success with perhaps more than one enquiry in three generating actual business. What is interesting about this personal market is that a great deal of the business walks in through the broker's door. Once he has established his position, recommendations from existing clients will lead to a continuing, and usually increasing, flow of business, provided he continues to do a good job.

In the industrial sphere, the position is quite different and it still seems a most inefficient process. One could estimate that under one in ten of approaches to customers is successful and with a different definition of the word 'approach', we could produce a success rate down in the 2 or 3 per cent category. It is fortunate that broking is basically a profitable business, or it would be impossible to finance such ineffective selling. The reasons for this ineffectiveness lie generally in lack of skilled marketing. The average broking account executive analyses his own success in terms of technical ability, personal charm, persistence or knowing the right people, and proceeds to carry through the same approach to clients whom he does not yet serve. In attacking an industrial account, there are two key factors. The first is timing and the second is the network of people involved in the sales decision.

In relation to timing, the best potential prospects are either dissatisfied customers – those who have become disillusioned with their existing broker's service – or those clients where changes in personnel or organisation raise the possibility of a change in insurance broker. By concentrating his attention on this point, the average broker could probably quadruple his effectiveness.

Looking at the organisational network involved in selling, one can make use of the work that has already been done in the field of industrial marketing and trace out the people actually involved in the broking decision. In industrial parlance, these will include at least three categories, namely the buyer (the insurance manager or person who actually gives the order), the user and the decision-maker. The user will be that part of the organisation concerned with the subject matter of the insurance. For example, the transport manager will be closely involved in most companies in marine insurance, but will not often take the marine insurance decision, although he can influence it considerably. The decision-maker may be a single individual, but for the bigger companies it is likely to be a group of individuals.

The actual mechanism by which companies make insurance-buying decisions or, more precisely, decisions to change their mode of insurance buying, is quite complex. For the broking salesman, it is important to establish whether he has a genuine prospect or, as is more often the case, he is being used as a stick to beat the existing broker into providing better service. The gathering of intelligence about buying intentions and buying decisions is part of the skills of every industrial salesman, but the broking world tends to lag behind in this respect. It may be that brokers' over-reliance on good social and personal relationships leads them to assume that every piece of information they are given is not only accurate but also the whole truth, when in fact it is often anything but.

There is not space in which to look at the whole picture of sales motivation, but quite often an inclination to change begins in an industrial company and is not carried through owing to lack of persistence, lack of perception and lack of imagination on the part of the broker attempting to sell his services. A good marketing approach would resolve most of these problems by encouraging the salesman to understand the market, his company's position in that market, and his potential client's problems and needs as well as the organisational structure and philosophy of that client.

The fourth part of the process is packaging. Many brokers might object to the use of the word 'packaging' in relation to their product or service, but it might be helpful to reflect on the importance of packaging in every other decision they make. The way in which a product or service is presented is a reflection of how the company feels about its customer or client. It can enhance their relationship or it can damage or destroy that relationship. Some years ago, a very large British industrial account changed hands in a situation where there was complete satisfaction with the account executive, but complete dissatisfaction with the quality of service provided by the office.

In packaging the broker is concerned with what the customer expects from him, how it is presented and the timing of that presentation. A report on changes might be the subject for discussion, in which case packaging does not mean the inclusion of a superb glossy cover – although equally the report should be tidily and confidently presented – but the manner of presentation. In particular it means the extent to which the report takes account of the preferences and problems of the client rather than the presenter's view of the skills and importance of his own organisation. Does the report take sufficient account of the short time available to the recipient to study it? If the opportunity presents itself, are audio-visuals used and do these audio-visuals reflect the character of the broker presenting them rather than that of the agency employed in their manufacture?

The same approach can be used in the renewal process. How serious is the preparation for the renewal discussions in terms of understanding the changes which are taking place in the client's organisation and business as well as in the insurance market? Apart from providing the opportunity for a long lunch, does the renewal discussion enhance the client's appreciation of the technical and other qualities of the broker? Does the broker deliver the insurance policies on time, correct and in good order?

One of the biggest problems in the broking world today is the increasing separation between account executive and technician. The account executive who masters the technicalities of the business will have a much stronger position with his client than the one who sees himself as captain of the team where everybody else does the work.

After-sales service is probably the weakest point of most broking operations today. It is hoped, however, that this will improve once the Financial Services Act comes into force, since a regular review of the client's needs in respect of long-term insurances is one of the Act's requirements. There have, in the past, been a number of reasons for this comparative weakness in many brokers' after-sales service. Shortage of skilled technical staff may be one, problems in insurers' offices may be another, but probably the main reason is lack of attention. The best means of selling most products and services is personal recommendation, and personal recommendation will be given on the basis, not of whether the user liked the product when he first bought it or whether he liked the salesman, but of how the product performed in service. For insurance broking this involves the day-by-day provision of technical advice and service, including the handling problems. Needless to say, in making this comment, cost has not been ignored.

What, then, is the position of marketing in insurance broking? It can be assumed that today most brokers know about marketing and have some idea of its relevance to them, but it can at the same time be argued there is as yet little conscious use of marketing techniques in insurance broking. The Financial Services Act may change this, since one intention of the Act is to enhance professionalism in the field of life assurance, unit trusts and pensions and it should therefore assist the marketing of insurance broking in these areas. There is very considerable scope for the organisations that take advantage of a skilled marketing approach in what is still a highly profitable market.

Chapter 16

The sub-broker's special schemes

JOHN S. SMEATON, FBIBA
Chairman, Fielding Smeaton Jones (Agencies) Ltd
Chairman, Motor Executive Committee, BIBA

INTRODUCTION

This could be said to be a chapter about salesmanship. Schemes basically are exclusive sales and originate from the inventiveness of the broker coupled with the flexibility, adaptability and co-operation of the underwriter.

Schemes range over the whole gamut of the insurance industry and therefore can be found in the fields of life, fire, motor or any one of the other segments that form the insurance world. Many of the schemes are designed specifically to meet the needs of a particular profession or industry.

Some schemes are solely operated and controlled, being exclusively set aside for the introducing or inaugurating broker. Other schemes allow for sub-brokers to send their enquiries for the class to the main controlling broker. Normally in these circumstances the 'client broker' retains control of the servicing of the policy. In this way he keeps in direct contact with his client and secures the most advantageous terms for him that are available in the market.

Schemes originate from the desire of the insurer or broker to produce an immediate potential volume of business. They can come from a collection of persons engaged in one pursuit – for example a motor club or a works association where the employees derive benefits therefrom – or, alternatively, from a collection of organisations within a specific industry such as radio and television retailers, farmers or those engaged in professional occupations.

There are many people within the insurance industry that have one day woken up with inspiration and thought that it would be a unique idea to launch a scheme for a particular group of persons, conjecturing how much business could accrue as a result. Some of these ideas are put to paper and eventually get off the ground; others fail. Schemes related to trades or professions are vastly interesting and additionally increase insurers' knowledge of the particular trade or industry – thus benefiting everyone concerned.

Schemes related to numbers of persons collectively operating together, as opposed to specific trades or professions, do not provide so much scope for the insurer or broker to innovate. Basically, this type of scheme represents a bulk-buying operation where increased discounts cater for premium reductions to the participants in the scheme. Broadly speaking, civil servants and bankers could be said to be within such a grouping as these classes have enjoyed reduced motor premiums for a considerable number of years. The railwayman's scheme for motor insurance goes back to the 1930s.

While the motor schemes in essence take a comparatively short period of time to launch, schemes for specific trades or industries – if they are to be viable at all – need 'in-depth' research into the processes or activities involved and the likelihood of unusual occurrences which could give rise to claims. Much technical reading is required on the theoretical data plus site visits on the practical side.

Sometimes you hear brokers remark in semi-joking fashion that what they really want is a scheme for all persons not in any other scheme. Frequently there is a spate of correspondence in one of the insurance journals regarding the merits or otherwise of a newly launched project on the market. The correspondence seems to become more heated when the particular scheme is on a closed-shop 'single broker only' basis.

It is no bad thing that a broker will sit down and think out an ingenious way of attracting more business to his company by this method. The only real complaint or criticism would lie in the case where the scheme itself was spurious or failed to give the adequate protection that was indicated.

However regrettable, it is a fact of life that there are many occasions when one is pipped at the post by the speedier inventiveness of others. One has to accept that there must always be a winner and a loser.

TYPES OF SCHEME

Motor schemes

Schemes for motor insurance divide into certain main categories. These are as follows.

Occupational schemes
Certain occupations are recognised within the motor insurance market as being eligible for reduced ratings. Civil servants, bankers and railway employees all have discounted rates available to them with most Lloyd's and some company underwriters. Originally these rates were available only to the white-collar workers within the professions but with nationalisation and the vastly increased range of civil servants now in the United Kingdom some underwriters have extended their acceptances to a much wider clientele to embrace new industries and the blue-collar employees. While the majority of insurers participating in these schemes used to produce quite separate civil service and bankers' scale rates – indeed, the bankers' rates were different from those of civil servants – the tendency nowadays is for a specific discount to be deducted from the underwriters' normal scale rates. Where such a reduction is taken, a lower commission is payable to brokers on this business.

Car clubs and works schemes
The normally acceptable and viable membership of such an organisation needs to be at least 100 participants in order to make this a worthwhile proposition for an underwriter. These schemes are not always profitable from an insurance point of view unless they are on a fairly substantial scale. There otherwise is a tendency for underwriters to be selected against by being offered the insurances of the substandard rather than the standard risks. Coming under this heading although not strictly within the framework of this chapter are the schemes for the Automobile Association and the Royal Automobile Club.

Schemes for certain drivers
Drivers who have passed the Advanced Motorists' Driving Test and members of the Veteran Motorists' Club are all eligible for discounted schemes. There are also schemes in existence for drivers who drive only a limited number of miles per annum or only within a certain radius of their homes.

Schemes for certain makes of car

There are in existence a number of schemes where motorists owning a certain specific make of car can obtain reduced premiums. These arrangements are not necessarily new. Indeed, long before World War II one was operated by a particular insurer whereby owners of Ford motor cars received an appreciable discount from their premiums. Some of these schemes exist for foreign cars, where the method of rating operation is normally to downgrade the vehicles one or two 'groups'.

For underwriters, these schemes have quite an attraction as often agreements are made with the manufacturers of the vehicles with regard to the availability of spare parts, specialist repairers and so forth.

Some of the schemes are available directly from insurers to members of the public and others arranged only through brokers. Those arranged through brokers are sometimes restricted to a single introducing broker outlet while others are available to the broking market at large. The governing factor in the latter case necessitates an agency with the company or underwriter.

Non-motor schemes

Under this heading a division exists between schemes arranged for normal peril insurances and those of an unusual nature designed for specialist trades or occupations.

Retailers' or shopkeepers' insurances particularly are suitable for schemes. A number of trade associations and unions have schemes specially designed to meet certain exigencies of their own trade or profession. Very often a master block policy automatically covering all members in a single document is arranged for the third-party liabilities and thus this cover can be omitted from the retailer's separate insurance.

Schemes have been devised that theoretically should result in a lot of business, but in practice this does not always prove to be the case. Some schemes have even been produced for trade journals within an industry whereby subscribers obtain lower insurance rates for their shop insurances.

Once the innovators get cracking, the hook on which the scheme is hung sometimes bears no insurance relationship to the perils being covered. Buying so many tins of polish, for example, does not really merit a reduction in one's household insurance premiums. For this reason, the British Insurance Brokers' Association has issued a statement saying that, while it accepts the principle of insurance schemes, nevertheless it feels that any departure from the normal rates, terms and conditions should be accompanied by a co-related insurance consideration. In other words, it feels very strongly that spurious schemes should not be encouraged but those that have an insurance connotation are not to be discouraged.

Brokers operating schemes frequently possess what is known as 'binding authorities' whereby not only can they rate the insurances but they can also issue immediately the necessary policies or certificates covering the risks. Others merely have what are known as 'line slips' whereby they operate a scheme but the individual insurances have to be submitted to the leading underwriter or underwriters in order that the special discounts and ratings can be agreed and the quotation offered for the risk calculated.

Support for any scheme launched by a broker – or, indeed, any insurer – must be of such a volume that it not only produces a satisfactory result for underwriters but also justifies the various extra discounts, terms and conditions provided by them.

It is for the foregoing reasons that once a scheme has been devised by a broker, particularly where an in-depth study has been made of the trade or profession enjoying the discounts, underwriters prefer that other brokers use the main broker's facility on a 'sub-broker' relationship. Often the main broker has spent a considerable amount of time and money and has carried out much detailed work into the background of the trade or profession before launching his scheme. Thus, already, the broker will know sufficiently the points to watch in the rating and the protections or precautions that may be required for the successful underwriting of each risk. He will also know the intention of the policy wording regarding unusual or excluded claims.

Mentioned earlier was the fact that some schemes remain exclusively operated by a single broker without the possibility of a sub-broker becoming involved in co-operation. The factor often influencing this decision can arise as a result of the keen terms negotiated by the placing broker which in themselves could be such that they leave no room for further financial involvement by a third party. Such further involvement could well render the scheme non-viable. The same position could arise where, for example, there were a limited number of prospects that could participate in the scheme and its viability depended on one broker securing the complete portfolio under his immediate control.

Economically, when a scheme is launched in the non-motor field, it is often far better for the sub-broker to utilise the services of the main broker rather than to be involved in the intense work that an alternative launch would command. One must also remember that the printing costs for proposal forms, policies or certificates can be a considerable expense, particularly as the success of the project so often depends upon the method of presentation. The writer is often amazed at the mediocre brochures and proposals circulated to the broking community which look as if they have emerged from some back-street printer and yet purport to advertise a gilt-edged venture. Without doubt the majority of these missives find their way directly into the wastepaper basket.

Where detailed thought goes into the preparation of proposal forms, making these clear and concise and readily understood, then the rewards start to build. Presentation, without doubt, is the keynote of success and this even extends to how the brochures and proposals are placed in the envelopes.

MARKET SCHEMES

There are already a vast number of schemes operating in the market. It might be helpful if a résumé of some of those available at the time of writing this chapter were set out with short notes on the contracts themselves.

It must be readily understood that all contracts are not of a permanent nature and they are obviously subject to review from time to time in the light of the experience gained. As a result, some of the schemes mentioned below may have disappeared by the time this book is published.

All-risks musical instruments
This is a facility for stars or other persons in the entertainment world. It meets a heavy demand for cover that otherwise is hard to obtain except on penal or onerous terms.

Betting shops
This scheme has many special extensions designed to meet the need of clients in this occupation.

Brucellosis
One of many insurances available from a firm of Lloyd's brokers operating in the farming world, providing very necessary protection for livestock owners.

Contact lenses
A specialist scheme to cover this quite extensively demanded cover. Facilities are available for both the micro-corneal and haptic lenses.

Continental car expenses for travelling abroad
Cover for the additional likely expenses that may be incurred while travelling abroad with a car.

Contingency for non-appearance
The loss of revenue or expenses incurred as the result of the non-appearance of an entertainer or speaker can be insured with suitable indemnities. There is often a measure of co-insurance here and the exclusion of financial reasons is quite normal.

Crop damage
A unique and wide-ranging cover for farmers available through a Lloyd's broker. Covers many of the perils to which farmers are subject.

Employer's protection insurance
A number of schemes operate providing an indemnity for employers with the Employment Protection Act in mind. Although fairly new in the United Kingdom, the cover has been available on the Continent and in the United States for many years.

Fish farm insurance
A tailor-made cover operating for fish farms – now a thriving industry – and a contract of a truly specialist class.

Foot-and-mouth disease insurance
Another of the special agricultural covers operated by a firm of Lloyd's brokers.

Fruitgrowers' insurance scheme
A scheme designed to protect fruitgrowers from many of the natural perils that overtake them in their industry.

High-risk fire and burglary insurances
There are special schemes available to accept this class of risk where the trade or past claims experience has proved too heavy for the normal market. Sometimes the risks call for added burglar or fire protection or a measure of co-insurance, making the insured very aware of the risks he is running.

Hotel insurances
A number of schemes are available for this class. Some have a conventional rating on sums insured while others are rated on the number of bedrooms.

Infringement of copyright, patents, trademarks, etc.
A scheme operated by a Lloyd's insurance broker covering infringement of rights.

Legal defence
An interesting cover available for individuals wishing to protect themselves against heavy legal costs in defence of their rights in common law.

Loss-of-use insurance for private cars and commercial vehicles
A contract available for car owners and fleet operators to provide an indemnity on a daily basis following breakdown or accident to their vehicles.

Seed contamination insurance
An ingenious scheme designed for seed producers.

Thatched dwellings
This is a contract operated by a firm of Lloyd's brokers which provides ready access to a sometimes otherwise difficult market.

Existing schemes are always disappearing and new ones growing; the above list is, therefore, by no means exhaustive.

INTERESTING ASPECTS

To illustrate the suggestion that schemes have a particular interest of their own we can study two examples, which are both now defunct but which clearly show the wide scope and detailed thought that is necessary in implementing a scheme.

The two schemes were both devised to provide an indemnity for fruitgrowers against the ravages of spring frosts. They were devoted in the main to top fruit, i.e. apples, pears, cherries and plums.

To devise a scheme and to sell it to the fruitgrowing community would be utterly impossible unless first of all one made a study of their business. To know the varieties of fruit, coupled with the way frost itself affects the orchards, was absolutely essential. From a most interesting book by Raymond Bush entitled *Frost and the Fruit Grower* (Cassell), one learned of 'blackeye' and 'frost drift' and, once this knowledge was assimilated, one was fit to enter the fray of talking to fruitgrowers with a sense of reasonable authority.

The first scheme involved the use of a clock thermograph. This was set four feet above the ground at the mean contour level of the orchard to be insured. The sum insured was limited to the average turnover of the grower's last three years' record. The insurance paid out the sum insured in the event of the temperature falling below a specified level for a period as shown on a set scale at any time between midnight on 10 April and midnight on 31 May.

The dates were preset and did not vary to take into account an early or late season. Thus, unintentionally, there was always the possibility that with a late season, where the fruiting of the trees was much delayed, one could have a severe frost without any subsequent damage at all to the crop and yet receive a 100 per cent pay-out under the policy!

The second scheme was based on an entirely different format. The rating took into account the siting of the orchard and the type of fruit grown, making allowance for the susceptibility of the earlier varieties of fruit to frost damage. Sometimes it was necessary to make a survey of the fruitgrower's holding and for him to implement any recommendations required thereafter – such as wind frost screening. The rating also took into account the standard of husbandry prevailing. The sum insured was based on a maximum agreed amount per bushel.

The insurance indemnified the insured in respect of loss of crop resulting from frost by the amount by which, as a direct result of such frost, the value of the actual crop fell below 80 per cent of that of the estimated crop at an agreed amount per bushel.

The scheme was a brilliant effort to place insurance on a scientific footing, albeit sometimes other natural perils prevailed, such as 'bad set' or lack of pollination, thus tending to increase the claims somewhat. The sum insured was paid out according to the estimated amount of actual frost damage. Cover commenced from the date of acceptance of the instructions from the fruit-grower and continued until the frost ceased. Thus one could appreciate that the policy took into account an early or late season – indeed, in one particular year frosts on 6 June cleared out one orchard completely!

Following a frost, the orchard was inspected as quickly as possible by the surveyor and a further visit was made at the time of the June drop. Finally the claim was assessed at picking time in September or October.

Here we had two examples of the ingenuity of brokers producing two very interesting schemes. Much investigation is necessary but the end result undoubtedly is very worth while.

Chapter 17

Insurance brokers' financial and management accounting

JOHN A. PHILPOTT, MA, ACA
Senior Manager, Ernst & Whinney

Accounting has been defined as 'the art of recording, classifying and summarising in a significant manner and in terms of money, transactions and events which are, in part at least, of a financial character, and interpreting the results thereof' (American Institute of Certified Public Accountants). This chapter provides an exposition of two main branches of the subject, financial accounting and management accounting, as they affect the business of an insurance broker.

FINANCIAL ACCOUNTING

Financial accounting embraces the bookkeeping function of recording transactions, and the periodic preparation of accounts and other statements from these records, to provide information for such parties as shareholders, creditors, bankers, the Inland Revenue and regulatory bodies.

Recording

The recording system may be based on handwritten ledgers or involve mechanised or computerised accounting. In any case the following underlying concepts apply:
1. Transactions are recorded for an entity, which in the case of a broker may be a sole practitioner, partnership or limited company, and this is regarded as separate from its owners.
2. Transactions are recorded in terms of money, as the only practical common denominator. Changes in the value of money give rise to problems in producing meaningful state-

ments from the data recorded, though this is of less concern to a broker than to a manufacturer.

3. Transactions are recorded on a double-entry system to reflect the dual nature of any commercial activity. If a business draws a cheque it will, apart from reducing its balance at the bank, either pay off a creditor, acquire an asset, incur an expense or reduce the owners' interest.

Brokers' accounts

A broker will normally raise accounting entries for general business premiums at the time a debit note is issued. The account of the client is debited with the gross premium due, and the account of the insurer with whom the business is placed is credited with the net premium. In the course of time these balances should be cleared by the receipt and payment of cash. The difference between gross and net premiums represents commission and is credited to a brokerage account which may be subdivided to identify separately income from different classes of business. At the end of the financial year, the balance on the brokerage account which has built up will be extracted from the books of account and included in the financial accounts, subject to any special accounting policy the firm may have.

In the case of life and pensions brokerage, the premiums rarely pass through the hands of the broker. It would be usual not to bring commission on such business into the books until a cheque has been obtained from the life company concerned, since cancellation of a policy would mean that the commission was never received.

When a broker receives claim payments from insurers he is simply acting as an intermediary through whom amounts are channelled to the ultimate insured. The accounting entries will reflect this by simply consisting of an equal debit in the insurance company's account and credit in the client's account. These will be raised when the claim has been agreed, and cleared when it has been settled by the insurer and paid on to the insured. In most cases there are no amounts of income or expenditure to be reflected in the annual accounts, though claim collection fees may arise.

Particularly in the London market, insurance brokers place significant amounts of business where the premium is denominated in a currency other than sterling. For each major foreign currency, it is normal practice to maintain a separate set of ledgers in the currency concerned.

All expenses incurred will be debited to the appropriate expense account. These accounts are classified over the major expenses of the business such as salaries, rent, postage and telephone in a manner suitable for generating the management accounting information required. A simple accounting system would be to make the entry at the time the expense is paid. In more sophisticated businesses the expense would be debited when the bill or invoice was received, and a creditor raised in the supplier's account. Payment then serves to clear the creditor balance.

Investment income will be credited to an appropriately designated account at the time it is received. In the case of interest received under the deduction of income tax the investment income should be grossed up by, and a debit balance raised for, the income tax suffered, since this can be set off against the tax assessment on the business.

Under the Insurance Brokers Registration Council (IBRC) and Lloyd's rules a broker will need to establish a separate bank account, known as an Insurance Broking Account (IBA) through which all receipts and payments in respect of insurance transactions can be made. An office account, to which transfers of brokerage can be made from IBA, will be necessary for the payment of expenses.

Annual accounts

The single most important report prepared from the accounting records is the document referred to as the annual accounts. Under the Companies Act 1985, a limited company is required to prepare annual accounts for the information of its members and file a copy at Companies House where the accounts are available for public inspection. For a broking sole trader or partnership such accounts are required by IBRC but would in any event be necessary for the owners of the business to agree their tax assessments with the Inland Revenue and to ascertain their own interests in the net assets of the business.

The principal components of the accounts are the balance sheet, which shows the assets and liabilities of the business and the owner's interest in it at a particular date, and the profit and loss account which summarises for a period (normally of 12 months) ending on the balance sheet date the brokerage earned, other income receivable and expenses incurred. Accompanying these would normally be a statement of source and application of funds, notes to the accounts giving various supplementary information, and reports by the directors and auditors. Where a broking company has subsidiary companies it is required to produce consolidated accounts, which are a summation of the accounts of all companies in the group after eliminating inter-company transactions and balances. A specimen profit and loss account and balance sheet are shown on pages 192 and 193.

Accounts are prepared upon what is known as the accruals basis. This means that brokerage, investment income and expenses are recognised as they are earned or incurred and not as they are received or paid. Revenue and costs are matched with one another and dealt with in the profit and loss account of the period to which they relate. The result of this is that expenses incurred but unbilled or unpaid by the year end, such as telephone calls or electricity, must be charged in the profit and loss account and a creditor raised. Conversely, expenses paid which relate to the next financial year are not charged in the present year's profit and loss account but are carried forward in the balance sheet as prepayments (included under the heading of debtors). Thus if rent has been paid in advance, the broker has an asset in the sense that he can use the premises for a number of months without further payment. Similarly, the cost of assets such as motor cars and office equipment having a limited useful life should be written off in the profit and loss account over their expected lives by way of a depreciation charge. A written-down value is included in the balance sheet.

The contents of the accounts of limited companies are specified by Schedule 4 to the Companies Act 1985. This Schedule prescribes formats for the balance sheet and profit and loss account, which set out the headings to be used in the accounts and the order in which the headings must appear. There is an overriding requirement for the accounts to show a true and fair view, and they must be audited by a qualified accountant.

Figures included in the annual accounts are not wholly objective since alternative accounting treatments of particular transactions are possible. The UK accountancy bodies have issued Statements of Standard Accounting Practice in an attempt to narrow the permissible treatments and to ensure disclosure of the significant accounting policies adopted. All accounts will normally be prepared on the assumption that the broker will continue in business for the foreseeable future, so that assets need not be written down to the amount they would realise in the event of a forced sale. But beyond this there is scope for many differences of opinion as to the particular year's profit and loss account in which various items of income and expenditure should be included.

Important accounting policies relating to insurance brokers include the following:

1. When brokerage income should be treated as earned. It may be regarded as earned at the comencement of every insurance on the grounds that the bulk of the broker's expenditure in connection with an insurance will occur at the time that it is arranged. Alternatively it may be spread over the full period of insurance, in which case the income will be apportioned between the profit and loss accounts for two or more years. Special treatments may be adopted for life and pensions commission, and on various long-term insurances.

2. Whether debtors and creditors relating to insurance business should appear in the balance sheet when the broker, acting as an intermediary, may not be the party to whom or from whom the amounts in question are legally due. It is normal practice for a broker placing general business to include these debtor and creditor balances on the basis of commercial substance – the balances have arisen and will be settled to and by the broker as part of a normal course of trading. Balances due to and from the same party in different ledgers or currencies will be netted off where it is the practice to make such set-off in settling the accounts.

3. Whether investments should be included in the accounts at cost or at market value.

4. What rates of exchange should be used for translating brokerage, assets and liabilities arising from business transacted in foreign currencies.

5. Whether goodwill arising on the acquisition of an existing broking business should be retained in the balance sheet as an asset.

Whichever accounting policies are adopted by a broker, they should be adhered to consistently from year to year.

EXAMPLE INSURANCE BROKER LIMITED

PROFIT AND LOSS ACCOUNT
FOR THE YEAR ENDED 31 MARCH 1987

	1987	1986
	£000	£000
TURNOVER	10,251	8,558
Operating costs	8,812	7,190
Operating profit	1,439	1,368
Investment income	330	262
PROFIT ON ORDINARY ACTIVITIES BEFORE TAXATION	1,769	1,630
Taxation	659	712
PROFIT ON ORDINARY ACTIVITIES AFTER TAXATION	1,110	918
Dividends	500	400
RETAINED PROFIT FOR THE YEAR	610	518

Explanatory notes to profit and loss account and balance sheet

1. Turnover represents earned brokerage.
2. Goodwill represents the amount paid for a business in excess of the tangible net assets acquired. It is effectively a payment for the existing business connection of a broker, and for the profits that connection is expected to generate.
3. The share premium account is built up from amounts paid when share capital is issued in excess of the nominal value of the shares. The use of this account is restricted: in particular, dividends may not be paid out of it.
4. Deferred taxation represents tax payable, for which there is no immediate liability because of temporary reliefs available, but which is expected to fall due in the foreseeable future.

EXAMPLE INSURANCE BROKER LIMITED

BALANCE SHEET AT 31 MARCH 1987

	1987	1986
	£000	£000
FIXED ASSETS		
Intangible assets – goodwill	671	671
Tangible assets	1,215	1,085
	1,886	1,756
CURRENT ASSETS		
Debtors	25,629	21,170
Investments	2,630	2,673
Cash at bank and in hand	4,532	4,331
	32,791	28,174
CREDITORS – amounts falling due within one year		
Trade and other creditors	30,192	26,268
Taxation	645	521
Proposed dividend	300	200
	31,137	26,989
NET CURRENT ASSETS	1,654	1,185
TOTAL ASSETS LESS CURRENT LIABILITIES	3,540	2,941
CREDITORS – amounts falling due after more than one year		
Long-term loans	422	601
PROVISIONS FOR LIABILITIES AND CHARGES		
Deferred taxation	47	21
TOTAL ASSETS LESS LIABILITIES	3,071	2,319
CAPITAL AND RESERVES		
Called-up share capital	1,500	1,500
Share premium account	150	150
Revaluation reserve	347	205
Profit and loss account	1,074	464

John Smith ⎫
G. Brown ⎭ Directors
7 August 1987

	3,071	2,319

Return to IBRC

A practising insurance broker or enrolled body corporate must send a Statement of Particulars together with a copy of the annual accounts to IBRC within six months of the end of the financial year. The purpose of the Statement of Particulars is to demonstrate compliance with the provisions of the Insurance Brokers Registration Council (Accounts and Business Requirements) Rules 1979.

These Rules specify solvency margin requirements for insurance brokers – i.e. amounts by which assets must exceed liabilities. There are three tests of this nature to satisfy:

(a)   insurance transactions assets at least equal to insurance transactions liabilities;
(b)   working capital of at least £1,000;
(c)   total assets to exceed total liabilities by at least £1,000.

The Rules provide precise definitions of the assets and liabilities which rank for the purposes of these tests. These definitions differ in a number of respects from normal accounting conventions; for example, liabilities payable within three years are treated as current and deducted from working capital whereas liabilities payable within three years or more are disregarded altogether.

The Statement of Particulars, which is a preprinted form, comprises the following sections:

Part I
Summary of assets and liabilities, analysing figures from the annual accounts in column 1 and applying prescribed valuation rules in column 2 in order to demonstrate the broker's solvency position at the end of the financial year.

Part II
Questionnaire concerning undue dependence on particular insurance companies.

Part III
Certificate by or on behalf of the insurance broker which confirms the correct completion of the Statement of Particulars and the maintenance of prescribed solvency margins throughout the financial year.

Part IV
Accountant's report on the Statement of Particulars.

Other considerations

There are other purposes besides the annual accounts and return
to IBRC for which financial accounting statements may need to
be prepared. These include the following:

1. Lloyd's broker's solvency test – a Lloyd's broker is exempt
   from the return to IBRC but must make a return to Lloyd's
   demonstrating compliance with the Lloyd's solvency rules for
   brokers.
2. Negotiation for a bank overdraft.

The format of the accounting records should be such as will
enable all appropriate financial accounting statements and management accounts to be prepared, and will facilitate day-to-day
operations such as credit control.

MANAGEMENT ACCOUNTING

Management accounting is concerned with the provision for
management of information about the economic operation of the
business to enable decisions to be taken and control to be
exercised.

Costing

Financial accounting statements provide a summary of the various items of income and expenditure but do not give any
indication as to the relative significance of each part of the
broking business in generating the profit or loss for the year.
While the accounting records may indicate how much brokerage
was earned by each department, they will not directly show what
proportion of the total expenses was incurred in generating the
brokerage for each class of business.

   Cost accounting, which can be regarded as an integral part of
management accounting, seeks to remedy this by laying down
principles for the classification and allocation of expenditure. A
broker may be organised as a head office with a number of
branches, or be divided into a number of technical departments
(such as motor, marine, life and pensions). In either case there
will be supporting service departments, such as claims, administration and accounts, that, while not giving rise to the receipt of
brokerage themselves, are essential to the operation of the
business as a whole. The basic costing technique is to define the

parts of the business to which costs can be charged (these are called 'cost centres'), to split total costs between cost centres on the most reasonable bases available and finally to apportion service department cost centres over the brokerage-earning cost centres.

This procedure will indicate to management any parts of the business that are operating unprofitably and enable performance to be monitored. The value of the information produced depends upon the validity of the assumptions made in splitting costs.

In many cases there will be no doubt as to the cost centres to which a particular expense ought to be attributed. To take the example of a broker operating from a single office, salaries, National Insurance contributions and pension costs for each employee are simply charged to the cost centre for which he works. The term 'allocation' is used where a cost or overhead results solely from the existence of a particular cost centre: other items that can be allocated are telephone rental charges, depreciation of specific assets, and travelling and entertaining costs incurred in generating a specific class of business.

All other costs must be 'apportioned' to cost centres on some equitable basis. For example, if a broker rents an office block, the annual rental will have to be split over all the departments in some way. One method would be to apportion according to the floor space occupied: other accommodation charges such as rates, lighting, heating and cleaning could be treated in a similar fashion. It is clear that there may be alternative bases of apportionment that are equally appropriate and when one turns to the apportionment of service department cost centres the choice of method is often extremely arbitrary.

Decision-making

Costing information can play an important part in showing that a problem exists about which a decision must be taken. It may be apparent from the cost accounts that a particular branch is running at a loss. However, further investigation is necessary before a decision to close it down can be taken. The courses of action open to the broker must first be defined; in the present case they may include reducing the staff or moving the branch to cheaper premises. Once all the options are known, steps can be taken to quantify the financial effects of adopting each of them. Considerable knowledge of the behaviour of costs is necessary.

Many costs will be fixed in some way: for instance, if a whole suite of offices has to be rented, reduction of staff will not result in a proportionate reduction in accommodation charges. As the time period examined increases, fewer costs have to be treated as fixed. Indirect effects, such as the increased cost of servicing business from a more distant office, and any redundancy payments that would arise, must also be considered.

Accounting information and techniques can demonstrate the effects of different courses of action, but it is still the prerogative of management to choose between them. Knowledge of the consequences will lead to a more informed decision, but if there is to be consistency in the decisions taken from year to year the broker ought to establish overall objectives for the business. These may be expressed in terms of profit, market share or return on capital employed, but whatever form they take it is important that they are made explicit. Once established, they can ensure that decision-making ceases to be a haphazard process and assist in the delegation of short-term decisions to a level below that of senior management.

Budgeting

An important set of management accounting techniques is concerned with the formulation of plans designed to achieve the business objectives. A budget can be defined as 'an economic plan for a period of time'. If long-term progress is to be adequately controlled, outline budgets for a number of years will have to be prepared in order to give advance warning of requirements for additional finance. But the most common form of budget is that prepared in detail for the forthcoming year. This will be based on an annual cycle: logically the brokerage budget ought to be prepared first, and then an expense budget drafted in the light of the activity levels implied by the brokerage budget. One of the main functions of budgeting is to ensure that the plans are consistent so that there are sufficient staff to deal with the business generated and adequate accommodation and back-up services.

Once the budget has been approved, it serves as a standard against which actual results can be monitored. The reasons for all significant variances must be investigated and, if a variance is unfavourable, appropriate corrective action taken. In exceptional circumstances, it may be found that the assumptions upon which the original budget were based have proved to be unrealistic because of, for example, an overall salary increase in excess of expectations. It would then be appropriate to amend the budget.

To achieve the aim of controlling progress, the budget must be subdivided into responsibility areas. These will to some extent correspond with the cost centres established for the cost accounting system, but further subdivision may be necessary to isolate the individual responsible for a particular item of income or expense. As far as possible, apportionment of expenses should be avoided in a system of budgetary control (though it is still necessary for costing purposes). Although the activities of the motor and life and pensions departments help to give rise to the need for an accounts department, the managers of these operating departments cannot directly control the efficiency with which accounting operations are carried out. Costs can be better controlled if it is left to the accounts department manager to explain all differences from the budget for his department.

The general principle to be observed is that individuals should be made responsible within the budgetary control system only for those items that they are capable of controlling. Such items as rent and depreciation of fixed assets may not be controllable by anybody, in the sense that they are the result of earlier decisions to obtain particular premises or fixed assets. These should be separately identified and taken to a 'special' responsibility area, simply to ensure that all outgoings are included in the system.

The budget also needs to be broken down into reporting periods, which would commonly be fixed at one month. Appropriate account would be taken of seasonal variations in brokerage, which might arise from treaty renewals due on 1 January, and the months in which particular expenses, such as rent and rates, are payable.

CONCLUSION

Financial accounting has a clear, legal background but is designed to satisfy the requirements of several different classes of person seeking information. Management accounting is a comparatively junior branch of the subject that has evolved to serve the particular needs of management. They provide complementary disciplines which play an important part in the overall business structure of an insurance broker.

FURTHER READING

Accounting standards 1986/87 (The Institute of Chartered Accountants in England and Wales, 1986).

French, Derek: *Dictionary of Accounting Terms* (The Institute of Chartered Accountants in England and Wales, 1985).

Harper, W. M.: *Cost and Management Accounting* (two volumes) (Macdonald & Evans, 1982).

Oakes, R. G. and Holmes, N. H.: *Business Briefing 6 – Insurance Brokers* (Institute of Chartered Accountants in England and Wales, 1985).

Wood, Frank: *Business Accounting* (two volumes), fourth edition (Pitman, 1984).

Chapter 18

The organisation and systems of an insurance broker's office

J. L. FLOWER, FCII
National Systems/Administration Director, Jardine Insurance Brokers Ltd

While increased mechanisation is inevitable, affecting the broker's needs for certain personnel, the underlying requirement of an efficiently organised office with skilled and experienced staff will remain unchanged. This chapter deals with some of the basic systems necessary to all brokers' offices whatever their size and the many and varied matters requiring close attention.

Many brokers' offices will have a computer to handle a large or small part of their operations. Reference has been made later in this chapter to the ever-increasing use of computers in the daily routine of a broker's office. However, it should be noted that the rapid advance of technology and the wide variety of systems available makes comment on any specific system difficult.

The purpose of every system is efficiency. To allow for growth all systems must be flexible and this chapter has been written so as to reflect this. It does not attempt to define a rigid way of organising an office, but in drawing attention to as many aspects as possible it is hoped that it will assist towards basic efficiency.

Systems are organised personnel with defined duties working to predetermined rules and it is therefore via these personnel as units that practical observations can be indicated.

SPECIALIST DEPARTMENTS

In their application to any particular broker's office each unit referred to under the following subheadings could be of several persons but equally in a small office one technician may wear two or more hats. To have specialists for every function of a broker's workload is impractical for all but the largest organisation.

Evolution and direction of development will usually dictate the emphasis on the particular skills required of each employee and whether the old divisions of fire, accident, motor, life and marine are used or the more recent categories of property, liability, transportation and the person.

General experience should be supplemented by personnel trained in a more specific field. Each stage of growth or staff replacement should be used to supplement or strengthen the team as required by changing practices in the insurance world and the composition of the broker's business.

The available technicians may well be divided into mixed skills sections each handling a range of clients, or in an office with a large connection in one trade a section may be devoted solely to clients in that trade. Where 'scheme' business forms an important part of the income specific personnel would probably be allocated to that work.

Using modern subdivisions, many of the particular matters relevant to the various classes of business are outlined in the following paragraphs.

The insurance of property and business interruption

A system must be established for the regular collection of clients' stock declarations where required for fire and/or theft policies, not only to ensure that annual premium adjustments are done but, more importantly, to keep a check on the adequacy of the sums insured. A similar system is needed for declarations necessary under book debts policies.

To adjust business interruption policies, auditors' certificates must be sent for after the known close of a client's financial year end. With correctly arranged cover there will no doubt be sizeable return premiums due to the client.

Any *bordereau* arrangements with insurers, whereby the broker is able to attach cover according to predetermined agreements, require the compilation of the relevant facts for onward transmission at the agreed intervals.

Particular reference material which should be made available to the technicians includes the *Rules for the Construction of Buildings* and the *Rules for Automatic Sprinkler Installations*, both obtainable from the Loss Prevention Council, 140 Aldersgate Street, London EC1A 4HX. Obtainable from the Fire Protection Association at the same address is their *Journal* and other technical information.

The insurance of liabilities

Declarations required from clients must be organised to comply with the terms of the policies. With any policies subject to a bonus for no or low claims, records must be kept to ensure such premiums are adjusted as claims may be outstanding for some years. A good system must be established for obtaining fresh proposal forms annually for professional indemnity policies. Where a change of insurer is envisaged or possible the client must be reminded of the need to record potential claims with the current insurers before expiry of the cover.

Insurances of transportation

A system must be established for the collection of monthly, quarterly or half-yearly declarations on motor fleet policies. Any motor rating guides held on behalf of insurance companies must be kept up to date.

A diary system is necessary for the issue of continuation motor cover notes. Cover note books must receive particular attention: they should be locked away when the office is unattended and a register kept of the receipt from and their return to insurers.

An adequate supply of certificates for marine open covers should be retained for onward transmission to clients as requested.

Insurances of the person

A system is necessary for obtaining annual recosting information for pension schemes; the speedy submission of salary lists ensures that the life cover is increased to the multiple of any higher salary agreed since the previous recosting. Pursuing the premium for passing on to insurers avoids any late payment charges to the fund.

Where individual pension arrangements have been made on a non-annual basis, a procedure should be established for making annual contact with the client to ascertain his ability and desire to make further one-off payments for his retirement. Those with annual arrangements must also be approached on increasing their provision for their retirement.

Most brokers' offices will issue travel certificates on behalf of one or more insurers and sufficient blank certificates must be kept for this purpose, particularly during the summer months.

Credit insurance and bonding

Apart from the need to obtain annual declarations, a system must be established to record the customers' credit limits agreed with insurers for each client.

For those clients requiring regular solvency bonds, the broker should obtain and submit to the surety company the annual accounts of the client as soon as they become available to maintain the facility for future bonds.

SERVICING AND DEVELOPMENT

Each commercial client and many private clients will need visiting at least once per year. This task may be undertaken by directors, partners, account controllers or departmental managers. It is the responsibility of all staff to keep the servicing executive advised of all matters relating to a particular client.

Although one or more members of staff may be specifically engaged on the development of new business, it is the duty of all employees to recognise and grasp every opportunity arising in this regard.

CLAIMS

The efficiency of a broker's business is more readily measured by the effectiveness of the actions of staff in dealing with claims, and the basis of such efficiency must be a good filing and recording system so that papers and information are speedily extracted.

A simple but effective system is for each claim to be numbered from a central record book and cross-referenced to a card index for clients maintained in alphabetical order. Files can then be retained in alphabetical or numerical order. For those clients with numerous incidents such as motor fleets' or employer's liability accident advices it may be necessary to establish a simple supplementary system.

Maintaining a record of settlement details has benefits in avoiding the need to refer for such information to insurers' records when so often it is required urgently. A diary system should be instituted to ensure requests for information are followed up. Where a *bordereau* underwriting authority is held, the appropriate records should be kept to recover settlements from insurers.

THE ARRANGING OF COVER

Enquiries from clients must be dealt with speedily. The full facts must be ascertained in order that a positive quotation for the correct cover can be provided. The facts can be conveyed to insurers by the 'slip' method – mainly used in the London market – or by letter, telephone or personal visit to the insurers.

The client's request for cover must be acted upon quickly with a confirmatory cover note or letter dispatched the same day where feasible. Telephone advices to insurers that cover has commenced on the terms quoted should be followed by a letter or broker form confirming the position.

All policies and endorsements must be checked to see that they provide the cover as requested by the client and tailored by the skill of the broker.

RENEWALS

The core of a broker's office must be the record-keeping system, which ensures that the renewal of each policy is attended to efficiently. It must be kept in date order either on cards or in book form, preferably loose-leaf.

Basic information should be recorded and kept up to date as amendments occur. This enables one to check that renewal papers are received from insurers and, if not, their absence can be investigated. After any necessary review of each policy the renewal notice should be sent to the client and an appropriate reminder system organised to ensure speedy completion of the operation.

With commercial and private clients who have several policies due on the same date the renewal invitations should be gathered together and an appropriate review procedure adopted including a consultation with the client, following which he can be debited with the renewal premiums.

GENERAL OFFICE PROCEDURES

Reception and telephones

The first impressions gained by a client or potential client are important and care must be taken to offer a polite greeting whether it is face to face or on the telephone. Sufficient information should be obtained from a telephone caller to ensure that the right person handles the enquiry.

How successfully telephones are used in an office will depend not only on the training of the telephonist but also on the training of the staff who deal with enquiries.

Filing

Insurance broking being an industry involving large quantities of paper, the need for an efficient and well-maintained filing system is paramount. The simplest system is often the best and is more capable of being maintained satisfactorily by inexperienced staff, although even the simplest system needs to be supervised by someone with experience and common sense. An alphabetical filing system fulfils the requirement for simplicity whether maintained in drawers or on shelving or in more sophisticated furniture.

Sufficient space must be kept for growth, and regular but infrequent thinning out is necessary under the control of an experienced member of staff. Microfilming is a useful aid to the reduction of stored paperwork. The files on outstanding matters should be kept separately to ensure that they can be reviewed regularly.

Typing

Whether a shorthand or audio system is used, the typing facility in a broking office needs control to ensure a smooth flow of the work. Either a supervisor is required or a senior person given the responsibility for the efficient processing of the workload.

All machinery must be regularly maintained and a steady replacement programme established. Portable dictation equipment can be a valuable aid, but such is the rate at which refinements in this and other types of equipment are being introduced that it would be meaningless to attempt to specify a typical system here.

Mail

It is not sufficient just to have the most junior member or members of staff opening and dispatching mail. Not only is there an auditing need to account for monies received through the post but also it is the area where inefficiency can be most easily noticed by the client. Supervision by an experienced person must be exercised.

Incoming

All incoming mail should be conveyed to the post desk or room immediately on receipt. If a particular letter is awaited, the intended recipient should have to seek it only in one place.

The main time for incoming mail will be the first thing each day when, after personally addressed mail is extracted and distributed, all envelopes and packages should be slit open. The supervisor should examine all post for cash, cheques, postal orders, etc., before the contents are sorted in accordance with agreed distribution. Personally addressed mail may contain important and urgent information. If the addressee is absent, an agreed procedure for opening should be arranged.

Where a second postal delivery is usual it should receive attention at a prearranged time and be dealt with in the same manner as the morning post. Many towns and districts have a local collection box facility; deliveries to it and collections from it should be timed to precede letter-opening arrangements in the office.

Outgoing

Apart from the occasional special dispatch, all outgoing mail should be made available to the postal staff in good time before the normal close of business hours. Not only will this avoid the irritation of after-hours work but also enable the duties to be performed with care.

Badly folded letters present a poor picture to the insuring public, and more than one envelope addressed to the same client on the same day will often result in some sarcasm. All mail intended by the sender to go first class must be clearly identified, and staff should be equipped with an appropriate postal weighing machine and postal rates to ensure the correct postage is affixed.

Despite the disproportionate expense when compared with other office machinery, a postal franking machine has advantages for all but the smallest office. Instruction must be given in its use to avoid incorrect franking, which again easily destroys client confidence in one's efficiency whether the mistake is an over- or under-franking.

PRINTING AND STATIONERY

Larger offices will have their own printing facility, but for most it is uneconomic and an outside printer's services are necessary. It is worth establishing a relationship with a printer who will become aware of one's requirements, particularly for the day when an urgent job is necessary.

A common leterheading should be used on all paper sizes, compliment slips and other printed material in order to reduce the cost of blocks or plates. Paper size varieties should be kept to as low a number as possible. For standard-size envelopes those of the window variety avoid supplementary typing and reduce postal handling duties. Larger envelopes should be stocked but not in too many sizes.

The use of preprinted 'tick in box'-type forms for routine correspondence with insurers is recommended as cost-effective. The extent to which similar forms can be used in correspondence with clients will be each broker's individual decision.

A regular check of stocks of stationery held should be instigated, with fresh supplies being ordered in good time.

ACCOUNTING

It is essential that an efficient system is set up for the collecting of insurance premiums and the passing of net premiums to the insurance companies. The exact terminology may vary from office to office, but the terms used below will be recognisable.

The invoicing of clients must be done promptly with copies retained for entering in the ledgers. A numbering system is recommended by the accountancy profession.

Where credit is allowed to selected clients, the entries should be made individually in the clients and insurance companies ledgers. Where it is a cash transaction then the entries should be made in the insurance companies ledger when paid.

A properly maintained insurance companies ledger minimises the reconciliation problems that will arise on the accounts with insurers, whether the broker settles with them on his own statement of monies due or by endeavouring to reconcile to insurers' statements of account.

Cash and cheques received should be entered in a day book, preferably as they are extracted from the post. All receipts should be entered in a cash book from which action is initiated to deal with cash clients' payments and credit clients' settlements. The bank paying-in book is prepared and the receipts banked daily or more frequently if appropriate.

All invoices should show the VAT number, and in cases where VAT is chargeable, such as for statutory inspections of lifting tackle, the charge should be clearly identified.

A system must be set up for sending regular reminders for premiums due. In particular, where credit has been given agreed time limits should be enforced.

Accounts personnel must also be equipped to handle salary payments, PAYE and National Insurance deductions, and other salary-related matters. Other expenses incurred by staff on the company's business must be reimbursed in a manner designated by management.

REFERENCE MATERIAL

Each broker's office should build up a library of textbooks for reference purposes, ensuring that they are replaced periodically to reflect changes which have occurred.

There are many and varied journals which can be obtained; each office will be aware of those from which it derives the greatest benefits. To be of value they must be seen by the greatest number of staff in the shortest possible time and should be circulated with this in mind.

ADMINISTRATION

Staff

The employment of staff has become more of a precise art as a result of the maze of employment legislation which more than ever before requires that the right person is obtained for a vacancy. In order to foster good employee relations it is essential that employers make themselves aware of what the legislation stipulates and follow the necessary basic procedures that are laid down.

Where a background of insurance experience is required, the specialist employment agencies are well worth approaching. Experience over a period of time will establish which agencies evaluate applicants before sending them for interviews. It can be very frustrating and time-wasting to be sent totally unsuitable candidates.

Advertising in the specialist insurance magazines and the careful use of national and local newspapers should be considered for specific skilled appointments. Jobcentres should also feature in the search for suitable staff.

Interviews are best conducted by one person who will develop his own technique in eliciting the information necessary on which a decision can be reached or a recommendation can be made. The persons to be most involved with the new employee should also be consulted.

When a decision has been arrived at, the offer of employment should be made in writing in a predetermined manner, restating many of the facts which will have been discussed during the interview and requesting an early decision in order that other applicants can be informed. References should be taken up and a contract of employment issued clearly defining the rights and duties of both parties.

No office can progress without regular training of both new and existing personnel. On-the-job training under supervision must be supplemented by specific in-house lectures and discussion sessions where those with particular expertise can expound their knowledge to other members of staff.

Conferences arranged by the BIBA, local insurance institutes and other bodies should each be considered for the practical benefit to be obtained, and staff should be encouraged to attend the various local specialist societies to expand their knowledge.

Few offices will be overstaffed and therefore most will be affected by staff on holiday, on courses, away sick or on maternity leave. To the extent that such absences can be controlled, care must be taken to ensure adequate staffing levels are maintained, utilising temporary staff where necessary. Planning must begin early for the main summer holiday period, which often causes the greatest difficulties.

Staff must be made aware of their duties when off sick. State benefits obtained should be dealt with in a previously agreed manner.

Secretarial

The company secretary in an insurance-broking firm has many essential duties common to all company secretaries. Responsibilities of recent origin particular to insurance brokers are fulfilling the requirements of the Insurance Brokers (Registration) Act, registering under credit law and preparing the information required for membership of the BIBA.

General administration

Apart from those matters specific to an insurance-broking office, there are many other procedures which require careful organisation to ensure that the facilities are available for the prime workload to be efficiently performed.

Security of the premises and the protection of records must be considered plus fire and accident prevention. A fire certificate must be obtained and fire-extinguishing equipment serviced, preferably by specialist contractors under a maintenance agreement.

Fire evacuation procedures must be established and advised to all members of staff, particularly new employees, and fire drills performed at regular intervals.

Computers and electronic data processing equipment

Much of the routine and tedious work in a broker's office can now be handled quickly and efficiently by a suitable computer system.

The efficiency of any electronic data equipment will depend as much on the quality of the hardware (equipment) and software (programs) as the personnel operating the system.

A typical good office computer administration system will contain full information on the broker's clients, both personal and corporate. It should contain full details of the client's various policies and be capable of handling all of the financial transactions that a broker carries out between both his client and the insurer.

The system should be capable of producing the broker's own personalised renewal documentation and at the same time automatically post the transaction into the client's account and the insurer's account.

Part of the record system would be a diary facility. The advantage of the computer diary over the desk diary for such things as cover notes and other follow up transactions, is that it cannot be missed. The entry remains in the computer until such times as it it physically deleted.

The automatic production of advice notes to insurers on changes within a policy is a facility contained in many computer systems, together with automatic letter writing facilities for routine memos between the broker and his client and the insurer.

The production of statistical management information should be a matter of routine, covering such areas as commission earnings by client, by insurer, by class of business, or any combination, together with other wide-ranging report facilities – all of which make the extraction of information for such things as IBRC returns and Professional Indemnity insurance relatively simple.

When considering computerisation, the broker should firstly analyse the type of business that he operates, i.e. personal lines only, commercial only, a combination of the two, life and pensions only, etc., as installing a computer system not designed for the broker's type of business can be an expensive error as there are numerous systems on the market, many with a bias towards a particular type of activity.

For members of the British Insurance Brokers' Association, one of the first steps in computerisation would be to obtain copies of computer factsheets from the Association.

Equipment

A broker's office is no different from any other, being highly dependent upon an increasing amount of electrical and mechanical aids – e.g. calculators and photocopiers – to provide the efficiency desired.

Space has limited the extent to which each aspect of the organisation and systems of an insurance broker's office can be covered, but it is hoped that the above forms a good insight into basic requirements on which each office can build with experience.

FURTHER READING

Smaller Firms' Systems Committee Report: A suggested office administration and manual accounting procedure (British Insurance Brokers' Association, 1979).

Training Manual for Insurance Brokers' Staffs (with updating service) (British Insurance Brokers' Association).

Chapter 19

The education of insurance brokers

RODERICK CLEWS FCII, FCIarb
Formerly Chairman, UK Operations, Glanvill Enthoven & Co. Ltd

The education pattern for insurance brokers has changed over the years, as indicated in the following summary.

THE CHARTERED INSURANCE INSTITUTE PROFESSIONAL EXAMINATIONS AND ACTIVITIES

Prior to World War II, the Corporation of Insurance Brokers held special examinations for the members and their staff, mainly because the Chartered Insurance Institute maintained separate Associateship papers for separate classes of business, and it was believed that an insurance broker needed a wide initial education and test.

The Institute did however provide for this in parts of the Fellowship examination, but this was not thought to be adequate. Additionally, in the early years of the Chartered Insurance Institute, insurance brokers were not allowed to join!

In 1946 the Institute introduced a general branch into the Associateship examination, which enabled the Corporation of Insurance Brokers to discontinue its own examinations.

With the formation of the British Insurance Brokers' Association and the passing of the Insurance Brokers (Registration) Act, there was a further impetus to provide more fully for the formal education of those destined to be managers of insurance broking firms.

A committee of the Chartered Insurance Institute, required to make recommendations for revision of the examination syllabus, included two BIBA representatives; as a result a new subject,

'The Management of Insurance Brokers', was included in the 1982 Fellowship syllabus. For the encouragement of the continued progress of those who have achieved Fellowship of the Institute, a Society of Fellows has been formed, the members of which will engage in research and more study.

The Insurance Institute of London has for many years promoted a committee and groups for advanced study. Any suitable member can apply to join a group, and many excellent papers have been published – some achieving worldwide acclaim – and have been translated into foreign languages (including Japanese!). This is an excellent method not only of contributing, but also of learning more about a specialist subject.

While there must be continuous development of education systems to cope with changing circumstances, these changes appear to have met the current needs of those able to enter the Chartered Institute system.

The educational achievements required for entrance to these examinations, one of which is to have passed two 'A' levels or the equivalent, have prevented many of those employed in insurance broking offices from entering. No doubt this comment could also apply to some employees of insurers.

Anyone employed in insurance can join the Institute as an ordinary member, but only those who have passed the appropriate examinations can receive designatory letters. There are currently two such grades of members. An Associate (ACII) has passed the first professional examination, and can then take another, more demanding one to become a fellow (FCII).

Membership, even for those not granted letters, can be very rewarding. Lectures can be attended, and one can take part in social events. The Institute has local affiliated institutes in most major towns.

EXAMINATIONS FOR THOSE WITH LOWER ACADEMIC ATTAINMENTS

The Education Committee of the British Insurance Brokers' Association considered the problem of those unable to enter the CII professional examinations, and were very conscious of the fact that such employees of many member firms were in positions where their lack of knowledge could seriously cause problems with clients and insurers.

The result was the promotion of a new examination called the

Certificate of Competence in elementary insurance knowledge. The first examination was held in 1983. All those operating in member firms can study for and sit this examination.

The Chartered Insurance Institute was for some time reluctant to embark on this form of examination. When its requirements were raised from an 'O' level standard to 'A' levels, there was much criticism, but to be fair to those concerned in decision-making, there were valid reasons for their view. It appears that many students were unable to cope with the standards required and were clogging up the system which, like all human endeavour, had limited resources both in tuition and examination efforts.

However, with the present emphasis on formal education, training and testing for all grades of ability, the Institute has now promoted a new examination called 'The Certificate of Proficiency'; there are no educational requirements for entry. The first examination was held in 1987.

Lloyd's has also introduced its own system. This is called the Lloyd's Introductory Test and emphasises practical matters involved in the Lloyd's market, as well as basic insurance knowledge.

These last three systems are not principally designed for those able to enter the Chartered Institute Associateship and Fellowship examinations, though the Lloyd's test is mandatory for those wishing to transact business in the 'Room' for the first time. All three provide some bridge to the Chartered Institute professional examinations by offering another route, through further tests, to registration as a student for the Associateship examination.

At the time of writing, the two-year Youth Training Scheme is in progress and the BIBA Certificate of Competence is being made to cater for the vocational needs of this system. However, insurance education at all levels is now available to anyone who decides to join the business of insurance broking.

THE INSURANCE INDUSTRY TRAINING COUNCIL

The Insurance Industry Training Council (IITC) was established in 1968 at the initiative of leading members of the insurance industry at a time when Industry Training Boards were being established throughout the economy. The Council is representative of the insurance community as a whole: the Insurance

Companies, the Industrial Life Offices, the Committee of Lloyd's, BIBA, the CII, the Confederation of Insurance Trade Unions and full-time teachers of insurance are all represented.

The Council exists to examine the training needs of the insurance industry and to promote improved methods of administering and conducting training. It pursues its aims by encouragement and advice.

Progress to the highest obtainable levels of professionalism is open to all.

Study is essential for those who wish to have a really satisfying career.

Full current details can be obtained by contacting the British Insurance Brokers' Association.

Appendix 1

The British Insurance Brokers Registration Council Statutory Code of Conduct

CODE OF CONDUCT DRAWN UP BY THE INSURANCE BROKERS REGISTRATION COUNCIL PURSUANT TO SECTION 10 OF THE INSURANCE BROKERS (REGISTRATION) ACT 1977

Words and expressions used in this Code of Conduct shall have the same meaning as are ascribed to them in the Act except that:

'insurance broker' means registered insurance broker and enrolled body corporate;

'insurer' means a person or body of persons carrying on insurance business;

'advertisements' or 'advertising' means canvassing, the offer of services or other methods whereby business is sought by insurance brokers.

1. This Code of Conduct shall serve as a guide to insurance brokers and other persons concerned with their conduct but the mention or lack of mention in it of a particular act or omission shall not be taken as conclusive of any question of professional conduct.

In the opinion of the Council the objective of the Code is to assist in establishing a recognised standard of professional conduct required of all insurance brokers who should, in the interests of the public and in the performance of their duties, bear in mind both this objective and the underlying spirit of this Code.

Matters which might relate to acts or omissions amounting to negligence will be dealt with, if necessary, by the Courts but the

Council acknowledges that gross negligence *or* repeated cases of negligence may amount to unprofessional conduct.

2.   The following are, in the opinion of the Council, the acts and omissions which, if done or made by registered insurance brokers or enrolled bodies corporate constitute unprofessional conduct: namely any acts or omissions that breach the fundamental principles governing the professional conduct of insurance brokers set out in paragraph 3 below.

3.   The principles mentioned in paragraph 2 above are as follows:

A.   *Insurance brokers shall at all times conduct their business with utmost good faith and integrity.*

B.   *Insurance brokers shall do everything possible to satisfy the insurance requirements of their clients and shall place the interests of those clients before all other considerations. Subject to these requirements and interests, insurance brokers shall have proper regard for others.*

C.   *Statements made by or on behalf of insurance brokers when advertising shall not be misleading or extravagant.*

The following are some specific examples of the application of these principles:

(1)   In the conduct of their business insurance brokers shall provide advice objectively and independently.

(2)   Insurance brokers shall only use or permit the use of the description 'insurance broker' in connection with a business provided that business is carried on in accordance with the requirements of the Rules made by the Council under sections 11 and 12 of the Act.

(3)   Insurance brokers shall ensure that all work carried out in connection with their insurance broking business shall be under the control and day-to-day supervision of a registered insurance broker and they shall do everything possible to ensure that their employees are made aware of this Code.

(4)   Insurance brokers shall on request from the client explain the differences in, and the relative costs of, the principal types of insurance which in the opinion of the insurance broker might suit a client's needs.

(5)   Insurance brokers shall ensure the use of a sufficient number of insurers to satisfy the insurance requirements of their clients.

(6)   Insurance brokers shall, upon request, disclose to any client who is an individual and who is, or is contemplating becoming, the holder of a United Kingdom policy of insurance the amount of commission paid by the insurer under any relevant policy of insurance.

(7)   Although the choice of an insurer can only be a matter of judgment, insurance brokers shall use their skill objectively in the best interests of their client.

(8)   Insurance brokers shall not withhold from the policyholder any written evidence or documentation relating to the contract of insurance without adequate and justifiable reasons being disclosed in writing and without delay to the policyholder. If an insurance broker withholds a document from a policyholder by way of a lien for monies due from that policyholder he shall provide the reason in the manner required above.

(9)   Insurance brokers shall inform a client of the name of all insurers with whom a contract of insurance is placed. This information shall be given at the inception of the contract and any changes thereafter shall be advised at the earliest opportunity to the client.

(10) Before any work involving a charge is undertaken or an agreement to carry out business is concluded, insurance brokers shall disclose and identify any amount they propose to charge to the client or policyholder which will be in addition to the premium payable to the insurer.

(11) Insurance brokers shall disclose to a client any payment which they receive as a result of securing on behalf of that

client any service additional to the arrangement of a contract of insurance.

(12)   Insurance brokers shall have proper regard for the wishes of a policyholder or client who seeks to terminate an agreement with them to carry out business.

(13)   Any information acquired by an insurance broker from his client shall not be used or disclosed except in the normal course of negotiating, maintaining, or renewing a contract of insurance for that client or unless the consent of the client has been obtained or the information is required by a court of competent jurisdiction.

(14)   In the completion of the proposal form, claim form, or any other material document, insurance brokers shall make it clear that all the answers or statements are the client's own responsibility. The client should always be asked to check the details and told that the inclusion of incorrect information may result in a claim being repudiated.

(15)   Advertisements made by or on behalf of insurance brokers shall comply with the applicable parts of the Code of Advertising Practice published by the Advertising Standards Authority and for this purpose the Code of Advertising Practice shall be deemed to form part of this Code of Conduct.

(16)   Advertisements made by or on behalf of insurance brokers shall distinguish between contractual benefits, that is those that the contract of insurance is bound to provide, and non-contractual benefits, that is the amount of benefit which it might provide assuming the insurer's particular forecast is correct. Where such advertisements include a forecast of non-contractual benefits, insurance brokers shall restrict the forecast to that provided by the insurer concerned.

(17)   Advertisements made by or on behalf of insurance brokers shall not be restricted to the policies of one insurer except where the reasons for such restriction are fully explained in the advertisement, the insurer named therein, and the prior approval of that insurer obtained.

(18) When advertising their services directly or indirectly either in person or in writing insurance brokers shall disclose their identity, occupation and purpose before seeking information or before giving advice.

(19) Insurance brokers shall display in any office where they are carrying on business and to which the public have access a notice to the effect that a copy of the Code of Conduct is available upon request and that if a member of the public wishes to make a complaint or requires the assistance of the Council in resolving a dispute, he may write to the Insurance Brokers Registration Council at its offices at 15 St Helen's Place, London EC3A 6DS.

Insurance Companies Regulations 1981 – SI 1981 No.1 654 (Sections 65 and 67)

PART VII

ADVERTISEMENTS, INTERMEDIARIES, NOTICES OF LONG TERM POLICIES, LINKED CONTRACTS AND REVOCATIONS

65. Contents of advertisements

1. This regulation applies to any insurance advertisement which:

(a) invites any person to enter into or to offer to enter into, or which contains information calculated to lead directly or indirectly to any person entering into or offering to enter into, any contract of insurance (other than a contract of reinsurance) with an insurer named in the advertisement the affecting of which by him would constitute the carrying on by him of ordinary long-term insurance business; and

(b) is issued at a time when the insurer named in the advertisement is not authorised to carry on that kind of business in the United Kingdom by or under section 3 or 4 of the 1981 Act,

but does not apply to any insurance advertisement if the insurer named in the advertisement is permitted to carry on ordinary long-term insurance business in the United Kingdom otherwise than by virtue of an authorisation to do so by or under the said section 3 or 4.

2. An insurance advertisement to which this regulation applies shall include the words 'An insurance company which does not and is not authorised to carry on in any part of the

United Kingdom business of the class to which this advertisement relates' and those words shall appear prominently:

(a)   immediately after or alongside the statement of the name of the insurer; or

(b)   if the name of the insurer is stated more than once in the advertisement, immediately after or alongside the most prominent of the statements of that name and for this purpose if two or more statements of the name are equally prominent that which appears first in the advertisement shall be treated as the most prominent.

3.   An insurance advertisement to which this regulation applies shall, if it states the name of any United Kingdom agent of the insurer named in the advertisement and that United Kingdom agent is not independent of the named insurer, contain a statement naming the insurer and stating that the United Kingdom agent is a person who is not independent of the insurer and that statement shall appear prominently:

(a)   immediately after or alongside the statement of the name of the United Kingdom agent; or

(b)   if the name of the United Kingdom agent is stated more than once in the advertisement, immediately after or alongside the most prominent of the statements of that name and for this purpose if two or more statements of the name are equally prominent that which appears first in the advertisement shall be treated as the most prominent.

4.   For the purposes of paragraph (3) above:

(a)   a person shall be deemed to be a United Kingdom agent of an insurer if he is a person who carries on any business in the United Kingdom in the course of which he performs functions for or on behalf of the insurer;

(b)   a United Kingdom agent of an insurer shall be regarded as not indepdent of that insurer at a particular time if at that time:

(i)   the United Kingdom agent or any partner, director, controller or manager of the United Kingdom agent is a partner, director, controller or manager of the insurer;

(ii)   the insurer or any partner, director, controller or manager of the insurer is a partner, director, controller or manager of the United Kingdom agent;

(iii)   the United Kingdom agent is a body corporate and the insurer has any interest in any shares or debentures of the United Kingdom agent; or

(iv)   the insurer is a body corporate and the United Kingdom agent has any interest in any of the shares or debentures of the insurer,

and for this purpose a person shall be deemed to be interested in shares or debentures of a body corporate if he is interested in them according to the rules set out in section 28 of the Companies Act 1967 with the addition, in subsection (9) of that section, of a reference to a scheme made under section 20 of the Charities Act (Northern Ireland) 1964 and to an authorised unit trust scheme within the meaning of the Prevention of Fraud (Investments) Act (Northern Ireland) 1940.   **[629]**

67. Intermediaries: connected persons

1.   For the purposes of regulation 68 below a person is connected with an insurance company if:

(a)   that person, or any partner, director, controller or manager of that person, is a partner, director, controller or manager of the insurance company or of any controller thereof;

(b)   the insurance company, or any partner, director, controller or manager of the insurance company, is a partner, director, controller or manager of that person or of any controller thereof;

(c)   that person or any controller thereof has a significant interest in shares of the insurance company or of any controller thereof;

(d)   the insurance company or any controller thereof has a significant interest in shares of that person or of any controller thereof;

(e)   that person, under any contract, not being a contract of employment, or under any other arrangement (whether legally enforceable or not) with the insurance company or with any associated company, undertakes not to perform any services relating to any class of insurance business (or any category thereof) for any insurance company other than the insurance company and, where the undertaking also relates to any associated company, the associated company:

Provided that an individual who gives an undertaking of the kind referred to above to any registered society shall not, by virtue of such undertaking, be a person connected with the society or with any company which is, within the meaning of section 150 of the Companies Act 1948 or section 144 of the Companies Act (Northern Ireland) 1960, a wholly owned subsidiary of the society.

2. For the purposes of paragraph (1)*(c)* and *(d)* above, a person shall be treated as having an interest in shares of a company if, by virtue of section 28 (other than subsection (3)*(b)* of the Companies Act 1967, he would be so treated for the purposes of section 27 of that Act; and the interest shall be treated as significant if it is such that notification of it would be required under section 33 of that Act.

3. A person who issues an invitation of the kind mentioned in regulation 68(1) below in respect of a contract of insurance which will be underwritten at Lloyd's shall, in respect of that contract of insurance, be connected with the insurance company to which that contract relates if that person or any partner, director, controller or manager of that person will take a share in the contract as a member of Lloyd's.

4. In this regulation:

'associated company', in relation to a body corporate, means a subsidiary or holding company or subsidiary of the holding company of that body;

'controller', in relation to a body corporate which is not an insurance company, means a person who is or would be, if he were a company, a holding company of that body;

'manager', in relation to a body corporate which is not an insurance company, means a person who directly or indirectly takes part in or is concerned in the management of the affairs of that body.   **[631]**

NOTES
    Commencement: 1 January 1982.

Glossary of insurance terms

Readers should note that the brief explanation given of each word or phrase in this glossary is not necessarily exhaustive and is intended to convey the general meaning rather than to provide a precise definition. For further information on an entry, readers should refer to the page number(s) given.

Abandonment: The insured surrenders all rights to his damaged property to the insurer when a total loss is claimed. Usually applies to marine insurance.

Accident: (1) A completely fortuitous mishap which is neither expected nor designed. (2) A class of business which includes motor, liability, personal accident and (sometimes) householders/owners comprehensive.

Actuary: A specialist in statistics and the theory of life expectancy, who applies mathematical probabilities to mainly life insurance.

Adjuster: See 'Average adjuster' and 'Loss adjuster'.

Agency agreement: Agreement between insurer and his agent, laying down the conditions of the relationship between the two parties. See pages 33–5.

Agent: A person or company who has authority to act for another (his principal).

Agent (Lloyd's): An individual appointed by Lloyd's to provide shipping and aviation information. There is a worldwide network of Lloyd's agents. Generally, both Lloyd's and company marine policies provide for a Lloyd's agent to conduct the survey and adjust claims in the event of loss or damage.

Aggregate: (1) Sum total. (2) In liability insurance, used to limit the overall liability of the policy to a specific stated sum, usually the limit of any one event.

Agreed value policy: A policy in which the insurers agree the value of the property to be insured. Proof of this value is normally in the form of an independent valuation and the value is stated in the policy. In the event of total loss, the insurers will pay the value as previously agreed. Also called a *value policy.*

All-risks: An insurance policy that covers all occurrences that are not specifically excluded in the policy (as against a policy covering specified perils).

Annuity: An income paid at agreed intervals by the life office to the policyholder, usually for his lifetime. Bought in two ways: (a) with a single, lump-sum premium, in which case payment is usually immediate; or (b) with a series of premiums, in which case payment is usually deferred, i.e. starts after a period of time has elapsed.

Arbitration: A procedure whereby an independent individual acceptable to both parties in a dispute is invited to make a judgement on that dispute leading to its resolution.

Arbitration clause: A provision found in most policies for the resolution by arbitration of any dispute as to the amount to be paid under a policy following a claim.

Assignment: (1) The transfer of the rights to a policy from one party to another. (2) The document or act making the transfer of the right.

Assurance (life): The term normally applied to life insurance.

Average (non-marine): Average applies where there has been under-insurance and a claim payment is scaled down in proportion to the degree that the sum insured bears to the total value at risk.

i.e.

$$\frac{\text{Claims}}{\text{payable}} = \frac{\text{Actual}}{\text{loss}} \times \frac{\text{Sum insured}}{\text{Total value of property insured}}$$

Average (marine): Partial loss or damage. Defined as:
1. *General average:* When a sacrifice is made or expenses are voluntarily incurred to preserve a venture, the loss or expense is shared among all the interests in the venture in proportion to the value of each. See page 122.
2. *Particular average:* Partial loss or damage affecting the subject-matter of insurance.

Average adjuster: One who assesses and apportions losses, mainly in marine insurance.

Avoid: To make void, to invalidate.

Benefit: A sum of money payable under a policy of insurance or assurance.

Bind: To put *on risk.*

Binding authority/Binding cover: An agreement under which a coverholder (usually a firm of insurance intermediaries) is authorised by an insurer(s) subscribing to the agreement to conduct business as if they were the insurer. The coverholder can:
1. accept risks on behalf of the insurer(s).
2. issue certificates of insurance to bind the insurer(s) without their prior consent;
3. collect premiums, instruct professional advisers and pay claims on the insurer(s) behalf. See page 48.

Bonus: A share of the profits of a life insurance company distributed to with-profits policyholders.

Bordereau: In reinsurance, a statement of business accepted and/or of claims paid.

Broker (insurance): An insurance intermediary registered with the Insurance Brokers' Registration Council. Acts on behalf of the insured and offers professional skills in advising on and arranging their insurances. Also acts as the insurer's agent.

Brokerage: (1) The commission which the broker receives from the insurer for placing business with them. (2) The business of the broker.

Capacity: The maximum amount of insurance the market, or individually an insurer, is prepared to accept in any one risk or series of risks.

Captive (company): An insurance company formed by a trading group, trade association or the like. Primarily for the insurance of the organisation's own risks, since large organisations may gain substantial advantages by establishing captive insurance companies to undertake their own insurance. See page 139.

Cede: The transference of a risk from one insurer to another.

Certificate of insurance: A document issued by insurers as evidence that an insurance contract exists. Certificates must be issued by law in relation to motor and employer's liability insurance.

Claim: A demand by the insured (or assured) for payment under his policy.

Clause: An individual paragraph or section of a policy or contract. See page 66.

Coinsurance: Where two or more insurers each issue a part of an insurance. Each of the coinsurers has a separate contract with the insured. In the United States coinsurance can either: (a) apply to non-marine average or (b) signify a form of participation in the cover by the insured on an agreed basis. See page 86.

Collection: The process of circulating Lloyd's underwriters or companies to obtain settlement of a claim.

Collective policy: A single policy document issued on behalf of a number of coinsurers. Each coinsurer authorises the leader to sign the document, accepting a predetermined percentage of the risk on his behalf. See page 83.

Commission: A payment made by the insurers to an intermediary for placing a particular policy with them. Is usually a percentage of the premium. See also 'Brokerage'.

Companies: Insurance companies, as distinct from Lloyd's underwriters.

Composite office: An insurance company which transacts a number of classes of business, normally including both life and non-life. See page 57.

Comprehensive policy: A policy with more than one section defining separate insurable interests at differing risks and conditions.

Condition: A provision which qualifies the operative clause(s) and exclusions in an insurance policy. A condition governs the validity of the contract and must be complied with by one or other of the parties concerned.

Condition precedent: A condition which has to be complied with for the contract of insurance to be operative.

Consequential loss: Financial loss of money resulting from a physical occurrence which is insured.

Consideration: The premium, i.e. the sum paid to purchase insurance.

Constructive total loss: Where the cost of repair and/or salvage value is greater than the maximum of the indemnities payable under the policy.

Contract of insurance: See 'Insurance'.

Contribution: The principle whereby if more than one policy covers the same loss for the same insured, each policy contributes to the loss in accordance with its rateable share. See pages 64–5.

Cover: (1) The amount and nature of indemnity available under a policy. (2) The events against which a policy affords protection. (3) A *binding authority*.

Cover note: An abbreviated document which stands in place of a policy prior to its issue and confirms insurance has been granted. For motor insurance, the cover note must include a certificate of insurance to comply with the Road Traffic Act requirements and is initially issued for a temporary period by the broker, awaiting a permanent certificate to be issued by the insurer. See page 120.

Coverholder: An agent or broker who is authorised by underwriters to bind business within predetermined limits and conditions, and in some cases to issue insurance documents.

Credit note: A document enabling a client or agent to be credited with a sum of money.

Days of grace: A period of time immediately after the renewal date allowed for payment of the premium. Cover is continued during this period as long as the premium is paid within it and there has been no indication of intention not to renew. Motor policies have no days of grace.

Debit note: A document enabling a client or agent to be debited with a sum of money.

Declaration: (1) A statement at the foot of the proposal form, signed by the proposer(s) to certify that the information given is accurate to the best of their knowledge. (2) A return of information by the insured, under a declaration policy, which requires a periodic valuation of fluctuating items insured, e.g. stocks, as a basis for adjustment of the premium.

Declinature: Refusal of an insurer to accept or renew a proposal for insurance.

Deductible: The first portion or percentage of a loss, specified in a policy, which the insured has to bear himself. If a claim comes to less than this amount, no payment is made by the insurers. Also called *excess*.

Direct dealing: In motor insurance, an arrangement under which UK non-Lloyd's brokers can deal direct with Lloyd's motor underwriters. See page 118.

Duty of disclosure: The responsibility of a proposer for insurance to tell all material facts about the risk before acceptance of the risk and at renewal, even when no specific question about the matter has been asked on the proposal form.

Employer's liability (EL): A class of business under which an employer may be insured against claims made against him by his employees. See page 106.

Endorsement: Any written addition to a policy which changes or varies the terms of the contract.

Endowment assurance: A type of life assurance where the sum insured becomes payable on death or at the end of a fixed number of years (at maturity), whichever is the sooner. See pages 73–5.

Exception: A peril or circumstance specifically excluded from the terms of a policy. Also known as *exclusion*.

Excess: The same as *deductible*.

Excess of loss: A cover whereby the first part of a loss is paid by another; i.e. an insured, an insurance company or a reinsured. It is in excess of an agreed maximum loss and usually up to a certain limit.

Exclusion: A condition of the insurance contract that limits its scope; also known as *exception*.

Ex-gratia: A payment made where there is no legal liability.

Experience: The past claims record of an insured. Usually shown as the premium, claims and outstanding losses prepared over varying periods of time.

Extension: An addendum or endorsement to an existing policy to cover an extra item, risk or period of time.

Facultative reinsurance: A contract where the reinsured can select which risks he cedes to the reinsurer.

Fidelity guarantee: Insurance taken out by a property owner against the dishonesty of persons to whom that property is entrusted.

First loss: A policy under which the sum insured is less than the total value at risk. The premium takes into account both the sum insured and the total value at risk. The average, if applicable, will apply to the total value, not to the sum insured.

Franchise: The minimum amount of loss necessary before the insurers will be liable. Once the franchise level is attained, the loss will be paid in full. For example, a policy containing a £100 franchise would pay in full if the loss incurred were £101, but would pay nothing if the loss were £99.

Friendly society: A mutual society established principally for the relief or maintenance of members or their relatives during sickness, infirmity, old age or widowhood. See page 57.

Fringe market: Consists of all those companies who have underwriting rooms within the City of London, underwriting mainly a broker account. See page 163.

Fronting company: An insurance company which accepts an insurance by prior arrangement with reinsurers who accept practically 100% of the policy. See page 162.

Green card: An international certificate of insurance issued to motorists for use abroad. No longer compulsory in EEC countries. See page 120.

Green card extension: Cover affected to bridge any possible gaps between the compulsory insurance requirements of the specified foreign country and the requirements of the UK Road Traffic Act. See page 120.

Home foreign: Insurance from overseas placed in the UK market. See page 163.

Indemnify: To make good a loss suffered by the insured.

Indemnity: The legal principle which ensures a policyholder shall be put in the same financial position after a loss as he was immediately before the loss occurred. See page 64.

Index-linking: Premiums/sums insured shall automatically fluctuate, usually according to: (a) the durable household goods section of the general retail price index (for contents insurance); (b) the house building costs index of the Royal Institution of Chartered Surveyors (for buildings insurance). The increase in premium is paid only at renewal. Index-linking can also apply to permanent health and life insurance.

Insurable interest: The insured's interest in the subject matter of the insurance. See pages 63–4

Insurance: A contract in which one party, the insurer, for a consideration (the premium) undertakes to indemnify the other party (the insured) to the extent of a stated amount (the sum insured) on the happening of a specified event that is contrary to the interest of the insured.

Insurance Brokers' (Registration) Act 1977: An Act of Parliament which provided for the registration of individual insurance brokers and the corporate bodies, and for the regulation of their professional standards.

Insurance Brokers' Registration Council: The regulatory body established under the Insurance Brokers (Registration) Act 1977.

Insurance broking account (IBA): A separate bank account for insurance brokers required by the Insurance Brokers' (Registration) Act 1977. This must be maintained at an approved bank to hold moneys in respect of insurance transactions, separately from other assets and moneys. It is intended to protect insureds and insurers by separating their premiums and claims from the broker's own moneys. The bank must agree that it will not be entitled to charge the broking company's debts against this account and there are restrictions on the handling of money within it. For full details, refer to Part III of the Insurance Brokers' Registration (Accounts and Business Requirements) Rules Approval Order 1979 No. 489.

Insured: The person/organisation covered by an insurance.

Insurer: A company or underwriter who accepts insurance risks, i.e. the party to a contract of insurance who is liable to pay claims arising under it.

Interruption insurance: A class of business relating to consequential losses following material damage, machinery breakdown or such events as murder, suicide and infectious diseases. See pages 86–8.

Knock-for-knock agreement: An agreement between motor insurers that, in the event of an accident involving their respective policyholders, each insurer shall cover the cost of making good the damage to their policyholder's vehicle, without regard to the legal liabilities. The agreement is between the insurers and must not prejudice the interests of their respective policyholders.

Layer: A stratum of cover: normally applied to each level of excess of loss cover.

Leader: The underwriter who places his line first on the slip and who is accepted by other underwriters as leading the risk. See page 165.

Legal expenses insurance: Provides cover to either individuals or companies and will pay for the defence in a legal action. Can also compensate for any expenses incurred at employment tribunal.

Liability: (1) Legal responsibility for injury to another person or damage to his property. (2) The sum insured.

Lien: Right on property to keep possession of it till debt due in respect of it is discharged. An insurance broker has a possessory lien over a policy if he receives it before the insured has paid him the premium.

Limit of indemnity: The maximum figure for which the insurer can be liable to pay under a policy of insurance.

Line slip: An agreement between a group of underwriters and a

Lloyd's broker whereby, in respect of a specific class of insurance business, certain named underwriters within that group may accept risks on behalf of all underwriters in the group in accordance with the terms of the agreement. See pages 48, 124–5.

Lines (written and signed): The sum or percentage written by the insurer which establishes the proportion of the risk accepted by the insurer. The written line is the maximum the insurer is prepared to accept and the signed line, the amount required to complete the order subject to the maximum of the written line.

Lloyd's agent: See 'Agent (Lloyd's)'.

Lloyd's broker: An insurance broker authorised by the Council to broke insurance business at Lloyd's and given access to the Underwriting Room there. As the London market does not generally deal with the public, the broker obtains the business for insurers, collects the premium on their behalf and undertakes a great deal of documentation work for underwriters.

Lloyd's of London: The market of individual insurance underwriters which is organised by the Corporation of Lloyd's in London and controlled by the Council of Lloyd's. The Corporation also provides ancillary services. Traditionally it is the world centre of marine, aviation and non-marine classes of insurance. The term 'Lloyd's' often is taken to include the brokers who bring business to the Lloyd's underwriters.

Long-term agreement: An agreement whereby in consideration of a premium discount, an insured agrees to offer renewal of a policy at existing terms for a specified number of years to the holding insurer. The holding insurer is not bound to accept and if the insurer wishes to impose stricter terms these need not be accepted by the insured, who then has the option of placing the business elsewhere.

Loss: Originally meant the amount lost (and therefore liable to be paid as a claim by underwriters) as a result of an event giving rise to a claim. The term is often used more generally to refer to the event itself or to the claim arising from the event.

Loss adjuster: An independent professional who assesses losses and negotiates the settlement of claims on behalf of the insurers. Generally a specialist in one class of insurance, the loss adjuster is paid a fee by the insurer. In the United Kingdom the relevant professional body is the Chartered Institute of Loss Adjusters.

Loss assessor: A person who specialises in negotiating settlements of claims on behalf of the policyholder and who is paid by the policyholder.

Low-cost endowment: A combination of endowment and reducing term assurance. See page 74.

LPSO (Lloyd's Policy Signing Office): The departments within Lloyd's which (a) check all brokers' work in processing insurances; and (b) process premiums received and collection of claims on behalf of underwriting syndicates. They also provide each syndicate with a statement of claims owing and premiums due. Each transaction signed in the LPSO is allocated a number and date, unique to this transaction.

LUNCO (Lloyd's Underwriters' Non-Marine Claims Office): An office in Lloyd's which co-ordinates the payment of claims when there are several syndicates involved.

Market: (1) All of the insurers who trade in a specific area (e.g. the London market). The term Lloyd's market refers to all the Lloyd's syndicates competing with each other for business in the Lloyd's Underwriting Room. (2) More specifically, the group of insurers who are on risk under any one insurance.

Master policy: A single contract in respect of a number of persons or interests. See page 165.

Material fact: Any fact or circumstance about a proposed risk which would influence a prudent insurer in deciding whether or not to accept that risk and, if so, on what terms.

Maturity: The agreed date at which payment of the sum insured falls due under an endowment assurance.

Moral hazard: The risk arising from the character and circumstances of the insured or his employees, including carelessness and dishonesty.

Mutual insurance company: An insurance company wholly owned by its policyholders, i.e. without shareholders. There being no shareholders, all profits remain the property of the company and/or policyholders. See page 57.

Name: An underwriting member of Lloyd's whose name appears on the list of those participating in any Lloyd's syndicate. The term active or working name may also be used.

New for old: Insurance where the payment of a claim for property lost or damaged is on the basis of replacement-as-new, i.e. without deduction for depreciation.

No-claim discount (NCD): A discount granted on a premium at renewal where there has been no claim in the previous period; usually applies to motor insurance. Also known as No-claim bonus (NCB).

Non-disclosure: Failure by the proposer of insurance or his broker to disclose a material fact or circumstance to the insurer before a risk is accepted or at renewal.

Off-cover: Insurance accepted under the terms of a contract or a line slip.

Ombudsman (insurance): Insurance industry official to whom any complaint about insurance can be taken.

On risk: The acceptance of an insurance by an insurer.

Peril: Any event which may be covered by or excluded from an insurance policy; a possible cause of loss.

Period of indemnity: Used in loss of profits insurance, now more commonly called interruption insurance. The maximum period from the date of the damage during which, if the business is affected by the damage, the policy protection operates. Both the sum insured and the rate of premium will vary, having regard to the period(s) of indemnity.

Permanent health insurance (PHI): A policy designed to pay an income during disability or long-term illness. The insured receives a regular income after a pre-agreed number of weeks following his becoming incapacitated. This continues until he is fit for work again or (normally) retired. See page 76.

Personal pension plan (PPP): A private pension arrangement in accordance with current legislation between an individual, who is not a member of an occupational pension scheme, and a life office.

Physical hazard: Physical feature associated with the subject-matter of insurance which introduces or increases the possibility of loss arising from peril.

Policy: The legal document of insurance, setting out its terms and conditions. See pages 65–6.

Policyholder: The person who owns the policy and who pays the premiums; usually the insured.

Portfolio: All or a definitive part of the insurances transacted by an insurer.

Premium: The payment made by the insured to the insurers in consideration of the protection afforded by the insurance.

Principal: Person for whom another acts as agent.

Products liability: The liability arising out of goods sold or supplied.

Professional indemnity insurance: Offers the professional protection against his legal liability to compensate third parties who have sustained some injury, loss or damage due to his own professional negligence or that of his employees.

Proposal form: The printed form on which a proposal may be made to an insurer, giving information required by the insurers when deciding whether to accept a risk and if so, at what premium. When agreed by both parties, it forms the basis of the contract between them. Proposal forms are not used for all insurance negotiations. See page 65.

Proposer: The person or company who wishes to effect an insurance cover. Once the application has been accepted and the contract brought into existence, the proposer becomes the insured.

Prospectus: A publication which describes the services offered by an insurer, e.g. a type of insurance. Does not include all details of conditions and exclusions.

Proximate cause: The effective cause of a loss or damage. See page 65.

Public liability (PL): A class of business which affords the insured protection against legal liability claims made against him by third parties. Used to be known as third party insurance.

Rate: The amount charged for each unit by which the total premium is calculated. Can be: (a) *rate per cent* i.e. premium expressed as percentage per £100 of the sum insured; (b) *rate per mille* i.e. premium expressed per £1,000 of the sum insured; or (c) *rate per capita* i.e. a headcount.

Reinstatement: (1) Repairing or replacing damaged property, rather than paying money for it. (2) Restoring the sum insured after it has been depleted by the payment of a loss, usually at an additional premium. Applies to both insurance and reinsurance.

Reinsurance: Transfer of all or part of the risk assumed by an insurer (the reinsured) to another insurer (the reinsurer). Reduces the total eventual liability of the insurer (the reinsured). Does not affect the rights or obligations of the insured. See Chapter 11.

Reinsurer: The company or underwriter who accepts a re-insurance risk.

Renewal: The continuation of a policy for a further period on payment of the appropriate premium.

Reserve for outstanding claims: The amount which insurers must set aside at the end of each accounting period (or hold in reserve) for claims known and unknown.

Reversionary bonus: A share of the life company's profits, added to the sum insured under a with-profits life insurance. It is payable only when the policy matures or is terminated by death, though the bonuses are added on to the sum insured every one or three years, depending on the company. The calculation is either: (a) simple – based on the sum insured; or (b) compound – based on the sum insured plus any bonuses already added. See page 71.

Risk: (1) The subject-matter of insurance. (2) The probability of loss. (3) Causes of loss covered by a policy.

Room (the): The area within the Lloyd's building in which the Lloyd's syndicates' boxes are situated and business is transacted.

Salvage: (1) The value of property recovered after it has been partially damaged by fire or other perils. (2) To save endangered property and to enhance the value of the damaged property. (3) In marine insurance, the cost of saving or recovering property exposed to a peril.

Settlement: The payment of a claim.

Short-tail: A term used to describe a risk in respect of which all claims are likely to be advised and settled within the period of cover or shortly after the cover has expired. Normally confined to physical damage risks.

Slip: A document submitted by a broker to underwriters, containing a summary of the cover proposed, as agreed between the broker and his clients and the underwriters.

Small-claims pool: A pool of funds contributed to by all the Lloyd's underwriting syndicates and out of which all small claims, which amount to less than £2 per syndicate, are paid.

Special perils: Risks added to a fire policy not normally contained within the printed wording of that document, e.g. the addition of water damage and impact.

Spread: Collectively, the underwriters on risk under any one insurance.

Strict liability: The defendant will be liable even though he has exercised reasonable care.

Subrogation: The insurer's right to take action in the policyholder's name against anyone who may be legally liable to the policyholder for all or part of the damage or loss. See page 64.

Sum insured: The extent of the insurer's liability.

Surplus line business: Business surplus to the capacity of the local licensed market or business which cannot be placed within the local filed terms and conditions. See page 161.

Surrender: The premature relinquishing of a life assurance policy in return for an immediate payment by the life assurance company.

Surrender value: The price which the assurance company is prepared to pay on the cancellation or discontinuance of a life policy.

Surveyor: A person qualified by knowledge and skill, who inspects buildings and their contents to assess and comment on the risk of losses and to check fire, theft and accident precautions.

Syndicate: A group of underwriting members of Lloyd's on whose behalf insurances are accepted. Each underwriter takes a proportion of the insurance for himself, without assuming liability for the proportions taken by other members of the group.

Term: The period of the insurance contract.

Term assurance: A low-cost, protection-only life insurance contract which pays out only on death within a specified period (the term). Also known as temporary insurance. See pages 68–71.

Terminal bonus: The bonus paid on completion of the period of assurance or on death. It is a declared percentage of the bonuses already declared on the policy and like these *reversionary bonuses*, is added to the sum assured.

Third party: Any person or corporate body other than the insured (the first party) or the insurer (the second party).

Treaty: A reinsurance contract between a direct insurer and one or more reinsurers, under which the insurer agrees to cede business and the reinsurers to accept it (within prearranged limits). Usually effected to cover the whole or a certain section of the reinsured's business.

Underwriter: (1) An insurance company official who determines whether to accept insurance and if so, on what terms. (2) An insurer (Lloyd's).

Underwriting agent: An individual or firm allowed by the Committee of Lloyd's to underwrite a class or classes of insurance business at Lloyd's. There are three different types of underwriting agent:
1. *Managing agent:* An underwriting agent who manages one or more Lloyd's syndicates.
2. *Member's agent:* An underwriting agent who acts in all respects for the name except for managing the syndicate.
3. An agent can combine both the above functions, in which case he is normally called a managing agent.

Unearned premium: The part of the premium which relates to that part of the period of the contract which has still to run from a given point of time, usually the last date of the accounting year.

Utmost good faith (uberrima fides): The duty imposed on both parties to the contract: the insured to disclose all material facts and the insurers to deal fairly with the policyholder. See pages 61–3.

Valued policy: see 'Agreed value policy'.

Void: Without legal effect.

Voidable: A contract which may be declared void at the instance of one of the parties to it (usually the insurer) if a condition is breached. If unchallenged, the contract is effective.

Waiver of premium: Provision that premiums do not have to be paid. On a life policy or permanent health policy this applies during prolonged periods of illness.

Warranty: A condition made by the insurer which must be exactly complied with. Failure by the insured to observe this discharges the insurer from liability, at his discretion. There are two sorts of warranty:

1. *Express warranty:* Usually an undertaking by an insured that: (a) something shall or shall not be done; or (b) a certain state of fact exists or does not exist. Express warranty is imposed for reasons of underwriting practice or risk control, is incorporated in a policy and must be strictly observed. If not, insurers could repudiate, notwithstanding the fact that such non-observance may not necessarily be material to the loss.
2. *Implied warranty:* This is found mainly in marine insurance and relates to the seaworthiness of a vessel and the legality of an adventure.

Whole life assurance: Life insurance which provides for payment of a certain sum only when the life assured dies. See pages 72–3.

With profits insurance: Life insurance where bonuses, which vary according to the company's profits, are added annually to the original sum assured and paid when the policy matures. See also 'Reversionary bonus'. See pages 71–2.

Wording: All the clauses and conditions in full specifying the terms and conditions under which the contract is issued.

Write: To accept the insurance risk.

Index